Critical Essays on D.H. Lawrence

In Honour of Dr. R.K. Sinha

Critical Essays on D.H. Lawrence

In Honour of Dr. R.K. Sinha

Edited by
Sunita Sinha

ATLANTIC
PUBLISHERS & DISTRIBUTORS (P) LTD

Published by
ATLANTIC
PUBLISHERS & DISTRIBUTORS (P) LTD
7/22, Ansari Road, Darya Ganj, New Delhi-110002
Phones : +91-11-40775252, 23273880, 23275880, 23280451
Fax : +91-11-23285873
Web : www.atlanticbooks.com
E-mail : orders@atlanticbooks.com

Branch Office
5, Nallathambi Street, Wallajah Road, Chennai-600002
Phones : +91-44-64611085, 32413319
E-mail : chennai@atlanticbooks.com

Printed in India at Nice Printing Press, A-33/3A, Site-IV,
Industrial Area, Sahibabad, Ghaziabad, U.P.

A Tribute to my Grandfather

In Loving memory of Dr. R.K. Sinha
M.A. (Pat) D.Phil. (Oxon),
Professor Emeritus, Head,
Department of English, Patna University

Dr. R.K. Sinha's doctoral thesis on *Literary Influences on D.H. Lawrence* was one of the pioneering works on D.H. Lawrence completed in 1949, under the supervision of Lord David Cecil, Professor of English at University of Oxford.

Preface

When you read Lawrence, it is hard to separate yourself from him and very easy to be enmeshed by his aesthetics, passions, and grand cultural shifts. That's the allure and danger of reading Lawrence. D.H. Lawrence was the most loved, oft quoted and passionately researched author, I grew up with. Under the tutelage of my grandfather Dr. R.K. Sinha, one of the most renowned scholars on Lawrence, it was but natural for me to be endeared to the "greatest imaginative novelist of our generation," whose fiction occupies a significant place within the canonical "great tradition" of the English novel.

"My aim, I repeat, is to win clear recognition for the nature of Lawrence's greatness. Any great writer who has not had his due is a power for life wasted," remarked F.R. Leavis, in *D.H. Lawrence: Novelist*. In the introductory chapter of his book, *Literary Influences on D.H. Lawrence*, which was published in the centenary year of Lawrence, Dr. Sinha also remarks, "It is time—all but two decades dead—his genius were given its due."

Three decades later, *Critical Essays on D.H. Lawrence: In Honour of Dr. R.K. Sinha* is a humble effort to revaluate the art and vision of the canonical literary figure of D.H. Lawrence and pay a glowing tribute to one of the most erudite litterateur, Dr. R.K. Sinha who emblazoned Lawrence's visionary genius in the most Lawrentian style.

In our family, in the love for literature that we all share, this distinguished scholar and great teacher lives on, the intellectual legacy lives on. In my mother, in my brother and sister. In me. And now in our children. And I cannot think of any better tribute than that.

Eighty-six years after his death, D.H. Lawrence continues to speak to the modern reader with the same forcefulness and freshness that impressed, and sometimes shocked, his contemporaries. The cliché of Lawrence as an enemy of intellect, as a disorganized thinker has been pervasive. As Wayne Booth spoke of "Lawrentian men of passion," "the irrationalist D.H. Lawrence", and "Lawrence's attacks on murderous intellect in the name of darker Gods." However, there was much to Lawrence than that. Without declaring a conclusive verdict on the ideological essence of Lawrence's oeuvre, we need to state that presenting him singularly as a preacher of love, passion, and instinctuality is not a complete assessment. Lawrence's ideology is not confined to love or sexuality, it embraces many aspects related to 'pantheism, individual and social fulfillment, the existence of a soul, the relationship of this soul to the divine force, and the possibility of the soul to survive the pressures of society unaltered.' To me, above anything else, Lawrence was a humanist. A man of great intellectual and spiritual energy, originality and personal magnetism, Lawrence was intensely responsive to the power and beauty of the living world. As Huxley aptly stated, "To be with Lawrence was a kind of adventure, a voyage of discovery into newness and otherness." As a writer, Lawrence combined in him Blake's mystical visions, Coleridge's penchant for the instinctive over the rational, Ruskin's romantic dissent against the ruinous effect of industrialization upon man, Nietzsche's doctrine of will, Freud's erotic mysticism Bergson's mechanism of intuition, Melville's and Whitman's celebration of nature.

Critical Essays on D.H. Lawrence: In Honour of Dr. R.K. Sinha is an enduring and comprehensive contribution to Lawrence's scholarship conveying a coherent, all embracing sense of Lawrence's achievement and critical reputation. The eighteen essays in this anthology focus on issues like human relationships, problematics of gender, psycho-cultural dynamics, autobiographical intent, sensual experience, battle of sexes, problem of form, colonialism, and philosophy of nature. All these essays instil a renewed faith in the challenge of Lawrence's work, making this anthology invaluable for Lawrence scholars and students.

Sunita Sinha

Contents

Preface .... *vii*

Introduction .... *xi*

Contributors .... *xxiii*

1. The Primitive Woman in Modernism 1
Katherine Lashley

2. From Heaven to Hell—On the Desire-driven Transitions Siegmund has Undergone in D.H. Lawrence's *The Trespasser* 12
Billy Bin Feng Huang

3. Character and Metonymic Colonialism in D.H. Lawrence's *The Rainbow* 35
Mbuh Tennu Mbuh

4. Retrospect, Introspect, Prospect: A Reappraisal of Human Relationships in the Novels of D.H. Lawrence 56
Anita Myles

5. The Lonely Pastoral 82
Carole Rozzonelli

6. Our Modern Marlowe: Lawrence as English Outsider and Cultural Insider to America's Literary Re-birth ... 92
Jeffery Moser

7. Atrophy in D.H. Lawrence's *Sons and Lovers* 113
Kenneth Usongo

8. D.H. Lawrence: Nature, Red Geranium and Sensual Experience 124
Joyashri Choudhury

9. The Battle of the Sexes: D.H. Lawrence and the Struggle for Modern Sexuality in *Lady Chatterley's Lover* 135
Charlotte Fiehn

10. The Problematics of Gender with Reference to the Philosophy of D.H. Lawrence 149
Jayeeta Ray

11. D.H. Lawrence and *Lady Chatterley's Lover* 165
Bhaskar Roy Barman

12. Instability of Form and Modernity of D.H. Lawrence's *Sons and Lovers* 181
Arpa Ghosh

13. Autobiography as Trajectory of Sublimation: D.H. Lawrence's *Sons and Lovers* 191
Reena Mitra

14. Psychoanalysis and D.H. Lawrence's *Sons and Lovers* 205
Enkelena Shockett

15. *Women in Love*: Between the Old and New 214
Mehar Fatima

16. *End of Another Home Holiday*: In the Light of *Rasavada* 224
Ratri Ray

17. Interrogating Psycho-cultural Dynamics in the Plays of D.H. Lawrence 232
Beena Agarwal

18. A Tale of Two Women (Sinning or Sinned Against) Anna Karenina and Lady Chatterley 247
Harish C. Gupta and *Tapu Biswas*

Index 259

Introduction

> *"My great religion is a belief in the blood, the flesh, as being wiser than the intellect. We can go wrong in our minds. But what our blood feels and believes and says, is always true. The intellect is only a bit and a bridle."*

"The world doesn't fear a new idea. It can pigeonhole any idea. But it cannot pigeonhole a new experience," remarked Lawrence. By experience Lawrence meant, of course, an experience of art. Experience speaks as no idea ever can. Detesting "beastly Kant", appealing to "phallic consciousness" and the "dark gods," D.H. Lawrence advocated the instinctive, the subconscious, the utterly spontaneous and the intuitive. Exasperated by the soulless clangour of machinery, stifled by the stultifying materialism, Lawrence emerged as an anti-intellectual fascinated by the dark gods of paganism, a modern rebel and a champion of instinctual life. To Blake's Newtonian single vision equivalent to blindness in the face of real life, Lawrence added his personal experience of the twentieth century estrangement from Nature, in the grip of machines. Like Wordsworth, Lawrence rebelled against the "tight little automatic universe" imposed by nineteenth century scientific materialism and wanted to go back to the "unenlightened" pagans.

Having read Nietzsche and Freud and encountered the work of the German expressionists, Lawrence became convinced that intellect was suspect and sexual repression the sole cause for the deterioration of English civilization. In particular, he blamed

Christianity for its repressive division of the self into spirit and flesh and its privileging of the spirit. To Lawrence, this was, "an attempt to deny the existence of, "a blood being, a blood consciousness, a blood soul, complete and apart from the mental and nerve consciousness." In this context, R.K. Sinha's remark seems revealing "But even when he extols the instinctual life in the uncivilized races, he is sharply aware of the danger of mere primitivism."

Torn like Baudelaire, between the flesh and the spirit, Lawrence believed that fulfilment cannot occur completely either in the Spirit or in the Flesh, both the spirit and the body must be regarded as 'Complementary Absolutes.' The inescapable reality of sex, the primacy of sensual passion as the primary motivating drive of all human activity in Schopenhauer, shocked Lawrence ruthlessly out of the Shelleyan etherialisation and led him to pursue a philosophy to liberate himself from "the mind forged manacles" of provincialism, puritanism and his mother's middle class morality.

Impatient with the aestheticism of the Moderns, Lawrence declared that his concern was with "man alive." Dying of tuberculosis in the winter of 1929-30, unable to walk, and rendered sexually impotent by his disease, he wrote:

> "For man, the vast marvel is to be alive. ....But the magnificent here and now of life in the flesh is ours, and ours alone, and ours only for a time. We ought to dance with rapture that we should be alive and in the flesh, and part of the living, incarnate cosmos."

According to Middleton Murry, Lawrence belongs to no school and no tradition, except the "tradition of himself." The intellect to him, was only a bridle. Work was produced by passion, like kisses; it was not composition. A fierce individualist as he was, his motto was, not surprisingly, "Art for My Sake." As a poet, a critic, a playwright, and as a novelist, he maintained his fierce individuality and refused to affiliate his inspiration to the mechanizing discipline of any school or literary coterie. Lawrence criticized novelists such as Flaubert and Mann whose novels are too "well-made" and who adhered too ardently to their craft. Lawrence trusted his own interpretation of the living, organic, or emotional form, which is not external or mentally enforced but develops in response to the necessity of the embracement of experience.

Lawrence's opinions earned him many enemies and he endured official persecution, censorship, and misrepresentation of his creative work throughout the second half of his life, much of which he spent in a voluntary exile, what he called his "savage pilgrimage". Wyndham Lewis suggested that "lack of thinking" was Lawrence's flaw. T.S. Eliot blamed Lawrence for "a distinct morbidity", thereby "rotten and rotting others". Against Eliot's plea for "extinction of personality" Lawrence's own individual voice sounds, 'jocularly abusive like a male friend's, or high-spirited and judgmental like a teen-age girl's, bounding always between the disjunct registers of the chatty and the rhapsodic'. Though Eliot points out at Lawrence's "incapacity for what we ordinarily call thinking" and remarks that, "demonic powers found an instrument of great range, delicacy and power in Lawrence," he concedes in *After Strange Gods*, "Against the living death of modern material civilization [Lawrence] spoke again and again and what he said is unanswerable." Bertrand Russell considered him "a positive force for evil" while D. Ferguson wrote that Lawrence's constant preoccupation with sex was "proof of his emotional immaturity." Even, John Middleton Murry, one of Lawrence's best friends, observed, "He [Lawrence] was always evil, always something to which he was tempted, and into which he feels. He was a fallen angel...and the darkness of sex into which he had fallen was an evil darkness" (Murry. 1954: 96-97).

However, F.R. Leavis has shattered the arguments of Wyndham Lewis and T.S. Eliot fairly and convincingly. Leavis emphatically insists: "What needs to be said is this: "Lawrence is, before all else, a great novelist, one of the very greatest, and it is as one of the major novelists of the English tradition that he will, above all, live". In the context of that "great tradition" stretching from Jane Austen to Lawrence, Leavis declaims, "Lawrence is incomparably the greatest creative writer in English of our time...

he is one of the greatest English writers of any time. Further, what is truly striking is the vehement defense of Lawrence by Richard Aldington: I have no hesitation in saying that most comment on Lawrence's books—especially those in newspapers—is worthless rubbish, turned out by people who have either not read him at all or read him so hastily, stupidly and unfairly as to amount to the same thing...the comment perishes; Lawrence's work remains and will remain (Aldington, 1976:1).

Though Lawrence's reputation as a writer was always immense, his work was often considered scandalous, even in his lifetime. Yet, when he died in 1930, *the Guardian* compared him to Tolstoy. Despite the shifts in his reputation over the years, Lawrence remains a crucial presence in the contemporary British fiction. On academic front he continues to evoke new lines of study among scholars. The diversity of approaches in the eighteen essays of *Critical Essays on D.H. Lawrence: In Honour of Dr. R.K. Sinha*, demonstrates how Lawrence studies have gained from the new critical readings. This anthology also achieves the internationalism of Lawrence studies for it consists of essays by scholars from Africa, France,Taiwan, America, India and Albania.

In her scholarly paper, "The Primitive Woman in Modernism," Katherine Lashley argues that four main writers of the modernist literary period perceive of the primitive woman and her sexuality differently. Claude McKay in his novel *Home to Harlem* (1928) and D.H. Lawrence in his novel *The Rainbow* (1915) show women appreciating their sexuality by removing their clothing. Nella Larsen in her novel *Quicksand* (1928) and Virginia Woolf in her novel *To the Lighthouse* (1927) show women carefully avoiding the primitive sexuality of women, because it is connected to marriage, child bearing, and child rearing—three tasks the independent women do not want.

In "From Heaven to Hell—On the Desire-driven Transitions Siegmund has Undergone in D.H. Lawrence's *The Trespasser*," Billy Bin Feng Huang uses Deleuze and Guattari's theorizations of desire to account for Siegmund's desire in D.H. Lawrence's *The Trespasser*. As Huang remarks, "First, Lawrence, like Deleuze and Guattari, also relentlessly criticizes how capitalist society represses human desires, which is also the central theme of *The Trespasser*. With a deeper argumentation, I believe we will discover that in this novel, Siegmund has actually undergone three Deleuzo-Guattarian transitions. He first 'liberates' his own desire, and then he 'represses' his own desire. In the process of 'deterritorialization,' he escapes his faciality and breaks from prescriptive familial and social relations in capitalist society. Then in the process of 'reterritorialization,' he returns to society and to his family, from which familial and social punishment ensues and results in his tragic suicide. He derives libidinous pleasure from his life with his mistress, which enables him to consummate the so-called 'full body without organs.' Then the love between him and his mistress begins to deteriorate, which causes him to end up experiencing the so-called 'cancerous body without organs.' If we can respectively retrace the three from-heaven-to-hell transitions and dialectically analyze their intertwined causalities, we can perceive Lawrence's critique of capitalism in *The Trespasser*."

"Character and Metonymic Colonialism in D.H. Lawrence's *The Rainbow*" by Mbuh Tennu Mbuh presents D.H. Lawrence as a complex writer whose colonial imagination constituted part of the conceptual need to destabilize the rationale of Empire. The paper analyses his controversial—and in many ways innovative—representation of colonial discourse by situating it within the consciousness of an individual, Anton Skrebensky in *The Rainbow*, who becomes metonymically relevant to the goals of Empire. At the same time, though, through Ursula Brangwen, he unintentionally provides the means to a Lawrentian counter-discourse in the narration of British colonial expansionism; a momentum that will accentuate, at least in contemporary intellectual debates around the subject, in the weakening of the status-quo in racial and class binaries. In the end, it will be evident that the manner in which characters negotiate sexual politics in Lawrence's work is intimately connected to a diagnosis of Empire and its inhibitive strategies.

In her essay, "Retrospect, Introspect, Prospect: A Reappraisal of Human Relationships in the Novels of D.H. Lawrence," Anita Myles remarks, " Recognized as one of the foremost novelists of the twentieth century, D.H. Lawrence has rightly been considered a trend setter. Ignoring the late Victorian novelistic style and surmounting negative criticism, he succeeded in unfolding new vistas in subject matter and technique both. In the works of Lawrence, autobiographical, social and sensual expositions co-exist establishing that his novels cannot be perused in isolation. His creative adventure begins with divulging personal life unhesitatingly which gets expressed in two manners—sexuality and the reflection of contemporary life—specially that of the working class, mostly concentrating on colliers, a universe that shaped his formative life. The precepts of human inter-relationships and interactions cannot be ignored while judging Lawrence as a novelist. Though personal reflections are evident in all his novels but the major focus centres on compatibility of human beings: man and man, man and woman and individual and society. This research paper "scans the novels of D.H. Lawrence in these lights, that is formative influences on him, the family and social environment in which he grew up, his experiences with the working class, the mental trauma due to Oedipus complex, his inner conflicts and contemplations about life in general, his experiment with themes and techniques and how he has left an indelible impact on later novelists. Keeping these facts in mind the reappraisal of the novels of Lawrence amalgamates the three aspects—the retrospective, the introspective and the future prospect."

"The Lonely Pastoral" by Carole Rozzonelli considers *Lady Chatterley's Lover* by D.H. Lawrence in terms of communicative impossibility, both social and in human relationships, within British society after the First World War. In particular, it would draw some lines of contiguity with a dystopian frame of representation, since the condition of England of the late nineteenth-century fiction. The division between the ruling class and the working people seems to be grounded on the Victorian dichotomy have-have not, whereas the sexual overflowing in opposition to hegemonic morality would perhaps anticipate, in a generalized and not individual way, the "free" moral in *Brave New World* by Aldous Huxley. Concerning the social issue, *Lady Chatterley's Lover* might be placed half-way, in its representation of the miners and the steel workers, between the degenerated machine-tenders of *The Time Machine* and the "moron" subalterns in *Brave New World*.

Jeffery Moser's essay, "Our Modern Marlowe: D.H. Lawrence as English Outsider and Cultural Insider to America's Literary Re-birth" points out through literary and biographical comparison with sixteenth-century English poet and dramatist Christopher Marlowe, that both Lawrence and Marlowe were writers situated within a unique cultural renaissance and which each helped to foster in their respective time, as their writings reflect. As he further elaborates, "Via review and overview of scholarly criticism and comparative literary analysis between the Elizabethan poet Marlowe and novelist, short-story writer, poet, playwright, and essayist Lawrence, each writer's social milieu is traversed with commentary. Reviews and corrections to each writer's mythographic and biographic constructions inform the criticism of their respective works. In particular, each writer's respective poetry is highlighted in order to discern the degree to which their critically assumed 'unorthodoxy' overshadows and prevents a clearer understanding of their literary contributions and poetic innovations, as well as revealing a more complex truth about each individual."

Kenneth Usongo's paper, "Atrophy in D.H. Lawrence's *Sons and Lovers*" shows how in *Sons and Lovers*, D.H. Lawrence depicts waste, the disintegration of humans. Through the leading characters in his novel—Walter Morel, Gertrude Morel, William and Paul—Lawrence explores the physical and emotional drain of these characters as they degenerate from being healthy and sexually vibrant persons into jaded individuals. The characters suffer from romantic frustrations as well as the harsh economic environment. The transition from an agrarian countryside to an industrial and capitalist milieu mirrors the physical and psychological decline of the Morel family, which Lawrence describes in terms of nature imagery.

"D.H. Lawrence: Nature, Red Geranium and Sensual Experience" by Joyashri Choudhury depicts Lawrence's love of Nature and his earnest search for beauty. As she remarks, "From a mining village in Eastwood, to the ugly man-made industrialized England, D.H. Lawrence was always looking for beauty in nature, even amidst the ugly surroundings the working classes were condemned to live in. Lawrence was deeply attached to the earth and nature. He was against the exploitation of both the human and natural resources. His works exemplify his deeply ecological consciousness. He was, in fact, the 'green novelist'."

"The Battle of the Sexes: D.H. Lawrence and the Struggle for Modern Sexuality in *Lady Chatterley's Lover*" by Charlotte Fiehn, "explores the representation of gender and sexuality in D.H. Lawrence's final novel, *Lady Chatterley's Lover*, arguing that it remains the most precise exploration of sexuality in the modern world that Lawrence offers in his fiction. Considering Lady Chatterley in contrast to Lawrence's other major novels, *Sons and Lovers*, *The Rainbow*, and *Women in Love*, the chapter argues that it is through Connie Chatterley, Clifford Chatterley, and Oliver Mellors that Lawrence develops the most extensive and the most precise portrait of struggling modern personalities and sexual identities, stressing not only the disconnection of modern man in his portrait of Clifford Chatterley, but also arguing for the possibility of recovery and reconnection through the relationship of Connie Chatterley and Oliver Mellors."

"The Problematics of Gender with Reference to the Philosophy of D.H. Lawrence" by Jayeeta Ray focuses on Lawrence's dictum that "the great relationship for humanity will always be the relation between man and woman."

Bhaskar Roy Barman's paper, "D.H. Lawrence and *Lady Chatterley's Lover*" focuses on D.H. Lawrence's last, many critics tend to say, and 'poorly written' novel entitled *Lady Chatterley's Lover*. Analysing the book intensively the author remarks, "Many scholars, particularly Lawrence scholars, sort of feel inclined to avoid discussing in detail this novel or rather rest satisfied by touching upon it when talking about the gamut of his literary work, characterizing it as a notorious novel. Its expurgated edition was published in 1928; it was published in full in England in 1960. The novel appears to me, I humbly confess, the most difficult of the whole gamut of his work to handle impartially, exploring and analysing it in intrinsic detail. We cannot bring ourselves to shut our eyes to the permeation of social evils and immorality and perversity into this novel. In Lady Chatterley's Love Lawrence, as the story of the novel suggests, shows himself determined to grapple efficiently with the problem of creating a resurrection story literally phallic, with a real man bearing the phallus. The sort of man assigned with the task of bearing the phallus is required to be a freed man, a man who has succeeded in throwing off the fatal chain and in isolating himself from the mob. In this novel Lawrence returns to his early archetype of non-conformity in the person of the gamekeeper, a kind of hermit, safeguarding his Garden of Eden. The hermit figure presented in the gamekeeper is not wholly satisfying, though. It is not possible to ascertain whether the hermit is escaping to or from life. There emerges out of the love between Connie and Mellors a glow which itself love in manifestation."

Arpa Ghosh's paper, "Instability of Form and Modernity of D.H. Lawrence's *Sons and Lovers*" presents Sons and Lovers as an impressive text which, "sets out to make a certain statement in the grand tradition of the Victorian novel. It does something more. *Sons and Lovers* is a novel with strong autobiographical elements. In the Victorian realist tradition the novel may be perceived as a triptych. The three women in Paul's life can be conveniently categorized as mother, angel and whore. The triptych stereotypes are heavily problematized. As Frank Kermode argues in his essay, "The Writing of *Sons and Lovers*" (21, Rylance: 1996) the novel is shaped not so much by an unfolding plot narrative (in the Victorian tradition) as it is by a pattern of 'symbolic and structural variations from episode to episode'. Lawrence's age marks the rise of the new individualism, of the cracking of old Victorian moulds. By means of narrative technique and style Lawrence holds this up. In the final count *Sons and Lovers* shines in its credo of honesty and commitment to the exigencies of the artistic text."

Reena Mitra's paper, "Autobiography as Trajectory of Sublimation: D.H. Lawrence's *Sons and Lovers*" argues wonderfully that the autobiographical content of the novel afforded him a strategy for coming to terms with life and with himself.

"Psychoanalysis and D.H. Lawrence's *Sons and Lovers*" by Enkelena Shockett focuses on D.H. Lawrence's *Sons and Lovers*. This piece of literature acclaimed for the perspectives opened up in reading it, is qualified as a masterpiece and worth to read and to discuss from various points of view. The author states, "As the paper collocates round Sons and Lovers this novel will be interpreted as a Freudian novel; even more my intentions will enrich and develop my projection also on how to measure the development of the stories and characters in the whole text and also how to evaluate the poetics utilized by D.H. Lawrence."

In her essay, "*Women in Love*: Between the Old and New," Mehar Fatima says that, "D.H. Lawrence voyages through a peculiar space and time wherein he encounters the 'vanishing apparitions' of the old, making way for something new to come. *Women in Love* struggles to live through the transition of multitude; of chasm, secrets, dreams, ambitions, fantasy, imagination, fear, madness, silence, chaos, anarchy, and void amidst the shadows, crossing between the past and future. However difficult to apprehend, it creates a wider scope for the readers to analyze the novelist's art in the work of fiction. The interpretation of the novel depends upon different and varied perspectives granting to reflection of its essential themes. Secrets of the mind and heart coiled in darkness, of relationships within and with others. The subconscious feelings; mingled with love and hate, become an energetic force which carry forward the novel in the development of relationships. Lawrence was making a new meaning of love by establishing a union between the couple where each [one] obligates to the other though sustaining the integrity of the person. We can feel the void somewhere, everywhere; an expression of the First World War, though we don't find any direct mention of it anywhere. It simply is rampant in the air, the actions, the food, and thoughts. In response to the multi-faced catastrophe of the Great War, one could sense the growing aspirations longing for change. Nothing could remain still, neither human nor nature. A part adieu to the fully accomplished world and a part effort to be reborn into a new becomes a significant theme of *Women in Love*. We discover Lawrence in search of some hope from the remains of the shattered individuals in the universal crisis. They are rescued and redeemed through love. However, the indeterminate ending; the incompleteness becomes a central component in the state of transition."

Ratri Ray's "*End of Another Home Holiday*: In the Light of *Rasavada*" is an attempt to analyse Lawrence's poem *End of Another Home Holiday* according to *Rasavada*. It is being assumed that the reader will have a working knowledge of this theory. Its intricacies will be clarified as and when necessary.

D.H. Lawrence's genius has universally been acknowledged for deconstructing the complexities of man and woman relationship including socio-cultural variables and their impact in human psyche. This perception of human life has been projected in his novels, short stories and even plays. He made efforts to explore a new idiom of theatre beyond the paradigms of aesthetics. "Interrogating Psycho-cultural Dynamics in the Plays of D.H. Lawrence" by Beena Agarwal is an analytical study of the socio-cultural dynamics projected in the plays of D.H. Lawrence. The use of theatre for the projection of psychological themes is unconventional and innovative. In this paper efforts have been made to study his thematic concerns, stage techniques, dialogues, language and symbols integrated in his plays that inaugurated a new era of theatrical tradition suitable enough to present on the stage, the 'invisible world' of human consciousness resisting against the well-defined convention of social paradigms and cultural recommendation. The findings of the paper will be a mile-stone to evaluate the psychological possibilities of theatre as it has been practised by Eugene O Neill, Arthur Miller and others.

Harish C. Gupta and Tapu Biswas in their scholarly paper, "A Tale of Two Women (Sinning or Sinned Against) Anna Karenina and Lady Chatterley" have taken a cue from the ever abiding question posed by Alexander Pope ('Is it, in Heaven, a crime to love too well?') and from D.H. Lawrence's own astute comment ('the monster was social, not phallic at all'), and believe that in the context of two extraordinary female characters, Anna Karenina and Lady Chatterley, ably created by two literary giants (one Russian; the other British), it was the social structure of the time, as even today, that could not come to terms with the fact that two individuals, being ladies, tried to exercise their right to seek their happiness. How [in a male oriented society] could ladies be allowed to have this liberty? If they were males that would have been another matter!"

The book is a humble effort to stimulate Lawrence's critics and scholars, and aims at presenting a vital, complex, multifaceted, original and provocative Lawrence. I wish to thank all my learned contributors for extending their support in every possible way. I also wish to thank Dr. K.R. Gupta for the confidence evinced in me and for seeing the book through the press.

Sunita Sinha

Contributors

Katherine Lashley, Ph.D. Candidate, Morgan State University, USA.

Billy Bin Feng Huang, Ph.D. Candidate, National Chengchi University, Taiwan (R.O.C.).

Mbuh Tennu Mbuh, English Department, University of Yaounde I, Cameroon.

Anita Myles, Professor, Department of English, D.D.U. Gorakhpur University, Gorakhpur, Uttar Pradesh.

Carole Rozzonelli, Associate Professor of English, ICT, Communications and Media Law, University of Lyon 2 – Lumière (France).

Jeffery Moser, British Renaissance Scholar and Ph.D./A.B.D., University of Denver, USA.

Kenneth Usongo, University of Denver, USA.

Joyashri Choudhury, Associate Professor, Head of Department of English, Khagarijan College, Assam.

Charlotte Fiehn, Offer holder at the University of Cambridge for 2015, and a current student at the Harrisburg Area Community College.

Jayeeta Ray, Assistant Professor (Senior Scale), in the Department of English, Rabindra Bharati University, Kolkata, West Bengal.

Bhaskar Roy Barman, South Bank of Girls Bodhjung Dighi, Banamalipur, West Tripura, India.

Arpa Ghosh, Head and Associate Professor of English, Vivekananda College for Women, Kolkata, West Bengal.

Reena Mitra, Professor of English in Amity School of Languages, Amity University, Lucknow, Uttar Pradesh.

Enkelena Shockett (Qafleshi), Ph.D., University of Tirana, Albania.

Mehar Fatima, Department of English, Jamia Millia Islamia, New Delhi.

Ratri Ray, Former Professor of English, Patna University, Bihar.

Beena Agarwal, Professor, Department of English, D.S. College, Aligarh, Uttar Pradesh.

Harish C. Gupta, Former Deputy Librarian, National Library of India. An enthusiast of Slavonic Studies, Recipient of 'Soviet Land Nehru Award'.

Tapu Biswas, Assistant Professor, Department of English, Visva-Bharati, Santiniketan, West Bengal.

1

The Primitive Woman in Modernism

Katherine Lashley

D.H. Lawrence and Claude McKay, writers of primitivist texts, use the primitivist discourse in order to challenge and expand upon the views of women's sexuality. These writers portray certain women as relying on their primitive natures and actions ultimately to show their strength and power as women, while learning to accept their female sexuality. Both Claude McKay in his novel *Home to Harlem* (1928) and D.H. Lawrence in his novel *The Rainbow* (1915) imagine primitive women, who through shedding their clothes to reveal their nudity, come to appreciate and accept their female bodies.

The idea of the Great Mother, which is connected to the primitive woman, is explained by Erich Neumann who observes that the primordial archetype of women or the Great Mother has contradictory elements—good and bad mother. Men particularly have difficulty representing the Great Mother. When men have finally been able to represent the primordial archetype of women, she becomes monstrous and inhuman (Neumann 12-13). Although Lawrence and McKay are men writing about primitive women, or the primordial archetype of women, one will see that these male authors, in the following scenes at least, positively represent the woman in her nudity.

D.H. Lawrence, in *The Rainbow*, positively describes the pregnant Anna who dances naked alone in her room. Alone, she sheds her clothing to expose her eight-month pregnant body. Naked, she dances about the room, moving her body by raising her legs and arms. When her husband enters the room, she wants him to leave. Upon his entrance and seeing her dancing, he desires her to stop dancing and clothe herself, yet she refuses to listen to him, preferring instead to continue dancing alone. Ultimately, his will prevails, and she dons her robe. Writing about sexual liberation in *The Rainbow*, Liang-ya Liou states that, "*The Rainbow* was denounced and tried for obscenity due to its sexual explicitness, particularly its representation of lesbianism" (Liou 57). One could argue that Anna's dancing hints at lesbianism, and therefore a number of readers find the image of the pregnant Anna dancing naked rather disturbing. The uncomfortable nature of this scene conveys the impact of a woman's ability to return to primitive behavior.

Neumann analyzes the image of the woman raising her arms: by raising her arms, she is engaging in a magical action representative of the priestess who desires to move closer to her goddess. A second interpretation furthers this vision of the priestess worshipping her goddess by claiming that she is having an epiphany, especially one where she meets the goddess (Neumann 116). Anna certainly exemplifies the image of the woman with raised arms in supplication and epiphany when she raises her arms as she dances. Her dancing naked while raising her arms intensifies the ritual of worshipping the Great Mother, especially as Anna takes on the image of the primordial archetype of women.

Anna, by dancing naked during her pregnancy, shows that she is finally comfortable in her female body, thus recovering her body from her husband, and pregnancy from the discourse that maintains that pregnancy is taboo and disgusting. When Anna removes her clothing, she removes the barrier between her body and the world around her. No longer do the clothes protect her body from potential injury. In addition to exposing her skin and pregnant belly to her surroundings, she further reveals her body by moving around freely and naturally—by dancing. The narrator in *The Rainbow* describes Anna, "And with slow, heavy movements she swayed backwards and forwards, like a full ear of corn, pale in the dusky afternoon, threading before the firelight, dancing his non-existence, dancing herself to the

Lord" (15). Anna heightens the intensity of her dancing by performing these actions before the fire, which adds to her sensuality. Physically, she moves her body in ways that expose her vulnerabilities, yet strengthen her spirit.

In writing about women and modernism, Bonnie Kime Scott observes that Lawrence invokes a pagan past and world in order to provide Anna with energy to support her desires. Lawrence invokes a pagan, preindustrial world for Anna by the removal of her clothing, which in turn removes the industrialization present within clothing production. Also, the removal of her clothing harkens back to the pagan, preindustrial days when people would not wear clothing, but simply interact with one another in their natural (primitive) form of nudity. Not only is nudity a life-sustaining force, but Anna also discovers that dancing is a life-sustaining force because of the vitality she feels in her body and spirit as a result of her dancing. By dancing, she shows that she no longer fears the criticism about her as a woman and as a pregnant woman. By dancing, she allows herself to become acquainted with her body and sexuality. She dances because the movements, which are experienced instead of imagined, allow her to familiarize herself with all the parts of her body. She experiences the beauty and wonder of her body, ultimately accepting her body and her sexuality.

Just as the absence of clothing no longer protects her from her surroundings, her clothing also no longer protects the viewer from fully visualizing her pregnant form. Now seeing her body the way it is without anything to conceal her pregnancy, the viewer is forced to confront that yes, she is pregnant and full of life. The fact that she is not ashamed of her body indicates that neither should the viewer be embarrassed. Yet, Liang-ya Liou believes that Lawrence illustrates Anna's female sexuality as lesbianism and perverted (58). I do not believe that Lawrence presents Anna's dancing as perverted, because Lawrence includes this scene primarily from Anna's perspective. The reader is first exposed to Anna's thoughts about her dancing before her husband's opinion is shared. Now, what can lead Liou and other readers to believe that Anna's dancing naked is perverted is exactly through the presence and opinions of her husband.

The narrator of *The Rainbow* describes how uncomfortable and painful it is to Anna's husband to watch her dance. Because of the torture he feels when seeing her dancing, he wants her to stop dancing and clothe herself. Female characters in *The Rainbow*, such as Anna, are analyzed by James Twitchell, who asserts that the woman's primal actions and passions can overwhelm their lovers, especially if the man does not direct the woman in her primitiveness (24). To an extent, Twitchell's analysis applies to Anna because Anna exhibits her primal passion through her dancing which does overwhelm her husband because he is not directing her primitive actions. However, Twitchell's analysis does not entirely apply to Anna because when she dances, she is not doing so to know or control her husband.

She dances in order to know and control herself. It is true that her primal passion is so strong that it overwhelms her husband, but that is because he recognizes the implications of her dancing. As he understands the meaning of her dancing, the husband, and not Anna, is to blame for human incompleteness, because Anna, by dancing, is complete in herself; her husband, however, being incomplete in his own identity, is actually to blame for being overwhelmed by her. In watching her, he recognizes that she accepts her body and that she does not need him in order to do so. He realizes that she does not need him to validate her body nor her existence. This revelation frightens him and causes him emotional distress, for if she does not need him, then why would she continue to remain married to him, or listen to him, or subvert herself to him? As a man, he needs to be needed by this woman, for without her his own sexuality and existence is called into question. He believes that if this woman—his wife—totally accepts her sexuality, then she will use the bare essentials of herself to overcome him. She will have learned to accept her female body and sexuality, thereby practicing an early form of feminism, and he will no longer have any control over her. As a woman using the power of her own mind and body together, she can do powerful things on her own, thus eliminating the need for him in her life.

When Anna dances for the Unseen, the Lord, she uses Christianity to support her inclination and desire to dance. By her female power alone, she could dance, and in actuality she begins in this way. Yet she becomes frightened of her own power as a primitive woman after her first instance of dancing. Peter Childs, explicating *The Rainbow*, observes that, "Lawrence portrays individuals driven by unconscious impulses and divided within themselves" (68). This happens with Anna as she is driven by the unconscious impulse to dance, yet once she realizes what her body can do and that her mind and heart enjoy the physical movements, she becomes divided within herself. Therefore, in order to combat her fear of the unconscious, primitive power of the woman's body, she embeds her dancing in Christianity. By situating her physical movements within Christianity and the Lord, she temporarily and cognitively finds solace by believing her dancing is in imitation of King David from the Bible before the Lord. Although she believes this, she also recognizes that this dancing is in fact a celebration of itself and its freedom and power. Her body's movements and confidence influence her mind, thereby bringing her almost full circle as she dances in rebellion against her husband. No longer does she dance solely for the Lord, but for herself, and for the idealized image of the primitive woman who is confident, strong, and free—a woman who does not need a man, or a husband or even a heavenly father.

Ultimately, Anna reclaims the primitive nature of woman by dancing. Although she relies on religion in order to give herself permission to experience the primitive parts of her female self, she makes a large leap in accepting herself as a woman. By struggling and resisting her husband's will, she proves to herself and to him that she can love herself in spite of his presence and domination. Bonnie Kime Scott believes likewise when she argues that "*The Rainbow* offers Lawrence's most affirmative views of matriarchy and of young women's development" (164). The affirmative views are vital for Anna, her daughter, and even for the women reading the novel, because of the influence Lawrence has on literature and culture. Because the mother (Anna) dances as a pregnant woman, before she is about to give birth to her daughter (Ursula) she transfers her fiery female spirit to her as yet unborn daughter. The mother Anna's confidence in her naked pregnant body transcends to the daughter Ursula who will continue in this new tradition of the glorification of female sexuality by engaging in uninhibited sexual intercourse with her own lover on the beach. Although the daughter Ursula's triumph of female sexuality and body is too involved for the scope of this paper, it is nevertheless necessary to recognize that the mother Anna's strength in female sexuality does not end with her, but lives and grows through her and her daughter. Thus, Anna and her daughter break the connection between the Great Mother and monstrosity; instead they are beautiful and powerful as primitive women.

Claude McKay, in his novel, *Home to Harlem*, provides a similar scene of female sexuality in relation to primitivism. Felice, the love obsession of Jake, tells him of two women from the West Indies who fight over a man by going outside, stripping off their clothes, and fighting with their bare hands and bodies. These two women fight, not concerned with the people gawking at them. Afterward, they clothe themselves and go about their day. A telling remark comes from two African American women who comment upon the way these women fight naked—that by doing so they do not rip or soil their clothing, which is a good thing. Now, Hazel V. Carby, in her 2013 article entitled, "Policing the Black Woman's Body in an Urban Context," states that "McKay situates his female figures in a very simplistic manner in various degrees of approximation to an uncontrolled and, therefore problematic sexual behavior" (749). Carby is correct when she observes that even these two fighting women are presented in a simplistic manner, but their sexual behavior is not problematic. Indeed, when the women disrobe, they are revealing their bodies, but they are not engaging in "problematic sexual behavior". Instead, these women show how the naked female body can be used for women's needs alone, without their sex factoring into their actions.

The two women, by removing their clothing, indicate that they are not afraid of exposing their flesh to each other while they fight. Indeed, by remaining clothed, they would not only be disguising their bodies, but protecting their flesh. Nevertheless, the removal of their clothing indicates that while the women will engage in the primitive act of fighting, they will utilize the primitive entirely by fighting naked. It appears that there could be nothing more primitive than fighting over a man, and their nudity appears to support this assumption. However, by removing their clothing to reveal their bodies, these women defy the masculine dictates of propriety. The male discourse desires the woman to be clothed, for her to hide her body. When the women are clothed, the man does not mind if they fight over him. However, with their nudity the women suddenly realize that it is not the man who holds control over the women and their bodies, but now the women themselves. The women forgo how men would want them to fight and instead fight in their own way. Now, not only do these women own their bodies, but they also own their fight.

By telling this story, Felice indicates that women have found a better way to fight. Felice thinks to herself, "A hen fight was more fun than a cock-fight.... The hens pluck the feathers, but they never ring necks like the cocks" (McKay 310). She recognizes that women may bite and scratch, but they do not involve guns and more life-threatening violence like men will. "However, she [Felice] was aware that in her world women scratched and bit into each other's flesh and men razored and gunned at each other over such things" (McKay 306). Also, one can interpret the two women's comments about fighting naked as reflecting Felice's own point of view. Otherwise, why would she include this information in the story? She does so in order to hint to Jake that she believes fighting naked is a good way for women to settle some of their differences. She indicates through her story and the women's comments that she believes that fighting naked is one way a woman can embrace the primitive about herself while still maintaining her respectability.

Respectability in society is important for Felice, and we see that her observation of the fighting women contributes to her reflection upon respect and freedom for black women. Kimberley Roberts observes that "On the one hand, he [McKay] seems to celebrate the sexual freedom certain women experience as an index of their ability to participate more fully and equally in the society at large. On the other hand, many of these women are configured as obstacles in the way of black male freedom" (120-21). Although Roberts does not discuss how McKay perceives the two fighting women, McKay certainly celebrates the fact that these women have the sexual freedom to settle their differences by fighting naked. These women bring their custom to the attention of African Americans in the United States, entering the African American society at large in Harlem.

After the fight, when the few female spectators say that this is a good way to fight because the clothes are not ruined, they mean that the women can still embrace the primitive aspects of themselves while still rising above the kind of primitive discourse imagined by men. These observers recognize that women fighting over a man is nothing new, yet they appreciate the way in which the women fight: naked, yet dignified, and by doing so these women leave the fight proudly. Women, by fighting clothed—the way a man would want them to fight—would definitely be catering to him and what he has deemed as acceptable. Yet these women disrobe, finding a way to fight without pleasing men, although the men who witness this fight are titillated because of the sight of the naked female body. The spectators admire these women because they witness that a woman can use the primitive parts of herself without submitting to man's desires.

These women also see the practicability of women fighting in the nude. "'It sure is better to disrobe like that, befoh battling,' one declared. 'It turn you' hands and laigs loose for action'" (McKay 310). They realize that this is no ordinary fight, but a battle, and they admit and recognize that there are times when they want to do battle as well. The use of the word "battle" indicates that a fight between women is just as important for women, even if the men do not think so. The above sentence uttered by one of the observing women indicates that these women realize the need for physical freedom to move in this battle. For if the women had fought clothed, their fighting strategies might have resembled a "cat fight," with the struggle appearing petty because blouses, skirts, and dresses would have hindered their movements. However, by being naked, these women take the fight seriously, strongly hitting each other, using the force of their bodies.

Jake's reaction to Felice's story indicates that he believes Felice is making too much of the fact that he is taking her away from another man whom he learns later is his friend, Zeddy. The narrator in *Home to Harlem* notes that, "But, unlike Felice, his [Jake's] thought was not touched by the faintest fear of a blood battle" (McKay 311). Jake does not conclude that Felice is making a connection between the women fighting over a man to Jake potentially fighting Zeddy over her. Jake's lack of concern for a potential battle indicates that he cannot be bothered by the story of the naked fighting women. This highlights his dismissiveness toward the subject of fighting. Jake cannot even be drawn out to voice his thoughts on the different way of women fighting. Indeed, Jake's total lack of response and the way that Felice's story is situated in the text can leave the reader unsure as to whether Felice actually tells Jake this story or if she merely reflects upon it herself. The lack of response from Jake, or Felice's reticence, bodes ill for their relationship in the future which the novel does not cover. If, for instance, Felice is unable to voice her concerns and opinions about women's thoughts and motivations, then at some point Felice just might find herself in a similar fight: exhibiting her primitive side through fighting, only this time with her lover.

McKay appears to emphasize the fact that the two women who fight naked, in a primal way, in an ancient tradition, do so because they are from the West Indies. Felice narrates that "After the challenge, the women had decided to fight with their clothes off. An old custom, perhaps a survival of African tribalism, had been imported from some remote West Indian hillside into a New York backyard" (McKay 308-09). McKay makes it clear to the reader that these women are not American, not even African American, but immigrants from the West Indies, thus hinting that these women come from a place with such primal and ancient customs still practiced even in the 1910s and 1920s.

Martha Jane Nadell, explaining the connection between modernism and race, asks an important question: "Did white—

and indeed non-white—artists fall prey to some of the same problems of European primitivism, engaging in fantasies of racial difference and stereotypes, exploiting the cultures of non-dominant populations, and drawing firm lines among different ethnic groups?" (Nadell 530). Unfortunately, it appears that the answer to Nadell's question when applied to *Home to Harlem* is "yes". McKay uses the racial differences and stereotypes of the West Indian women in order to include this scene of the two women fighting naked. However, when one considers the scene, one realizes that it would not work, and indeed could instigate even more judgments of whites against African Americans if the fight occurred between African Americans. Although McKay is "engaging in fantasies of racial difference" by making these women West Indian, he actually manages also to redeem this scene by providing Felice, the African American women commentators, and the readers with the perceived benefits of allowing women to fight naked. Here, he ultimately glorifies the West Indian women and offers encouragement for African American women to find ways in which they can adapt the primitive actions of the West Indians for their own use as African Americans in the United States. Thus, McKay also deconstructs the connection between the Great Mother and monstrosity by posing the primitive woman as the ideal for African American women.

Both of these scenes—Anna dancing and the two women fighting—show that these women accept their female bodies in their nakedness. These women have been conditioned to perceive their bodies as cursed and primitive, yet they recognize the beauty and power of their bodies. The authors of these scenes, D.H. Lawrence and Claude McKay, are writers before their time. Through their writing, they take the prevailing notion of the curse of female sexuality, and they portray the female body in ways that demonstrate that female sexuality is not cursed but beautiful, clever, and ultimately on a higher intellectual level than the male counterpart. Lawrence exalts the improvised dance movements of Anna as better than the choreographed movements approved for her by her husband. McKay posits the women's way of fighting naked with only their bodies as less injurious than man's way of fighting with weapons. By employing female characters who use their naked bodies in different, unexpected ways, Lawrence and McKay herald the coming years when writers, readers, men, and women will accept and appreciate the female body.

These male writers, though writing from their own male perspectives on women, actually help other men reexamine the boundaries of acceptable female behavior by writing daring women into their novels. Lawrence and McKay have contributed to the stereotypes of women, yet they have also contributed in their own small ways to the advancement of how women and women's bodies are viewed sexually.

Works Cited

Carby, Hazel V. "Policing the Black Woman's Body in an Urban Context." *Critical Inquiry* 18.4 (1992): 738-55. *MLA International Bibliography*. Web. 21 February 2013.

Childs, Peter. *Modernist Literature: A Guide for the Perplexed*. New York: Continuum, 2011.

Lawrence, D.H. *The Rainbow*. 1915. New York: General Books, 2009.

Liou, Liang-ya. "The Problematic of a Politics of Sexual Liberation: D.H. Lawrence's *The Rainbow* and *Women in Love*." *Studies in Language and Literature* 7 (1996): 57-87. *MLA International Bibliography*. Web. 20 February 2013.

McKay, Claude. *Home to Harlem*. 1928. Boston: Northeastern UP, 1987.

Nadell, Martha Jane. "Modernism and Race." *A Companion to Modernist Literature and Culture*. Ed. David Bradshaw and Kevin J.H. Dettmar. Malden, MA: Blackwell, 2006: 527-34.

Neumann, Erich. *The Great Mother*. Trans. Ralph Manheim. Bollingen Series XLVII. Princeton: Princeton UP, 1983.

Scott, Bonnie Kime. "Lawrence, Forster, and Bloomsbury: Male Modernist Others." *Refiguring Modernism: The Women of 1928*. Vol. 1. Indianapolis: Indiana UP, 1995: 162-86.

Twitchell, James. "Lawrence's Lamias: Predatory Women in *The Rainbow* and *Women in Love*." *Studies in the Novel* 11 (1979): 23-42. *MLA International Bibliography*. Web. 20 February 2013.

2

From Heaven to Hell—On the Desire-driven Transitions Siegmund has Undergone in D.H. Lawrence's *The Trespasser*

Billy Bin Feng Huang

Introduction

> Lawrence shows in a profound way that sexuality...is a matter of flows.
>
> Deleuze and Guattari, *Anti-Oedipus*, 351

For D.H. Lawrence, capitalism is the archenemy of human desire. F.R. Leavis believes that Lawrence is asserting his Lawrentian human values against his materialistic environment (*For Continuity,* 186). Here, his so-called 'human value' refers to the release of the human body, or the liberation of the human desire. In *D.H. Lawrence and Body Mystical*, Frederick Carter points out that for Lawrence, "his body was a mystically sealed document..., stamped with the superscriptions of the powers of bondage in the world. Above all, he was urgent to seek its release" (18). In his "The Therapeutic as Mythmaker," Philip Rieff perceives Lawrence's "belief in human erotic desires". According to Rieff, "what ties Lawrence close to an ancient reforming tradition is his belief that the decisive function in man is will or desire—not intellect" (57).

Capitalism and desire not only figure prominently in the Deleuzo-Guattarian tradition but also are two interrelated key concepts. Èric Alliez, in reviewing *Anti-Oedipus,* states that the liberation of desire will inevitably occur in capitalist society, and capitalism will in turn repress these decoded and deterritorialized flows ("Anti-Oedipus—Thirty Years On (Between Art and Politics)," 164). On the other hand, for Deleuze and Guattari, desire "produces connections and arrangements that are real in their function and revolutionary in their sprawling multiplicity" (Boundas, Introduction, 12). That is, for Deleuze and Guattari, desire should be liberated from the capitalist society, or even revolutionize it, regardless of the latter's effort to repress the former. In this paper, Deleuze and Guattari's desire-related theorizations will be used to account for Siegmund's desire in Lawrence's early novel, *The Trespasser*. My aim is to retrace the three from-heaven-to-hell, desire-driven transitions Siegmund has undergone in *The Trespasser*. After dialectically analyzing the intertwined causalities of the three transitions, I hope to get a new perspective on *The Trespasser*, a novel that has rarely been critically acclaimed.

Deleuze and Guattari vs. D.H. Lawrence: Desire, Family, and Capitalism

> From Hardy to Lawrence, from Melville to Miller, the same cry rings out: Go cross, get out, break through, make a beeline, don't get stuck on a point.
>
> Deleuze and Guattari, *A Thousand Plateaus*, 186

Lawrence binds desire, capitalism, and family together in a rather straightforward manner. First, Lawrence has stated, "The great relationship, for humanity, will always be the relation between man and woman" ("Morality and the Novel," *Phoenix*, 531). Barry J. Scherr, in his *D.H. Lawrence Today*, praises Lawrence as "the priest of love, the great sexual liberator, the love rebel" (405). In *The History of Sexuality,* Michel Foucault, quoting Lawrence, says that it is now a priority to realize sex. "Today the full conscious realization of sex is even more important than the act itself" (157). In addition, Peter Widdowson has observed that Lawrence spares no effort in "articulating life-values in a destructive industrial/materialistic civilization" and "rebelliously challenging and subverting...

the repressions and conventions of bourgeois society" (*D.H. Lawrence*, Introduction, 4). That is, Lawrence is convinced that capitalism has perpetrated a major crime of repressing mankind's natural desire for sexuality. Hence, he has never ceased to argue that human relations should be naturalized, and that above all, falsified ethics in this industrialized society should be transcended.

As for the family, Lawrence's distaste for marriage is rather evident. In *Women in Love* he writes:

> The hot narrow intimacy between man and wife was abhorrent.... It was a whole community of mistrustful couples insulated in private houses or private rooms, always in couples, and no further life, no immediate, no disinterested relationship admitted: a kaleidoscope of couples, disjoined, separatist, meaningless entities of married couples. (226)

Interestingly, Freidrich Nietzsche, almost in the same vein, gives a similar comment on marriage, "Reverence for each other, as for those willing with such a will, is what I name marriage.... Alas, this poverty of the soul in pair! Alas, this filth of the soul in pair! Alas, this wretched contentment in pair! Marriage they call this,...these animals entangled in the heavenly net" (*The Portable Nietzsche*, 182). Daniel J. Schneider explains the parallelism of their viewpoints on marriage, "both men (*Lawrence and Nietzsche*) are distrustful of conventional love and marriage, which threaten to destroy the heroic soul in the 'greater man'" (*D.H. Lawrence,* 48, *italics mine*). This is why a bunch of Lawrence's novels, such as *The Trespasser*, *Lady Chatterley's Lover*, deal with the motif of familial escape.[1]

Deleuze and Guattari have a much more sophisticated way of clustering together their ideas of desire, capitalism, and family. However, here I intend to condense their complex theorizations into a few main points. First, as we know, Deleuze and Guattari have articulated their outcry against the Lacanian idea that desire originates from a lack. Instead, they argue that desire should be viewed from a machinic perspective:

> Desire does not lack anything; it does not lack its object.... Desire and its object are one and the same thing: the machine, as a machine of a machine, and the object of desire is another machine connected to it.... Lack is a counter effect of desire; it is deposited, distributed, vacuolized within a real that is natural and social (*Anti-Oedipus,* 26-27).

Then Deleuze and Guattari further put forward their conceptions of desiring-machines and desiring-production. In the case of the former, Deleuze and Guattari believe that they are "binary machines, obeying a binary law or set of rules governing associations: one machine is always coupled with another" (5). And from this machinic assemblage, as Deleuze and Guattari would call it, desiring-production flows (6). Afterwards, Deleuze and Guattari have theorized tremendously about desiring machines and desiring production. However, my emphasis is how desiring production can be juxtaposed with social production. First of all, speaking of production, Althusser and Balibar argue that "mode of production" is fundamentally a "relation between relations" (*Reading Capital,* 224). For them, every mode of production is made possible by a network of social relations. Deleuze and Guattari apparently think it's the same case with desiring production, for they do say that "social production is purely and simply desiring-production itself under determinate conditions" (29). By and large, Deleuze and Guattari have combined Freudianism and Marxism, perceiving the similarity between desiring-production and social production. Even so, they are not parallelizing them unconditionally; they are more interested in how the latter represses the former:

> Psychic repression is such that social repression becomes desired...psychic repression is a means in the service of social repression. What it bears on is also the object of social repression: desiring-production.... The family is the delegated agent of psychic repression, or rather the agent delegated to psychic repression.... (119)

Deleuze and Guattari point out that on the social and psychic levels, desiring-production is similarly repressed. Above all, this social and psychic repression operates through the agency of the family. In other words, the family is the locus where social production psychically represses desiring-production. Thus, family becomes a minion of capitalism, as Eugene W. Holland argues:

> Just as the nuclear family interposes the power of the father between the infant and the mother as its means of life, market society interposes the power of capital between the worker and the earth as its means of life. ("Schizoanalysis, Nomadology, Fascism," 85)

In short, this is the case scenario Deleuze and Guattari propose: capitalism assigns the role of the worker to the father of the nuclear family. In turn, the father exercises his power on his wife and infant. This is how Deleuze and Guattari have critiqued the Oedipus complex, or the process of oedipalization. For them, this is how social production designates the family to "the recording of social production," or "as a system of reproduction of the producers" (120). To be more specific, with the daddy-mommy-me triangle, the Oedipus complex ensures that the sociodynamics of the capitalist market can determine the homologous psychodynamics of the nuclear family (Holland, 85).[2] Only by then can the family be a fully productive unit in, will "appear to be due to capital...and seem to issue from the womb of capital itself" (Marx, *Capital*, 827).[3] As far as Deleuze and Guattari are concerned, the Oedipus complex is a capitalist myth they wish to explode, or a capitalist façade they want to tear down.

The above is a simple comparative framework of Lawrence and Deleuze and Guattari. Sketchy as it may be, it attests to the compatibility of the Lawrentian and Deleuzo-Guattarian traditions. (No wonder in exploding the Oedipal myth, Deleuze and Guattari draw on Lawrence's imagings of the mother, the fiancée, or the mistress, claiming that they are "dependents of Oedipus, even in their reversals and their substitutions" (366). Most of all, it proffers a solid rationale to my following enterprise of tracing the three Deleuzo-Guattarian desire-driven transitions in *The Trespasser*.

The Three Desire-Driven Transitions Siegmund has Undergone in *The Trespasser*

> A philosophy's power is measured by the concepts it creates, or whose meaning it alters, concepts that impose a new set of divisions on things and actions.
>
> —Gilles Deleuze,
> *Expressionism in Philosophy: Spinoza*, 321

There is no doubt that 'desire' is a one of the key notions in the Deleuzo-Guattarian tradition, and that Deleuze and Guattari have invested it with multiple meanings.[4] Therefore, sometimes it may be difficult to pinpoint its precise definition. For instance, Ian Buchanan, in "Power, Theory, and Praxis," claims that Deleuze and Guattari's so-called 'desire' may range from the length of skirts to the style of music (24). Philip Goodchild adopts a narrower definition: desire is a sexuality, and it should be located in sexual relations. He further points out that for Deleuze and Guattari, desire is a spontaneous attraction between heterogeneous terms resulting in the incorporation of each other into their modes of existence (*Deleuze and Guattari*, 41). Goodchild's definition explains why Deleuze and Guattari's desire-related theorizations are especially applicable to the treatment of a text dealing with erogenous relationships, such as *The Trespasser.*

One crucial aspect of the Deleuzo-Guattarian politics of desire is the liberation and deterritorialization of desire. In *Anti-Oedipus*, Deleuze and Guattari describe such a case scenario, "...at times, the movement through which desiring-production is continually overcoming the limit, becoming deterritorialized, causing its flows to escape, going beyond the threshold of representation..." (313). Torkild Thanem and Stephen Linstead agree that desire can be liberated or deterritorialized, "Power then operates through stratification and conjugation whilst connection destratifies as it occasions mutual deterritorialisation between desire—literally releasing them into each other" ("The Trembling Organization," 46). Likewise, Goodchild first emphasizes Deleuze and Guattari's aim to "liberate desire by reinvesting it within the social formation that produced it".

Then he claims that a deterritorialized desire "leaves behind the constant nature given by its previous strata in order to cross a boundary and become something entirely different" (146). In a sense, for Deleuze and Guattari, as desire breaks loose from its previous social strata or relations, it is liberated and deterritorialized. From this point emerges the possibility of the politics of desire.

In *The Trespasser*, Siegmund has doubtless liberated his desire and deterritorialized himself. In the beginning of *The Trespasser,* Helena "had come as a pupil to Siegmund, first as a friend of the household...then the two went walks together... (until) he [*Siegmund*] had lost himself to her" (18). Eventually, a week later, when he lay resting his head on her lap, in Richmond Park, she said:

> "You are so tired, Siegmund." She stroked his face, and kissed him softly. Siegmund lay in the molten daze of love...." You are so tired, dear. You must come away with me and rest, the first week in August."
>
> His blood had leapt, and whatever objections he raised... he allowed to be overridden. He was going to Helena, to the Isle of Wight, tomorrow. (19)

David J. Gordon is more specific. In his "Lawrence as Literary Critic," he points out that in his novels Lawrence actually challenges various social limits, which "are to be defined only by the points beyond which the soul and relationship lose their subtlety and fluidity" (20). Only by removing these limits can Lawrence "permit all desires their full natural expression" (28). Rick Rylance thinks that *The Trespasser* "dramatizes what became major Lawrencean themes, including the need to seek release from inhibiting social obligations, the discovery of personal authenticity through sexual passion..." ("Ideas, histories, generations, and beliefs," 23). Both their observations confirm that the liberation and deterritorialization of Siegmund's desire is thematicized in *The Trespasser*. By and large, freeing human desire from various social shackles remains a typical Lawrentian theme. Translated into the Deleuzo-Guattarian language, it denotes the liberation and deterritorialization of desire. *The Trespasser* is no exception. Siegmund, a music teacher, has fallen in love with Helena, his pretty student. At last, Siegmund succumbs to his libidinous desire and flies to the Isle of Wight. That is, Siegmund's deterritorialization ensues from his liberation of desire.

My analysis would only scratch the surface if I didn't take into consideration the circumstances under which Siegmund's affair with Helena occurs. First, Siegmund is a music teacher with meager earnings, and he lives in a shabby residence:

> The room was drab and dreary. The oilcloth was worn into a hole near the door. Boots and shoes of various sizes were scattered over the floor, while the sofa was littered with children's clothing. In the black stove the ash lay dead; on the range were chips of wood, and newspapers, and rubbish of paper, and crusts of bread, and crusts of bread-and-jam. (15)

Ai Min, Ch'eng, Cheng Wen, Wang, and Fei Yang associate Siegmund with capitalism. They have pointed out that he is portrayed as a victim in the machinic society, where art is relegated to merely cheap amusement (*The Trespasser,* Introduction, 7). Consequently, his insufficient salary can barely sustain his family or satisfy his wife, "who had been brought up like a lady, educated in a convent school in France" (20). Ch'eng, Wang, and Fei Yang have addressed a somewhat hidden issue in *The Trespasser*, namely, the value of money in capitalist society, and how it impacts the individual. In fact, S. Zizek thinks that in capitalist society, money isn't just a social convention but a physical embodiment of value (*The Sublime*, 31). That is, capitalism has physically equated money with value, whether it is the value of something or someone. P. Virno is more specific. He asserts that as capital turns to the productive power of science, knowledge, and communication, it must deterritorialize these powers as well, keeping them locked in particular locales (*A Grammar of the Multitude,* 37). According to Virno, the intelligentsia, like Siegmund in *The Trespasser*, can also contribute their productive power to capitalism in particular places, such as the opera house. Of course, their productive power should be measured by money. Virno's viewpoint can be compared with Deleuze and Guattari's:

> The person has become "private" in reality, insofar as he derives from abstract quantities and becomes concrete in the becoming-concrete of these same quantities. It is these quantities that are marked, no longer the persons themselves: *your capital or your body capital*, the rest is not important, we'll always find a place for you within the expanded limits of the system.... (*Anti-Oedipus*, 25)

By 'quantities' or 'capital,' Deleuze and Guattari refer to the profits one's labor can generate. That is, Deleuze and Guattari view money not only as a yardstick for one's value but also as a criterion by which one should be intepellated into capitalist society. In the case of Siegmund, the value of his profession, or even his whole existence, is determined by his petty earnings. In other words, in order to exploit his musical expertise for lucrative purposes, capitalism incarcerates Siegmund in his line of work.

This analysis only partially accounts for how Siegmund has ended up as a music teacher. Deleuze and Guattari call it the process of facialization:

> A child, woman, mother, man, father, boss, teacher, police officer, does not speak a general language but one whose signifying traits are indexed to specific faciality traits. Faces are not basically individual; they define zones of frequency or probability, delimit a field that neutralizes in advance any expressions or connections unamenable to the appropriate significations. (*A Thousand Plateaus* 167-68)

For Deleuze and Guattari, 'faciality' connotes a structure or a network of relations sanctioned by capitalism. It also prescribes a course of action the individual mustn't deviate from. To put it simply, it is purely a social idea. In *Difference and Repetition*, Deleuze defines the social idea as "a system of multiple ideal connections between differential elements," or "a social multiplicity—in other words, by the varieties of these differential relations" (186). As I've mentioned above, capitalism has given Siegmund a career as a cheap-paid music teacher. However, this is only part of Siegmund's facialization.

According to Deleuze and Guattari, he is also facialized to be a father or a husband. These identities constitute his "multiple ideal connections" or "social multiplicity," or Rylance's so-called "inhibiting social obligations" of Siegmund's, or the suffocating realities of his life from which he desires a flight. This is the root cause of Siegmund's deterritorialization. Chris Land thinks of deterritorialization as a means to reverse the process of facialization, "In this sense a deterritorialization of the human is an explicitly political move...rejecting the Othering process that enables the domination and overcoding of faciality on the human side..." ("Becoming Cyborg," 126). Siegmund's 'flight plan' is very simple: he explores the possibility of another identity. In *The Logic of Sense*, Deleuze explains 'univocity' as the idea that all events are compatible; they are "inter-expressive" (177). Foucault illuminates Deleuze's concept of univocity:

> The univocity of being, its singleness of expression, is paradoxically the principal condition which permits difference to escape the domination of identity, which frees it from the law of the Same as a simple opposition within conceptual elements. (Michel Foucault 192)

What Foucault basically means is that pursuing one's univocity of being is a means to escape one's dominant identity. This is precisely what Siegmund does. As if recoursing to the unvocity of his being, he escapes his dominant identities and pursues a different one, namely, Helena's lover. That is, Siegmund has de-facialized himself.

After Siegmund and Helena flee to the Isle of Wight, they eventually construct an Elysian world for themselves. For instance, one night on the islet, Siegmund utters:

> "It's the finest night I have seen," said Siegmund. Helena's eyes suddenly filled with tears, at his simplicity of happiness.
>
> "I like the moon on the water," she said.
>
> "I can hardly tell the one from the other," he replied, simply.

> "The sea seems to be poured out of the moon, and rocking in the hands of the coast. They are all one, just as your eyes and hands what you say, are all you." (40)

Then he says:

> "I feel at home here," he said; "as if I had come home, where I was bred."

She pressed his hand hard, clinging to him.

> "We go an awful long way round, Helena," he said, "just to find we're all right." He laughed pleasantly. "I have thought myself such an outcast! How can one be outcast in one's own night—and the moon always nailed to us—and the sky half her time in rags. What do we want!" (41)

Here, what Lawrence gives his readers is a typical we-have-each-other case scenario between two lovers. In "Psychology and Art in *The White Peacock* and *The Trespasser*," Schneider comments on this scene:

> A general law of psychic life in Lawrence's fiction is that love, under the right conditions, transforms the individual: the old self dies in the darkness of the unconscious, and a new self may be born, eager to adventure into the unknown and to achieve maximum of being. (288)

In short, Schneider believes that both Siegmund and Helena have taken their lives to a higher level as if they were reborn. It is noteworthy that Siegmund's rebirth is due to the liberation of his desire. In other words, what he does is more than letting his desire run its own course. He lets his desire construct a world where he and Helena are consistently connected with each other. In the Deleuzo-Guattarian language, it is the case of "the full Body without Organs". First, in *Anti-Oedipus*, Deleuze and Guattari have defined "the Body without Organs" as a mechanism that "serves as a surface for the recording of the entire process of production of desire" (11). That is, it is a virtual dimension where the production of desire operates. As for "the full Body without Organs," Niels Albertsen and Bülent Diken first gives a simple definition to this term, "a plane of consistency without which no social, mental or physical order would exist" ("Society with/out Organs" 231). Goodchild gives a more detailed account of it:

> The socius of desire, the full body without organs, recalls Deleuze's empiricism: relations are external to their terms. The social field is like a set of film images, and desire is the director who constructs relations through montage.... Desire dismantles the images, tracing lines of flight through new connections, in an attempt to... construct its own consistency and plane of existence. (203)

There is no doubt that Siegmund and Helena, flying to the Isle of Wight, have escape their "facialities," or external social relations. Most of all, their libidinous desires for each other have directed their new life, which not only gives them supreme erotic pleasure but also makes them feel as if they owned the world. From Deleuze and Guattari's perspective, they have successfully constructed their own plane of consistency, namely, "an absolute level at which all things are grasped according to the immanent relations that constitute them" (Goodchild 219).

Unfortunately, Siegmund and Helena's case scenario of "the full Body without Organs" doesn't last long. In Chapter 11 of *The Trespasser*, Helena realizes that "she must be slowly weighing down the life of Siegmund. There was a long space between the lift of one breath, and the next. Her heart melted with sorrowful pity" (82). This problem between them goes on:

> Then he [*Siegmund*] came to the hour of Helena's strange ecstasy over him. That, somehow, had filled him with passionate grief. It was happiness concentrated one drop too keen, so that what should have been vivid wine, was like a pure poison scathing him. But his consciousness, which had been unnaturally active, now was dulling. (85-86, *italics mine*)

Schneider has given his comment, "In her possessiveness, she [*Helena*] creates her dream lover.... Siegmund has relinquished himself to her; but her gloating over him in this ecstasy of possessiveness poisons the relationship.... Indeed, he is almost destroyed as a self-responsible individual..." (291, *italics mine*). Clearly, as Helena's love for Siegmund has transmuted into possessiveness, Siegmund's love for Helena has deteriorated into anxiety. Their once burning flame of romance has already become a burden neither of them can carry.

As his 'party' with Helena is over, Siegmund is heading back home. On the train, he is reflecting on his dilemma:

> But when I am, comparatively, free, I cannot live alone. I shall want Helena—I shall remember the children. If I have the one, I shall be dammed by the thought of the other. This bruise on my mind will never get better.... And Helena—I should have nothing but mortification. When she was asleep I could not look at her. She is such a strange, incongruous creature. (158-59)

For Siegmund, it is a lose-lose situation: his relationship with Helena has already become a tormenting encumbrance; that is, even if he stays with Helena, his wife will be filled with suffering and mortification. My point is that what has become of Siegmund is a typical case scenario of "the cancerous Body without Organs":

> Desire turns to repress itself because of the unbearable affects and intensities it produces; representation is ultimately a way of sheltering from unbearable affects. Primary repression is a functioning part of desire; but when it becomes unbearable, primary repression may turn back upon itself to repress itself....In practice, this means that an intensity will 'turn on itself' to 'repress' its social conditions of production.... (Goodchild 85)

Indeed, Siegmund's desire for Helena does grow 'cancerous,' beginning to produce unbearable affects. In the end, repression has become his last resort. Siegmund has no choice but to go back home.

After Siegmund's return, he is met with "the coldly self-righteousness anger of an injured wife" (Draper, *D.H. Lawrence*, 37), namely, Beatrice's contempt and hostility. His wife, Beatrice, keeps reminding him of "who is going to be responsible for your children, do you think?" (189), or calling him a "coward," a "miserable coward," or a "miserable thing" (190). Eventually, Siegmund thinks to himself:

> But Beatrice, his young children, without him—? He was bound by an agreement which there was no discrediting to provide for them. Very well, he must provide for them. And then what? Humiliation at home, Helena forsaken, musical comedy night after night. That was insufferable—impossible. Like a man tangled up in a rope, he was not strong enough to free himself. He could not break with Helena and return to a degrading life at home: he could not leave his children to go to Helena.
>
> Very well, it was impossible! Then, there remained only one door which he could open in this prison corridor of life. Siegmund looked round the room. He could get his razor, or he could hang himself. (209-10)

Tragically, Siegmund's affair with Helena ends with his suicide. Before I get into an adequate discussion of it, I must pick up where I left off. As I've mentioned previously, Siegmund's elopement with Helena is a deterritorialization, or a defacialization. On the other hand, as he breaks loose from his family, he has dismantled the daddy-mommy-me triangle in his family, which means that he has commenced a process of deoedipalization. For Deleuze and Guattari, the Oedipus complex secures the family as "the form of human matter or material that finds itself subordinated to the autonomous social form of economic reproduction" (*Anti-Oedipus* 263); therefore, Siegmund's breakaway, or deoedipalization, simply indicates that he has halted his social productivity, or that he is no longer an economically functional member in capitalist society. It perfectly explains why his inability to provide for his family can become a major concern that keeps haunting him on the eve of his suicide. As I've mentioned previously, the value of Siegmund's existence in capitalist society is assessed by his low income as a music teacher. Low though his income may be, the idea of becoming an unproductive individual genuinely terrorizes him into coming home.

On Siegmund's return, he has repressed his own desire and reinserted himself into the restrictive society and re-embraced the trammels of his previous relations. It is doubtless his reterritorialization. In one respect, Siegmund's reterritorialization is foreseeable from a Deleuzo-Guattarian perspective. Ian Buchanan states that according to Deleuze and Guattari, every deterritorialization will be accompanied by a reterritorialization ("Practical Deleuzism and Postmodern Space" 144). However, Siegmund's reterritorialization is more than a certainty. Roger Ebbatson in his *Lawrence and the Nature Tradition* observes the consequence of Siegmund's elopement, "*The Trespasser*, in his boldly erotic style, anatomises man's cutting-off of himself from the earth and his subsequent entombment" (66). By "his subsequent entombment," Ebbatson surely refers to Siegmund's suicide following his reterritorialization.[5] At the same time, he also suggests that Siegmund's deterritorialization is doomed. Graham Martin observes that in most of Lawrence's novels, the hero's disengagement is usually a crucial theme. However, "such a disengagement usually leads nowhere" (47). Interestingly, Martin's observation coincides with Todd May's viewpoint about the Deleuzo-Guattarian reterritorialization, or a line of flight (*Gilles Deleuze* 38). May warns us of the hazard of deterritorialization, "Follow a line of flight and you do not know where it leads" (153). Siegmund follows through his line of flight, and it leads him to his death.

In *The Trespasser*, Siegmund's family is the primary force that pulls him back into society, stopping his deterritorialization. Because the family is an institution subservient to capitalist society, we can say that capitalism has blocked Siegmund's line of flight. In *Dialogues,* Deleuze and Claire Parnet assert that desire "is in itself an immanent revolutionary process". Therefore, organizations of forms will incapacitate desire (96). Here, by "incapacitating desire," they mean repressing desire, or resorting to reterritorialization to compensate the merely relative deterritorialization (136). Deleuze and Parnet point out that deterritorializations may be of different magnitudes. Relatively weaker ones are bound to be neutralized, in which case reterritorialization usually becomes a principal weapon of capitalism. Manuel DeLanda reminds us that a "merely relative deterritorialization," or an unsuccessful one, does have a punitive consequence. DeLanda argues that any act of disobedience shouldn't go unpunished and transgressors must be made an example of, lest the morale of those who obey should be threatened ("Deleuzian Social Ontology and Assemblage Theory" 259). That is, after reterritorialized, the once deterritorialized individual has to face punitive consequence. This is exactly Siegmund's case. After his return, his punishment is effected within his family, taking the form of his wife's reproach and sarcasm. That is, his family has become 'a site of discipline'. This is because in capitalist society, the family isn't just a subservient institution. The logic of capitalism is fully inscribed in the fabric of the family. Functionally, it is a form of organization that miniaturizes capitalism society (Holland, 85).

A Recapitulation

> "Lawrence" has been something of a rallying point for humanists, unwilling to abandon the binaries of author and work, or psychoanalysis and literature, or form and meaning.
>
> —Earl G. Ingersoll, *D.H. Lawrence, Desire, and Narrative,* 168

So far I've dialectically analyzed the intertwined causalities of the three heaven-to-hell, desire-driven transitions Siegmund has undergone in *The Trespasser*. A recapitulation of them can certainly help me to readjust my dialectical focus. In capitalist society, Siegmund has been facialized to be a meagerly-paid musician and an unaccomplished father. Then, his encounter with Helena has motivated him to liberate his desire and deterritorialize himself. His quality time with Helena has taken him to the level of the full Body with Organs. Later, his relationship with Helena has gradually growing burdensome. Eventually, he has no choice but to repress his desire and return to his family. On the one hand, this is the case scenario of the cancerous Body without Organs. On the other hand, his return is his reterritorialization.

All in all, Siegmund has undergone the transitions from liberation to repression of his desire, from deterritorialization

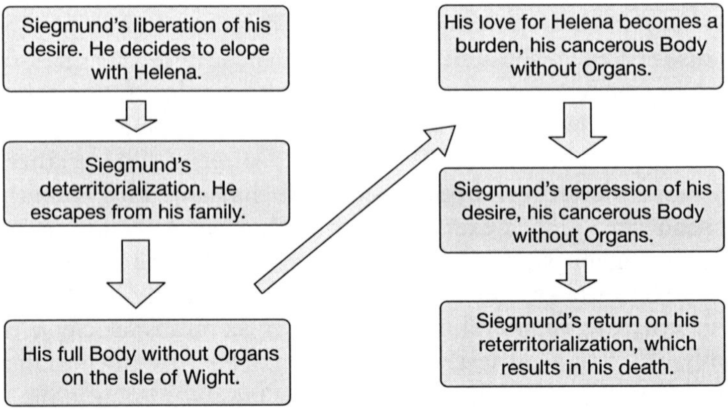

to reterritorialization, and from the full Body without Organs to the cancerous Body without Organs. The three transitions can be illustrated in this diagram on next page.

With this diagram, I have unearthed a Deleuzo-Guattarian subtext of *The Trespasser*, a novel that has rarely been critically acclaimed. John Worthen thinks *The Trespasser* is written only to impress. It should be criticized for its ostentatious prose or its lack of the mimetic density of realism. (*D.H. Lawrence* 23). In explicating the modernist counter-revolution against Wagner, Stoddard Martin thinks of *The Trespasser* as turgid, moody, and oppressively overwritten (*Wagner to 'The Waste Land'* 168-69).[6] Here, through a reading of the Deleuzo-Guattarian subtext in *The Trespasser*, I hope to construct an interpretive framework within which Siegmund's affair could be seen as an unsuccessful crusade against capitalism. Draper states that Siegmund, "a man of individuality, a musician and with a musician's temperament, revolting against the petty cares and monotonies of life with the woman he married at seventeen, wrenches himself free from her and his four children" (*D.H. Lawrence* 46). Tony Pinkney notices Siegmund's failed attempt to break free, and such a possible escape route will subsequently be further explored in Lawrence's later works, such as *The Rainbow* (*D.H. Lawrence* 54). Both Draper and Pinkney emphasize Siegmund's attempt to explore a possibility of flying away from the repressive social assemblages.

Above all, failure as it is, it must be glorified because it betokens Siegmund's courage. Schneider thinks that in *The Trespasser*, Lawrence, with "a scientific clarity," depicts the hero's "proud integral selfhood to fight against the dead world of convention" (*D.H. Lawrence* 120, 132). That is, in *The Trespasser,* Lawrence has presented to us an ordinary man's straight route of escape from capitalism, or his simple plan to fight the rigorous relations of capitalist society. As he fails, he is simultaneously martyred. This is how Lawrence critiques capitalism in *The Trespasser*. Tracing the three desire-driven transitions simply enables us to perceive the strength of Lawrence's critique.

Conclusion

I read Lawrence of course as an English novelist.

—Raymond Williams,
The English Novel:
From Dickens to Lawrence

In *Gilles Deleuze: An Apprenticeship in Philosophy,* Michael Hardt traces some of the Deleuzean thinking back to Spinoza. According to Spinoza, a between-body encounter can be characterized by two passive affections, joyful passive affections and sad passive affections. In the case of the former, one meets a body with compatible internal relationships; in the case of the latter, it's quite the reverse (93-94). Hardt tells us that Deleuze, drawing on Spinoza, centralizes desire should operate between two individuals. Lawrence, one of the most English novelists for Raymond Williams, also tends to thematicize how erotic desire is repressed in the capitalist society of England. In *The Trespasser*, Siegmund has an affair with Helena, and finally, he elopes with her. From a Deleuzo-Guattarian perspective, behind his elopement are actually three heaven-to-hell, desire-driven transitions: his transitions from liberation to repression of his desire, from deterritorialization to reterritorialization, and from the full Body without Organs to the cancerous Body without Organs. Once we dialectically analyze their interrelationships, we can see how Lawrence attacks capitalism in *The Trespasser*.

Notes

1. For instance, George Levine, in "*Lady Chatterley's Lover,*" regards Clifford Chatterley as "a construction of modern civilization." Then he states, "Clifford's world is the world of the machine." This world is "merely an animated corpse; the world belonging to the irrational and mythic energies of nature...is the only truly human reality". That is, Levine suggests that the conventional marriage in Lady Chatterley's Lover is a rigorous and lifeless formality that deserves to be dismantled. See George Levine, "*Lady Chatterley's Lover,*" *D.H. Lawrence*. Ed by Harold Bloom (New York: Chelsea House Publishers, 1985): 234.
2. Similarly, Guattari and Antonio Negri have illuminated on the Oedipus complex in a similar manner. They assert that capitalism uses it as a way to inject antiproduction into every private sphere, such as the family. Thus, desire will be invested as the only available mode of production. See Felix Guattari and Antonio Negri. *Communists Like Us*. Trans. by Michael Ryan (New York: Semiotext(e), 1990): 25.
3. In terms of the relationship between production and capital, Marx, in his *Grundrisse,* has said that no production is possible without an instrument of production, and that capital is also an instrument of production. "Therefore, capital is a general, eternal relation of nature." See Karl Marx, *Grundriss,* Trans. by Martin Nicolaus (Middlesex: Penguin, 1973): 86.
4. Speaking of the creation of concepts, John Marks, in *Gilles Deleuze: Vitalism and Multiplicity,* notes that for Deleuze, "philosophy always arises out of concrete historical problems." Eugene Holland, in "Karl Marx," points out that in Deleuze's opinion, "'concept-creation' involves responding to problems arising outside philosophy, by adapting selected concepts and new elements to new situations". See John Marks, *Gilles Deleuze: Vitalism and Multiplicity* (London: Pluto Press, 1998): 42. And Eugene W. Holland, "Karl Marx," *Deleuze's Philosophical Lineage.* Ed. by Graham Jones and Jon Roffe (Edinburgh: Edinburgh University Press, 2009): 148.
5. John E. Stoll ascribes Siegmund's suicide to his failure to retain his masculine identity and survive. In his opinion, the root cause of Siegmund's tragedy is his passivity. See John E. Stoll, *The Novels of D.H. Lawrence: A Search for Integration* (Columbia: University of Missouri Press, 1971): 45-46.

6. Of course, some critics also think that such negative criticism doesn't do *The Trespasser* justice. For instance, Melvyn Bragg, quoting the *Westminster* review, thinks "*The Trespasser* remains a book of extraordinary beauty and power". See Melvyn Bragg, Introduction, *The Trespasser* (Frogmore: Granada Publishing, 1982): xv.

Works Cited

Ai Min, Ch'eng, Cheng Wen, Wang, and Fei Yang. Introduction, trans *The Trespasser.* By D.H. Lawrence. Taipei: Lin Yu Cultural Enterprise, 1995: 1-6.

Alliez, Éric. "*Anti-Oedipus*—Thirties Years On (Between Art and Politics)." *Deleuze and the Social.* Ed Martin Fugsang and Bent Meier SØrensen. Edinburgh University Press, 2006: 151-68.

Althusser, Louis and Etienne Balibar. *Reading Capital*, trans. B. Brewster. London: New Left Books. 1970.

Bragg, Melvyn. Introduction, *The Trespasser.* By D.H. Lawrence. Ed Elizabeth Mansfield. New York: Cambridge University Press, 1981: vii-xvi.

Bouchard, Donald F. ed *Michel Foucault: Language, Counter-Memory, Practice.* By Michel Foucault, trans. Bouchard and Sherry Simon. Ithaca: Cornell University Press, 1977.

Boundas, Constantin V. Introduction. *The Deleuze Reader.* Ed Boundas. New York: Columbia University Press, 1993: 1-23.

Buchanan, Ian. "Practical Deleuzism and Postmodern Space."*Deleuze and the Social.* Ed Martin Fugsang and Bent Meier SØrensen. Edinburgh University Press, 2006: 135-50.

———. "Power, Theory, and Praxis."*Deleuze and Politics.* Ed Buchanan and Nicholas Thoburn. Edinburgh: Edinburgh University Press, 2008.

Carter, Frederick. *D.H. Lawrence and Body Mystical.* London: Dennis Archer, 1932.

Deleuze, Gilles, and C. Parnet. *Dialogues,* trans. H. Tomlinson and B. Habberjam. New York: Columbia, 1987.

Deleuze, Gilles, and Félix Guattari. *Anti-Oedipus: Capitalism and Schizophrenia,* trans. R. Hurley, M. Seem and H.R. Lane. Minneapolis: University of Minnesota Press, 1983.

———. *A Thousand Plateaus,* trans. Brian Massaumi. Minneapolis: University of Minnesota Press, 1987.

Deleuze, Gilles. *Expressionism in Philosophy: Spinoza,* trans Martin Joughin. New York: Zone Books, 1990.

———. *Difference and Repetition,* trans. Paul Patton. New York: Columbia, 1994.

DeLanda, Manuel. "Deleuzian Social Ontology and Assemblage Theory."*Deleuze and the Social.* Ed Martin Fugsang and Bent Meier SØrensen. Edinburgh University Press, 2006: 250-65.

Draper, R.P. *D.H. Lawrence.* New York: St. Martin Press, 1964.

———. *D.H. Lawrence: The Critical Heritage.* New York: Barnes & Noble, 1970.

Ebbatson, Roger. *Lawrence and the Nature Tradition.* Sussex: Harvester Press, 1980.

Foucault, Michel. *The History of Sexuality,* vol. I, trans. Robert Hurley. New York: Pantheon Books, 1978.

Goodchild, Philip. *Deleuze and Guattari: An Introduction to the Politics of Desire.* London: Sage Publications, 1996.

Gordon, David. "Lawrence as Literary Critic." *D.H. Lawrence.* Ed Harold Bloom. New York: Chelsea House Publishers, 1986: 19-29.

Guattari, Felix, and Antonio Negri. *Communists Like Us,* trans Michael Ryan. New York: Semiotext(e), 1985.

Hardt, Micheal. *Gilles Deleuze: An Apprenticeship in Philosophy.* London: UCL Press, 1993.

Holland, Eugene W. "Schizoanalysis, Nomadology, Fascism."*Deleuze and Politics.* Ed Ian Buchanan and Nicholas Thoburn. Edinburgh: Edinburgh University Press, 2008.

———. "Karl Marx." Deleuze's Philosophical Lineage. Ed Graham Jones and Jon Roffe. Edinburgh: Edinburgh University Press, 2009.

Ingersoll, Earl G. *D.H. Lawrence, Desire, and Narrative.* Gainesville: University Press of Florida, 2001.

Kaufmann, Walter, ed. *The Portable Nietzsche.* New York: Viking Press, 1954.

Land, Chris. "Becoming-Cyborg: Changing the Subject of the Social?"*Deleuze and the Social.* Ed Martin Fugsang and Bent Meier SØrensen. Edinburgh University Press, 2006: 112-31.

Lawrence, D.H. *The Trespasser.* Ed Elizabeth Mansfield. New York: Cambridge University Press, 1981.

———. "Morality and the Novel." *Phoenix II: Uncollected, Unpublished and Other Prose Works by D.H. Lawrence.* Ed Warren Roberts and Harry T. Moore. New York: Viking, 1970.

———. *Women in Love.* New York: Random House, 1950.

Leavis, F.R. *For Continuity.* Cambridge: Minority Press, 1993.

Levine, George. "*Lady Chatterley's Lover.*" *D.H. Lawrence.* Ed Harold Bloom. New York: Chelsea House Publishers, 1986: 233-39.

Martin, Graham. "D.H. Lawrence and Class." *D.H. Lawrence.* Ed Peter Widdowson. New York: Longman Publishing, 1992: 35-48.

Marks, John. *Gilles Deleuze: Vitalism and Multiplicity.* London: Pluto Press, 1988.

Martin, Stoppard. *Wagner to 'The Waste Land': A Study of the Relationship of Wagner to English Literature.* London: Macmillan, 1982.

Marx, Karl. *Capital: A Critique of Political Economy,* Vol. 3, ed Friedrich Engels, trans. Samuel Moore and Edward Aveling. London: Lawrence and Wishart, 1972.

———. *Grundrisse,* trans. Martin Nicolaus. Middlesex: Penguin, 1973.

May, Todd. *Gilles Deleuze: An Introduction.* Cambridge: Cambridge University Press, 2005. New York: Chelsea House Publishers, 1986: 31-58.

Pinkney, Tony. *D.H. Lawrence.* Hertfordshire: Harvester Wheatsheaf, 1990.

Rylance, Rick. "Ideas, histories, generations and beliefs: the early novels to *Sons and Lovers.*" *D.H. Lawrence.* Ed Anne Fernihough. Cambridge: Cambridge University Press, 2001.

Scherr, Barry J. *D.H. Lawrence Today: Literature, Culture, Politics.* New York: Peter Lang Publishing, Inc., 2004.

Schneider, Daniel J. *D.H. Lawrence: The Artist as Psychologist.* Kansas: University Press of Kansas, 1984.

———. "Psychology and Art in *The White Peacock* and *The Trespasser.*" *D.H. Lawrence.* Ed Harold Bloom. New York: Chelsea House Publishers, 1986: 275-96.

Stoll, John E. *The Novels of D.H. Lawrence: A Search for Integration.* Columbia: University of Missouri Press, 1971.

Thanem, Torkild and Stephen Linstead. "The Trembling Organisation." *Deleuze and the Social.* Ed Martin Fugsang and Bent Meier SØrensen. Edinburgh University Press, 2006: 39-57.

Virno, Paulo. *A Grammar of the Multitude,* trans. I. Bertoletti, J. Cascaito, and A. Casson. New York: Semiotext(e), 2004.

Widdowson, Peter. Introduction. *D.H. Lawrence.* Ed Widdowson. New York: Longman Publishing, 1992: 1-27.

Williams, Raymond. *The English Novel: From Dickens to Lawrence.* London: Chatto and Windus, 1971.

Worthen, John. *D.H. Lawrence and the Idea of the Novel.* London: Macmillan Press, 1979.

Zizek, S. *The Sublime of Ideology.* New York: Verso, 1989.

3

Character and Metonymic Colonialism in D.H. Lawrence's *The Rainbow*

Mbuh Tennu Mbuh

Introduction: *Sons and Lovers* and Colonial Feelers

Sometime in 2006 I attended a D.H. Lawrence Society evening in Eastwood, during which Professor Neil Roberts gave a talk on "Lawrence and Mexico"—a logical follow up to his work, *D.H. Lawrence, Travel and Cultural Difference* in which mention of India is peripheral at best, even when there are insightful references to the parallel writings of E.M. Forster and Rudyard Kipling. This "neglect" may be explained by the fact that the subcontinent does not fall into Lawrence's formal travel itinerary, and so further explains why Roberts refers to Ceylon—which was synonymous to Lawrence's Indo-vision at the point of fleeing from Europe—only in relation to Lawrence's ideas about Mexico. Besides, Roberts seems not to see any correlation between travel, at least for Lawrence, and the British Empire of which India was a major location. After the talk, I was introduced to Professor Roberts by my PhD research co-supervisor, Dr Sean Matthews, who was also the Director of the D.H. Lawrence Centre at the University of Nottingham. During our brief chat Professor Roberts wanted to know from me if there was evidence of postcolonial activity in *Sons and Lovers*. I was slightly startled because of the obvious domestic and national outlook of the novel, which my research interest had suggestively appropriated, with the rest of Lawrence's oeuvre, into a postcolonial frame. Yet, it is possible, as I pointed out eventually in my thesis, that Lawrence was already exploring the English peripheries, so to speak, of the colonial mentality, in which case we even have to go back to his first novel, *The White Peacock*, to find evidence of how the rest of his writing was an obsession with how the movement from feudalism into industrial capitalism at home exhausted itself and sought new energies from beyond Europe. The shift in Lawrence's early writing from feudalism to industrial capitalism is thus perceptive mainly because industry and not land became the marker of difference—difference that was neither domesticated nor defined within communal confines. The rise of the industrial class posed a greater threat to social harmony because of its aggressive propaganda that colluded with the colonial agenda; that is, a new and more pervasive form of subjugation of the masses beyond national boundaries.

In this case, while Lawrence is not really a colonial writer, and by implication, not even a writer of empire—in the sense in which we will read Rudyard Kipling—colonial and imperial themes fuse into a complicated trajectory in his work and give it another unique character in modernist experimentation. Unlike formal colonial writing which stages the voice of an emerging western hemisphere creating spaces of convenience for itself elsewhere, the Lawrentian complication instead indicts colonial historiography and its narcissistic influence. That voice in colonial literature is naturally arrogant, caught up in its self-blinding conceit and the inability to imagine parallel worlds that may be superior to its vision. Colonial writing disclaims nothing within its consciousness, and fosters a replication of its identity across the prospected territory. Lawrence was opposed to this foisting consciousness, and even his valediction of Englishness can hardly be sustained as a form of Kiplinesque jingoism. In his novels, vestiges of this personality abound, but are characteristically undercut by the narrative.

The elastic definition of postcolonialism today, by which its "anti" sentiments accommodate diverse constituencies even within cosmopolitan strongholds, makes Lawrence a pioneer in many ways, not least because he bracketed the fates of Africa and India into a single personality, that of Anton Skrebensky in *The Rainbow*. A metonymic character in Lawrence's work, Skrebensky personifies both the perverse propaganda of empire and its wilting manhood, and makes it possible for even the early Lawrence to be postcolonially interesting. *Sons and Lovers* (together with the more tentative *The White Peacock*) can thus be considered as Lawrence's depiction of English civilisation on the verge of embryonic changes that either influenced or were themselves conditioned by England's colonial ambitions. Accordingly, Lawrence's writing becomes a blend of characters who sowed the seeds of empire and those who fought to prevent these from taking root. Because the former are in the minority—notably Skrebensky and then Gerald Crich in Women in Love—their colonialist dreams are destroyed or at least threatened by "mass" resistance to the dominant voice. As such, Lawrence, according to the implications of Elleke Boehmer's model in Colonial and Postcolonial Literature for defining the postcolonial moment, "critically scrutinise[d] the colonial relationship" and aptly anticipated decolonisation by "demand[ing a] symbolic overhaul, a reshaping of dominant meanings" (3). Lawrence's work, from such analysis, evinces anti-colonial sentiments from "home" as a strong subtext and thereby anticipates the "empire writing back" model of Ashcroft et al. His overall concern is to challenge the mentality that gave birth to such an osmotic relationship in the first place.

Sons and Lovers therefore offers a significant insight into the observed lifestyle that repulsed Lawrence and forced him to imagine characters who either strive for or recoil from the colony. While this imbalance formed the crucible of the Settler colony, it is clear that Lawrence recognised the practical possibility, if not necessity, of going abroad for a livelihood, away from home constraints of an increasingly inhibitive capitalist economy, long before he wrote *Sons and Lovers*. In the autobiography, there are passing but revealing references to King Solomon's *Mines and the Arabian Nights' Entertainments*, references which if read as allusions, describe Lawrence's imminent response to how the imperial space was being interpreted to the "home" audience. In *Writing Under the Raj* Nancy L. Praxton underscores this, when she points out the ironic manner in which John Burke's speeches countered "more familiar eighteenth-century conventions about the lawless sexuality of Oriental men and women that found expression in popular harem tales like *The Arabian Nights*" (37-38); just as "late nineteenth-century adventure stories marketed for boys began to shade into 'romances' written presumably for more adult male readers, as Rider Haggard indicated when he dedicated King Solomon's Mines to 'to all the big and little boys who read it'" (qtd in Praxton 138).

Very early in his writing therefore, Lawrence seems to have been aware of two solutions, which offered themselves to the hero who is eventually overwhelmed by a feeling of alienation: he either escapes for what Wright Morris refers to as "the true Territory ahead", based on Lawrence's concept of "the pure present", (156); or submits to death. I adapt Morris' view to the territory of empire, which was also the experimental ground for the development of the radical Lawrentian self. For Paul Morel, escape and death suddenly fuse after his mother's death when "his soul oscillated, first on the side of death, then on the side of life, doggedly," (*SL* 456); and then unable to patch up things with Miriam, he wonders about his destination and "what would be the end of him" (*SL* 463). Consequently, one of his most perilous struggles in the novel is to separate the death and escape instincts, and then disentangle himself from their grip. When he leaves Miriam for the last time, he wanders away, clutching at anything that will save him from the final fall. His "derelict" walk down the road is in fact a dilemma of choice whether to submit to death or stray from a society that no longer has personal meaning for him. When he turns back toward the city, he at once rejects the ease, if not cowardice, of surrendering to death, and of leaving say for the colony. It is a "victory", which only Mellors will repeat, in a different context, in Lawrence's novels. In-between *Sons and Lovers* and *Lady Chatterley's Lover*, Aaron (*Aaron's Rod*), Richard (*Kangaroo*) and Birkin (*Women in Love*) unconvincingly and—for themselves—unsatisfactorily enact the escape alternative, while Gerald fulfils the death wish.

To move from *Sons and Lovers* to *The Rainbow* in this manner is also to see Skrebensky as a continuation of the tradition of the imperial hero in English fiction, with Lawrence as its unwilling inheritor. Generally, however, critics read

Skrebensky as a dispensable complement to Ursula's identity, and point out how "it would strain the ingenuity of any reader to find a rainbow or even an arch or doorway of any sort in the sparse account of Anton Skrebensky's ignominious marriage to an unnamed colonel's daughter at the very time that Ursula, his long-term lover, is probably pregnant" (Virginia Hyde 15). This is the general trend of anti-Skrebensky criticism, in which his personality is submerged in Ursula's, and ends where their partnership crumbles. In Lawrence's *Men and Women* Sheila Macleod asserts: "It is Skrebensky's lack of belief in himself which leads to his addictive, helpless behaviour and in turn to his destruction. Skrebensky has been asking for it, Ursula only acting according to the obverse side of her womanliness in response" (156). But such overstretched conclusions which vindicate Ursula are instead more applicable to the much later Gerald-Gudrun relationship in *Women in Love*. For all his flaws, Skrebensky is as much a victim as he is honest with himself—or lack of self. His "destruction" at the end of the novel is only partial, and not as fatal as Gerald's, probably because the one is still initiating what the other is already evidence of.

Yet, what is "destroyed" in Skrebensky is a component of his personality that easily adapts to social convenience. Similarly, Nicholas Marsh draws an analogy between Lot in the Bible and Skrebensky, and concludes: "...the consequences of Lot's story make an added, bitter reflection on Anton's character: the remainder of Lot's life produces only evil and perversion, as he lies with his two daughters in drunkenness, producing children born out of incest. This suggests a scathing and disgusted comment on the nullified, unproductive future Anton goes into at the end of the novel: his empty dedication to the army, and his makeweight marriage of convenience to the colonel's daughter" (155-56). There is hardly any evidence, beyond Ursula's scepticism, to prove that Skrebensky's future is "nullified, unproductive", while his ultra-patriotic spirit may indicate, without really affirming it, "his empty dedication to the army". He and his interests have largely been confined to Ursula's vaulting sensibilities, to demonstrate what Hyde typically identifies as "Lawrence's intended display of the marriage institution's failure to have meaning and thus to form an arch, like an ark, nurturing the future symbolised by the child." My preoccupation here will not be with the tensions generated by Skrebensky's incompatibly doomed relationship (although this will be implied all along), but with how these tensions become a stepping stone for his unknown and representative exploits in India. This is important because to read imperial structures in Skrebensky's preference for India also requires the filling-in of some spaces in the narrative, which thematically, Lawrence evokes without emphasizing.

The Individual, Nation, and Empire

In his "Introduction" to *The British in India: Imperialism or Trusteeship*? Martin Deming Lewis rhetorically underscores the controversial representation of India in England:

> Was British rule in India destructive or creative? Was its essence the exploitation and the impoverishment of the country for the benefit of alien rulers? Or, in contrast, did British rule serve to infuse a new dynamism into the hitherto stagnant and backward society, and to lay the essential groundwork for India's ultimate modernisation? (viii)

This bias juxtaposition of what the imperial mission covertly aimed at with the insinuation of what was propagated, is the relatively ignored subject of the closing pages of *The Rainbow*. To go beyond the predictable representation of Skrebensky, it will be realised that the civilising propaganda and the dispossession that accompanied it were part of the scheme that justified European expansionism. And, ironically, Skrebensky who personifies this ambiguity, finds his greatest strength where he seems to fail conventionally. Highlighting his inadequacy as a man and a lover needs to be balanced with the other side of his personality as the extended metaphor for colonial conquest in English fiction. He is the 20th century version of Daniel Defoe's Crusoe or Emily Bronte's Heathcliff, and only slightly less intimate with Conrad's Kurtz. Unlike his predecessors who portrayed character to underscore a change in one's "station" that sustained individual and national economic identity, Lawrence is very careful not to idealise the change. He instead shows it as directly implicated in the social, economic, and political conditions that the characters are engaged with. In fact *The Rainbow* and to an extent *Women in Love* can be read as anti-idealisations of the type of empire such as L.S Amery celebrates in India and Freedom:

> No romance can compare with the story of the handful of Englishmen...who, beginning as mere traders and merchant settlers, [had] in barely two centuries built up the majestic structure of an Imperial system under peace, order and good government are secured for three hundred and fifty millions of human beings inhabiting what is in essence a continent of its own. (quoted in Lewis, vii)

This praise is similar to Skrebensky's rhetoric of the patriotic citizen who is dulled by "civilised" conceits. His aristocratic background already poses a threat to the relationship he engages with Ursula only because he grows above his postcolonial ancestry. He has been brought up to be conscious of his origins and status, with the father not only adoring him but also communicating with him in Polish, a medium that is comparatively "archaic" and consequently more of a status-marker than the colloquial English language of his new home. As a "quick, observant, restless" child "with a glance of interest at everything" (*RB* 185), Skrebensky's preference for a military career is a logical follow-up to this upbringing—to embrace and serve the empire of his new status. Ursula therefore risks everything when she counts on her emotions as bargain with an aristocratic man of action who sees himself as the very personification of empire.

But it is also possible to see Skrebensky's affair with Ursula, and the way he treats her and she him, as the ironic realisation of the expansionist dreams of the Brangwen women. They are dreams that indicate the instinct behind empire building, away from the absorbing communality of the Marsh Farm. It is a juxtaposition of "the heated, blind intercourse of farm-life" with "the spoken world beyond," where the latter is projected as a "far-off world of cities and governments and the active scope of man". All the attributes that define the women's aspirations are masculine, already anticipating Ursula's frustrating encounter with the man's world. They visualise a world beyond the Farm in which "men moved dominant and creative, having...set out to discover what was beyond, to enlarge their own scope and range and freedom" (10).

Granted that such dreams could still have been realised within a humanly healthy context such as Lawrence later speculates in "Nottingham and the Mining Countryside," and Lady Chatterley, their further qualification makes them vulnerable to the muscling instinct that corrupted the colonial encounter in the form of "the battle...far off, being waged on the edge of the unknown" (11). Because the Brangwen men successively fail in this regard, it is Ursula who ironically shows the potential of participating in the man's world, with the hope of feminising it through a kind of mothering pedagogy. This is how her alliance with Skrebensky would have been an important complement in charting out the imperial route, if Skrebensky's fate to fulfil it was not diametrically opposed to hers. It is a relationship whose fulfilment, if it were to be possible, makes love a necessarily secondary consideration, and in fact only significant for as long as it gives the colonial encounter a homely appearance.

Realising these defects, Ursula counters the envisaged blurring of boundaries between woman and the (Indian) colony, when she is identifiable with the colony in order to justify colonial representations. What she resists is the intended transformation of her body into geographical space for a metaphorical "shallow penetration", as Loomba suggests, based on the "remote control[led]" colonial administration (111). As Praxton further remarks, it was the challenge from reformist groups to the "social and sexual contract that prevailed in Regency England" which transformed India into "an imaginative space where women's ideal place in the nation could be envisioned and where vexing problems concerning women's freedom, consent, sacrifice, and desire could be reconsidered" (38-39). The problem here is that Ursula is too unstable in her emotions to be attributed a definite social definition.

Their first encounter is something of a perfect match, emotionally, when Ursula seems to recognise a soul mate in Skrebensky. With his "very greyish eyes that waited until they were called upon, before they took expression" Skrebensky is an "unknown", which as Stephen J. Milko notes, "brings with him another set of Lawrentian motifs" (*Towards Women in Love*, 161). Ursula then has to seek him out, after which "[s]he felt proud, her spirit leapt up to life" (*RB* 269). Shortly after this they have a discussion about Skrebensky's profession, at the end of which Ursula makes her well known statement that he "seem[s] like nothing" to her (289). According to H.M. Daleski, this description is valid because Skrebensky "accepts his place in [the world] with a mechanical and unadventurous complacency" (*The Forked Flame* 108). However, like much of the criticism on him, this too is limited by its consideration of Skrebensky's "place" as a stereotype of social expectations in which Skrebensky "has no real identity" since "[h]e is content to belong, amorphously, 'to the nation'" (109).

This is where the other side of Skrebensky's personality has to be brought into the equation, to show that Ursula does not actually (as Daleski insists), "[strip him] of his essential nothingness" (112) postcolonially, otherwise he will not forsake her so terminally. Using Ursula's terms to define Skrebensky already condemns him, vulnerable as he is, to the subjective mode of her expectations. What she notices but refuses to recognise, as part of Skrebensky's personality is his excessive patriotism that overshadows his human character. He is the ideal personification of Rupert Brooke's persona in "The Soldier", hailing the possibility of death in occupied lands as the mark of patriotism. For Skrebensky, it will be an honour to sacrifice his life for the nation, yet to do this he fails to qualify as the cavalier of Ursula's dreams, one who "could get out, dismount into [the] enchanted land where nobody had ever been before" (*RB* 283). This is because the impulse in him does not see the love of woman and the love of country as synonymous, not even as complementary. Rather, the one inhibits full realisation of the other and the "nothingness" in Skrebensky—a convenient modernist-absurdist terminology—undermines the nature of the dominant force that pulls him toward more fulfilling spaces.

The difference between him and Ursula lies basically in the manner in which they learn and then adapt what they have learned to their changing environment. The son of Polish emigrants, Skrebensky's soldierly vocation makes him a robotic arm of the expansionist nation, and goes to South Africa to confront his fate. As an army engineer, Skrebensky compares his task to that of a nigger with a slavish enthusiasm that obviously sees any long-term romance with woman as unnecessary luxury. On her part, and partly sharing Skrebensky's ancestry, Ursula prefers a form of education through which she becomes impatient with the arrogant propaganda of colonial education. Innately, the distance between them can only grow, even when they are together, since the apparent mutuality is only the gloss of imperialism. Given Skrebensky's militaristic individualism and Ursula's insatiable expectations in opposition, even long before their final split, the two suffer from a protracted realisation that their essential selves cannot really meet beyond Ursula's unarticulated emotions: she suffers because of an inability to violate physical worlds, while he celebrates their violation as the very basis of his being.

Between the two, conventionally, Ursula lies to herself and to him more than Skrebensky does to her and himself, since she envisages a subjective attainment of "a self which is harmoniously reconciled between its male and female elements" (Daleski 112). In contrast, Skrebensky's preference objectifies masculinity and its manifestation in some physically active space like war or the colony, whether in South Africa or India. In this case Ursula's criticism of Skrebensky, that he was not man enough seems to be a contradiction of terms. She had earlier been jubilant that she too had contributed her brick to the structure that man was building, but suddenly scared by the expanding frontiers and emotionally stifling prospects of that world, she turned down Skrebensky's invitation to accompany him as wife to India. To be man enough for her privileges the "night goal" over a "day goal", and because Skrebensky is deficient in this, Ursula rightly (but also in an escapist way) sees his enthusiasm for India as inseparable from the perversity of imperial arrogance. If his movement to India is the logical conclusion to a trajectory from feudalism to conquest in the man's world, then it is a step that will provide only partial satisfaction, since it ignores, for Ursula, the complementary "night goal". Since Ursula's conception of the man's world is limited by her expectations, "demand[ing] from Skrebensky a kind of maleness he is incapable of giving" (Daleski 117), she is doomed to be collateral to Skrebensky's amoral strategy.

But Ursula also seems to recognise a rival to her love in the colony that attracts Skrebensky. The anger and frustration at his "failures" as a lover, like the indifference that results from jealousy, are worsened by Skrebensky's inability to assure her as expected of a lover and knight about to depart for conquest such as we see in the Cavalier poet, Richard Lovelace's "To Lucasta: Going to the Wars": "I could not love thee, dear, so much,/ Loved I not Honour more," (Lieder et al. 451). Ursula's final decision against even the lover in Skrebensky, results from this lack of chivalric acknowledgement of love through heroic exploits. Ursula's resistance can also be seen as the anti-feminisation of the colony then associated with what Praxton describes as, "an allegory of rape that defines Western desires to know the Orient and its people as revealing a universal lust for domination" (39), reminiscent of Edmund Burke's 1772 description of "the colonial relationship between England and India as poised between rape and courtship":

> 1767, he declared, marked the year when the "administration discovered that the East India Company were guardians to a very handsome and rich lady in Hindostan. Accordingly, they set parliament in motion; and parliament...directly became a suitor, and took the lady into its tender, fond, grasping arms, pretending all the while that it meant nothing but what was fair and honourable; that no rape or violence was intended; that its sole aim was to rescue her and her fortune out of the pilfering hands of a set of rapacious stewards, who had let her estate to run waste, and had committed various depredations." (Praxton 1)

Ursula dreadfully sees herself as a medium through which such schemes could be negotiated; and refusing to facilitate the transposition of such values, she makes The Rainbow to pose a threat to the establishment's programme. Thus, an alternative reading of Ursula's denunciation of Skrebensky's envisaged itinerary in India will reveal a significant criticism of imperial manoeuvres with which *The Rainbow* also concerns itself as a sub-text. If, as Daniel Albright notes in *Personality and Impersonality*, Skrebensky's condition at the end of the novel is one in which he "has been reduced to a shell without a core" (28), Ursula's vested criticism also acknowledges the one-sided nature of Skrebensky not as an end, a "nothingness", but a continuity no matter how perverse. Skrebensky feels incomplete in the social world and seeks the exotic as a means of reviving his vitality and ensuring his dominance.

In *The Dark Sun*, Graham Hough remarks that "[t]he attraction and the failure between Ursula and Skrebensky ought to be a mystery, but in fact it becomes a muddle". This is because, apparently, "Lawrence is trying to make some equation between the limitations of Skrebensky's mind and his physical failure as a lover" (69). As I have already suggested, this is a representative view from which we can expand on "the limitations of Skrebensky's mind". His failure in this regard demystifies the mystery and foregrounds his imperialist instinct, the only secure outlet for a "muddled" mind that has to define its reality as a self-conscious effort to appear as what it is not—that is, actively alive. The activity here becomes the appropriation of alien territories to compensate for the inadequate personal and national personality as embodied by Skrebensky. The colonel's daughter who easily fits into the formal space of a "Mrs Skrebensky" completes the muddle in a way which Ursula would never have been able to, and in so doing, according to Mary Procida, "encapsulate[s] the complex, often contradictory nature of the experiences" lived by the wives of colonial masters. For Procida, such women were merely wives, and not "independent career wom[e]n" and consequently, "intimate personal identification" with the husband's profession was also an identification "with the British imperial presence in India" (*Married to the Empire* 1).

Many critics have commented on the "darkness" that threatens Skrebensky at the end of the novel, even if it is limited generally to his libidinal instinct. While he encourages this conclusion by dreading the night and preferring daylight when he can vigorously engage himself conventionally, this is more of a confession of his nature than an acknowledgement of his failure or weakness, since Ursula passionately prefers a "night goal". The darkness, which Skrebensky dreads—that of his passional life directly associated with his bedroom—is an alternative to the wild, externalised darkness of the colony, which he replicates through his profession. Such darkness could be accommodated in ideological terms, but never really domesticated or, as Ursula hopes to do, possessed. The darkness which he craves ultimately demands a denunciation of emotional engagements that basically distract so that for him, Ursula remains "the darkness, the challenge, the horror" from which "[h]e turned to immediate things" (*RB* 447). The "immediate" describes his envisaged engagements in India, and marriage simultaneously becomes a formality of convenience to screen off "the challenge of his own soul". Love has nothing to do with his precipitated marriage, and the passion, which Ursula expected of him, will become a vital asset for colonial administration.

Skrebensky's contingent wife therefore provides a metaphor of how his colonialist/imperialist interests abstract matrimony into an "equation" where "limitations of [the] mind" and "physical failure as a lover" necessarily complement the stage-managed socialisation in India where she will mingle with other "subjugated" women, merely "get[ting] along", and dependent on Skrebensky's raised salary (423-24). This imaging of India as a space of colonial convenience is one where marriage is also perceived as a public commodity for Skrebensky. Yet, not public in terms of being "in range with all the things which nullified him, and from which he was…entirely dissociated", but rather as "his social wife [and]…part of that complication of dead reality" which transforms the "social wife" into "almost a material symbol" (419). Skrebensky is thus threatened by the loss of his conventional self, while Ursula wishes to freeze time and space, almost selfishly, in the Donnean sense of what now appears as an escapist bliss. This prevents or limits her participation in the darkness beyond the "tissue of romance... round them" and explains why her recurrent desire "to go" before now, was not related to physical space but rather to some indefinable zone, a complex of emotional and psychological space, always limited by inevitable interference of physical demands.

Metonymy as Cultural Currency of Empire

We can argue then that the individual who represents a centrist ideology such as Skrebensky, also represents the cultural currency which Lawrence challenges. While India is not part of *The Rainbow's* formal structure—considering that it marks the beginning of Lawrence's exploration of the imminent collapse of European culture which he was to conceptualise, however controversially, in more apocalyptic detail in *Women in Love*—Skrebensky's enthusiasm toward the subcontinent indicates how his own courtship of its "darkness" reflects the expected fulfilment he could not bring Ursula to be reconciled with; his verbalised manhood benefits the Empire, wherein he finds his fulfilment. As such India provides functional darkness for Skrebensky, a more militant alternative to that offered by Ursula. She has been "tempted" by India, based on consideration of the place as a "strange, strange land" but after rationalising her feelings she concludes that "India was no more attractive...than Nottingham" (439). And fighting in Africa, Skrebensky had remained a lively memory to her, but back in England Ursula associates him with "the new world...waiting for her" with him as "the key, the nucleus to the new world" (409).

The problem which arises from this, and which ultimately destroys their relationship, is their divergent definition of "the new world". For Ursula, it is the fairyland of her dreams personified by her idealised image of Skrebensky, whereas he knows the reality of that world as anything but romantic. His animal-like description "in a low, vibrating voice" of "Africa, the strange darkness, the strange, blood fear" significantly hints at the nature of this world, and the misconceptions attributed to it: "in Africa [darkness] seems massive and fluid with terror—not fear of anything—just fear. One breathes it, like a smell of blood. The blacks know it. They worship it, really, the darkness. One almost likes it—the fear—something sensual" (413). This is the "civilised" Skrebensky talking, and consciously he tries to rationalise the "soft and natural" quality of English darkness of which he is the perverse personification. His later attitude toward Ursula proves this, and like Conrad's *Kurtz*, he simply transposes this unto the African darkness in a self-betraying way, and becomes the perfect "key, the nucleus to the new world".

In his analysis of this passage, Milko qualifies the reference to "the new world" and its significance so that "in a sense [Skrebensky] is [that world], for Ursula must get to know the familiar beasts of darkness better. This far Skrebensky can certainly take her; he now has exotic African experience with which to tantalise" (Milko 171). The problem with such analyses, as I have already suggested, is the fact that Skrebensky's "darkness" and his desire for the dark beyond is essentially sexualised. To "tantalise" is a very limited appreciation of what can now be described as the Skrebensky mystique in the remaining pages of the novel, and consequently dilutes the impact of his imperialist personification. While it is appropriate to relate his sexual life (in terms of its inadequacy) as a complement to his zealousness to dominate "others", critics usually tend to over-emphasize the former. Yet, it will be interesting to see India (or Africa) as more than a mere referential piece of evidence of the other component of Skrebensky's personality. As Murry points out, it is important "to understand that the killing of the intrinsic male in [Skrebensky], and his unhesitating acceptance of service to the State, are complementary" (84). Here, the relationship will be that of Skrebensky and India/Africa and not, as is often the case, one of reading India/Africa through his sexual failure. Otherwise, Milko's reference to Skrebensky's "escape into secure banality" (181) only suggests, without finally underlining, the nature of his "banal" engagements.

The latter part of Murry's uncertain sexualisation footnoted above, as to whether the "darkness [is] beneficent, or... horrible?—creative, or destroying?" (90) suggests the potential in Skrebensky as a colonial administrator. According to Marvin Mudrick, "the bourgeois imperative...defended the materialist order against its gravest threat" in Anglo-Saxon fiction for two centuries, an "imperative" that was "against human normality" ("The Originality of *The Rainbow*" 56). This is where Skrebensky is handicapped, as he prepares for duties in India, trying to justify what is evidently abnormal. Ursula becomes his opponent and ridicules his professed goodwill abroad as nothing but bullying. She had already exposed what for her was wrong with the appropriation of territory, camouflaged as democracy, wherein Skrebensky, according to her, "will be one of the somebodies there":

> "You think the Indians are simpler than us, and so you'll enjoy being near them and being a lord over them", she said. "And you'll feel so righteous, governing them for their own good. Who are you to feel righteous[?] What are you righteous about, in your governing[?] Your governing stinks. What do you govern for, but to make things there as dead as they are here?" (427-28)

Such scathing criticism of the imperialist mission, which is complemented by Allen J. Greenberger's assertion in *The British Image of India* that "[t]he chief reason for the British to be in India was that it was their mission or their duty" (21), explains Ursula's rejection of the status of "being Mrs Skrebensky, even Baroness Skrebensky, wife of a lieutenant in the Royal Engineers, the Sappers" (439). Her anticipated position was partly the result of a cultural "proscription", which, according to Mudrick, "deprive[d] English fiction [of] normal women" whose "sphere of decision...in Western civilisation at least, has always been love and marriage". As a consequence, "the woman [who] is not permitted to take into account the most serious impulse of her private existence...may surrender to domesticity" (57). No wonder Ursula prefers to be simply "Ursula Brangwen, spinster, school-mistress". Thus, Skrebensky's failure arises from the fact that Ursula does not wait to be "permitted" before asserting herself; that is, does not wish, as Anne McClintock suggests, to "serve" the "ambiguous complicity" like most colonial women, "discreetly at the elbow of power as colonial officers' wives, upholding the boundaries of empire and bearing its sons and daughters" (*Imperial Leather* 6).

Critics have variously commented on the link between the First World War, consequent imperialism, and its impact, for Lawrence, on human relationship. In *Class, Politics and the Individual*, for example, Peter Scheckner draws attention to the fact that "on the verge of world war, British capitalism destroyed the basis for successful personal relationships within family and between men and women" (49). As such, Lawrence was convinced that "neither personal relationships, nor family, nor love, nor community could survive industrialism and imperialism" (56-57). These comments specifically address the action of the latter part of *The Rainbow*, its ambitions and frustrations. Ursula is key to dismantling this imperialist scheme and even if her effort remains at a textual level, it is still insightful to the way Lawrence was already envisaging an anti-materialist awareness in post-empire. In this way, Alan Friedman rightly points out in "D.H. Lawrence: Pleasure and Death" that

> the militaristic Skrebensky embodies all that Lawrence then hated about the masculinist culture that produced the Great War out of loyalty to "potent unrealities" like "the nation". The failed love between Skrebensky and Ursula is explained largely by passion represented as dominance and submission, triumph and destruction, rather than harmony and integrity. (210)

From here, and given the ominous future that awaited her in acquiescing, Ursula's rejection of Skrebensky anticipates anti-colonial struggles and exposes the logic of feminising the colony. Her denunciation blends into and counters what Ben Knights describes in Writing Masculinities as the "phallogocentricism" in "novels and polemical writings [of] an hysterically male (and white) supremacist programme," which culminates in the paradox of Lawrence's "account of masculinity" as "inevitably rais[ing] questions about the nature of male being and male power" (88). Ursula becomes the tentative representation of a consciousness that was to be radicalised against class and racial conceits by Connie in Lady Chatterley.

Conclusion

This complex characterisation in Lawrence is significant in relating individual relationships and the sexual politics which they engage in, to a diagnosis of empire. Skrebensky, who personifies the cultural evolution of England into imperialism, fails Ursula; but his failure becomes an analysis of the vulnerability of the type of maleness and its purported power which colonialism conceptualised. Skrebensky's significance here as a liminal character lies in the fact that he hovers over boundaries from which he simultaneously recoils emotionally, and for which he aspires "professionally". The one illustrates the failure of his "male being" while the other is a fitful attempt to assert "male power" beyond its relational application to woman in the masculine world of the early Brangwen women.

As the furthest realisation of such dreams, Ursula understands this complication in a rare moment of stiffness against the world of Skrebensky's unmitigated potentials: "why must she be bound...by the world?" (455). Her self-awareness also depicts an understanding of Skrebensky's dual representation, of which she possessed only half. The sentimental component of that world could not finally satisfy her own emotional and psychological drives, while the inscrutable soldier forever eluded her. This is a concession to and a critique of the man's world once it violates organic essences of the Lawrentian world and overwhelms every form of sentimentality. The situation between the two has reversed from its previous state when Ursula ridiculed the world-assimilated Skrebensky—hoping to rescue him into her emotional space—to one in which, realising the absolutism of that world, she instead fights "to be free of him and his world" (456).

Read as a novel that borders on colonial experiences, then, *The Rainbow* offers a different perspective for postcolonial speculations. It is concerned with individual experiences that overlap with and describe the established convictions of both colonial exploration and empire building. Inasmuch as it depicts Skrebensky's quest for and justification of heroic exploits in colonised spaces, the novel also deals with how he becomes the isolated victim of his desires in a more composite way than say Kurtz's unilateral representation. This characteristic in Skrebensky arises from Lawrence's ability to conceive of characters who accept and yet doubt, question and be questioned, and show their convictions as undermined by knowledge of the fact that the appropriated values of non-Europe are not wholly inferior. In this way, *The Rainbow* helped to generate, and still does, a counter-discourse that was/is disturbing to both centrist and marginal consciousnesses at liminal moments of "post" and "neo" isms.

Works Cited

Albright, Daniel. *Personality and Impersonality: Lawrence, Woolf and Mann*. Chicago: The University of Chicago Press, 1978.

Ashcroft, Bill, Gareth Griffiths, and Helen Tiffin. *The Empire Writes Back*. London: Routledge, 1998.

Boehmer, Elleke. *Colonial and Postcolonial Literature*. Oxford: Oxford University Press, 1995.

Daleski, H.M. *The Forked Flame: A Study of D.H. Lawrence*. London: Faber and Faber, 1956.

Friedman, Alan. "D.H. Lawrence: Pleasure and Death" in *Studies in the Novel*, Vol. XXXII, No. 2 (Spring 2000): 207-28.

Greenberger, Allen J. *The British Image of India: A Study in the Literature of Imperialism*, 1880-1960. London: Oxford University Press, 1969.

Hough, Graham. *The Dark Sun: A Study of D.H. Lawrence*. Guildford, Surrey: Duckworth, 1956.

Hyde, Virginia. "Kate and the Goddess: Subtexts in The Plumed Serpent," *D.H. Lawrence Review*, 26, 1-3 (1995-96): 249-74.

Knights, Ben. *Writing Masculinities: Male Narratives in Twentieth-Century Fiction*. Basingstoke: Palgrave, 1999.

Lawrence, D.H. *Lady Chatterley's Lover* (ed. Michael Squires). Cambridge: Cambridge University Press, 1993.

———. *Sons and Lovers* (eds. Carl Baron and Helen Baron). Cambridge: Cambridge University Press, 1992. (As referred as SL).

———. *The Rainbow* (ed. Mark Kinkead-Weekes). Cambridge: Cambridge University Press, 1989.

———. *The Plumed Serpent* (ed. L.D. Clark). Cambridge: Cambridge University Press, 1987.

———. *Women in Love* (ed. David Farmer, Lindeth Vasey, and John Worthen).

Lewis, Martin Deming, (Ed.). "Introduction," *The British in India: Imperialism or Trusteeship*. Boston: D.C. Heath and Company, 1962: vii-xiv.

Loomba, Ania. *Colonialism/Postcolonialism*. London: Routledge, 1998.

Lieder, Paul Robert, Robert Morss Lovett, and Robert Kilburn Root (eds). *British Poetry and Prose: From Beowulf to Blake*, Vol. 1. Cambridge, MA: Riverside Press, 1938.

Macleod, Sheila. *Lawrence's Men and Women*. London: Paladin Books, 1987.

Marsh, Nicholas. *D.H. Lawrence: The Novels*. New York: St. Martin's Press, 2000.

McClintock, Anne. *Imperial Leather: Race, Gender, and Sexuality in the Colonial Contest*. New York: Routledge, 1995.

Milko, Stephen J. *Towards Women in Love: The Emergence of a Lawrentian Aesthetic*. New Haven: Yale University Press, 1971.

Morris, Wright. "The Territory Ahead" in Granville Hicks, *The Living Novel: A Symposium*. New York: The Macmillan Company, 1957: 120-56.

Mudrick, Marvin. "The Originality of *The Rainbow*" in Moore (ed.) *Lawrence Miscellany*. London: Heinemann, 1961: 54-81.

Murry, J. Middleton. *D.H. Lawrence: Son of Woman*. London: Jonathan Cape, 1980.

Praxton, Nancy L. *Writing Under the Raj: Gender, Race, and Rape in the British Colonial Imagination*, 1830-1947. New Brunswick, NJ: Rutgers University Press, 1999.

Procida, Mary A. *Married to the Empire: Gender, Politics and Imperialism in India*, 1883-1947, Manchester: Massachusetts UP, 2002.

Roberts, Neil. *D.H. Lawrence, Travel and Cultural Difference*. London: Palgrave, 2004.

Scheckner, Peter. *Class, Politics, and the Individual: A Study of the Major Works of D.H. Lawrence*. London: Associated University Press, 1985.

4

Retrospect, Introspect, Prospect: A Reappraisal of Human Relationships in the Novels of D.H. Lawrence

Anita Myles

David Herbert Lawrence, a protuberant figure of the English literary world especially of the twentieth century unequivocally stated that the subject matter of his writings was essentially the relations amid men and women which could conveniently be elaborated as the man-woman relationships generally considered as power fights, family relationships and interactions among human beings within specific social groups. To quote from *The Norton Anthology of English Literature:*

> The theme of all Lawrence's novels is human relationships, the ideal of which he restlessly explored with shifting emphasis throughout his career; such relationships can be all too easily distorted by the mechanical conventions of society, by notions of respectability and propriety, by all the shams and frauds of middle-class life by the demands of power, or money or success. ("The Twentieth Century" 1734)

The discordant relationship between his parents resulted in adverse psychological effect on him. The indelible marks stamped on his personality as the result of childhood experiences get efficaciously reflected in his novels. W.W. Robson aptly observed that the childhood of the son of a Midland miner and a woman of marked character in a country village transformed by the mining industry provided the plot of *Sons and Lovers* (1913) and *The Rainbow* (1915), with insight into the emotional and moral problems arising between husband and wife and also between child and parent, in a working class environment.

Readers encounter the complexity of many concrete human situations in his fiction. *The White Peacock* (1911) deals with the conflict between man and woman; *The Trespasser* (1912) continues with his attack on women; *Sons and Lovers* (1913), an autobiographical novel focuses on the relationship between mother and son; *The Rainbow* (1915) and *Lady Chatterley's Lover* (1928) discuss sexuality candidly; in *Women in Love* (1920) he expressed his views about human life. As a child Lawrence witnessed the humiliation suffered by his father so he frequently wrote about the plight of men with little education or men who were dominated by women in their lives. Incidentally, a strong streak of latent homosexuality was evident in Lawrence which could have been the result of his observation of the life of miners. Mary Eagleton and David Pierce claim that miners under the pressure of their work cultivated a powerful closed community leading to intimacy among them. Lawrence made it more explicit by using a language which implied homosexual relationship.

Being conscious of the class division in society Lawrence's prose and poetry both assert his working class origin not only in theme but also in style specially the skilful use of dialect and the power to conduct an argument often contrasting the working class with the middle class. For instance, he observed that working class couples had violent quarrels, tended to sulk for long periods but soon compromised whereas middle-class families avoided rows though the basic emotions were missing. Due to the impact of modernization Lawrence pleaded for primitivism. Emphasizing this aspect in the novels of Lawrence G.S. Fraser observed:

> Lawrence's great strength was in instinctively putting a finger on what is alive and what is dead. His weakness was not allowing enough place for the life of the intellect in his total picture of man. Man is at once something more, and something less happy, than a harmoniously working animal. He is rational

as well as passionate and imaginative. In modern society he can no longer live by ritual; but he still dreams of Eden, and his dream, transmuted through an imagination like Lawrence's, help to keep him\alive (127).

Kangaroo (1923) and *The Boy in the Bush* (1924) substantiate this view where Lawrence used material from his visits to Australia exalting the values of primitivism and denouncing the artificialities of modern life. Apparently enough the characters in his novels project his own personality and view of life having striking similitude with their creator.

Throughout his career as a novelist Lawrence was concerned with the theme of either contentment of individuality in a relationship or its violation. In Lawrence's work satisfaction often involves the crossing of class and cultural borders, where the absence of fulfillment is frequently the result of resisting this. In several of his novels one comes across a woman in a relatively superior social status emotionally drawn towards a man of lower social rank, or in some cases towards a foreigner, obviously an autobiographical trait for Lawrence was born in this situation, he married into it and so inevitably this became his favourite theme.

The writings of D.H. Lawrence express his inner feelings—his frustrations, complexes and sufferings and as appropriately inferred by Graham Hough it is not erroneous to brand his work autobiographical. Lawrence's mother exercised a tremendous influence on him because due to the unhappy relationship with her husband she turned towards her sons and consequently the 'adolescent emotions' in Lawrence were warped culminating in recurring incapability of maintaining healthy relationship with the opposite sex. Once he remarked that he loved his mother like a lover believing that they had a bond of pre-natal origin which could never be broken making it difficult for him to find a compatible mate in any other woman. This aberrant love for his mother created a psychological imbalance in Lawrence. In every woman he sought the image of his mother and if he did find a woman of his choice he tended to dominate her. Diana Neill has rightly perceived this aspect in Lawrence's relationship with his wife, Frieda who was intensely possessive having a strong and even violent nature. Diana Neill elucidates:

> Lawrence was driven by his own neurotic disposition to seek in her both a mother-substitute and a woman he could dominate. Frieda was neither and their marriage gave Lawrence little peace of mind.... (273)

Undoubtedly, Lawrence suffered from an Oedipus complex in the Freudian sense though he tried to overcome this complex by recreating his past experience in his novels especially in *Sons and Lovers*.

Lawrence looked upon the modern civilized woman as his sworn enemy who could deprive him of his manhood. Since he had actually witnessed the sad plight of his father who suffered the over dominance of his wife, Lydia, Lawrence would get hysterically violent at the very thought of a dominating woman. This aspect is evident in his novels. For instance, in *Aaron's Rod* he writes:

> I hate her when she will make of me that which serves her desire.... She may love me, she may be soft and kind to me, she may give her life to me. But why? Only because I am hers. I am that which does her most intimate service. She can see no other in me. And I may be no other to her. (243)

The above lines substantiate Lawrence's view that the chief cause of all human unhappiness is the discordance and the disparity between men and women.

Lawrence desired human relationships to be evaluated and explained not only psychologically and imaginatively but also scientifically believing that these relationships are realistic and meaningful. For this purpose he employed Einstein's theory of relativity as a model. In his monumental non-fictional work *Fantasia of the Unconsciousness* (1922), the novelist dwells in detail upon his own comprehension of the theory of relativity applying it to explore human relationships. In the beginning of the essay, he avers:

> I am, but also you are you, and we are in sad need of a theory of human relativity. We need it much more than

> the universe does. The stars know how to prowl round one another without much damage done. But you and I, dear reader, in the first conviction that you are men and I am you, is owing to the oneness of mankind, why, we are always falling foul of one another, and chewing each other's fur. (72)

Einstein had declared that the universe is governed by one absolute principle emphasizing at the same time that life continues progressively in relation to several factors interconnected to and interdependent upon each other. Agreeing with this notion Lawrence proclaimed:

> But I also feel most strongly, that in itself each individual living creature is absolute: in its own being. And that the things in the universe are just relative to the individual living creature and that individual living creatures are relative to each other. (191)

Thus if man thinks himself to be 'absolute' or self-sufficient to survive in isolation, he is bound to suffer leading to the collapse of the entire social system. Being a social animal, as Aristotle stipulated for human beings, we must develop a spirit of tolerance and co-existence. Lawrentian doctrine reiterates this point that human interrelationships within the family or outside it be it between man and woman or man and man is essential for a happy existence and this supposition finds ample expression in all his novels. Gerald Holton comments rationally, "When literary critics use science in their work they make a new alloy" (30). Rachel Crossland has appropriately alluded in her paper entitled "What D.H. Lawrence Understood of 'The Einstein Theory'".

> The new alloy which Lawrence created in the early 1920's combining what he read of Einstein with what he read by James along with his own ideas on human individuals and relationships, was his 'theory of human relativity'. Lawrence's highlighting of our need for such a theory in *Fantasia* and the subsequent explorations of relatives and absolutes in relation to human individuals in *Kangaroo*, suggest that Lawrence did indeed find

> in his reading of Einstein the 'suggestive thought' that the latter had hoped for his readers, a thought which resonated in some way with Lawrence's own understanding and vision of the world, and of human relationships in particular. (31-32)

The critic's observation stresses that Lawrence combined his personal ideas with some existing novelistic theories and with Einstein's system in order to prove that proper human relationships can be maintained as a two-way process. In this connection it is also noteworthy that predominance of the subject of sex in the novels of Lawrence is not merely due to any glorification of sex but it has been utilized creatively in the context of explaining bonds of human relationships.

Initially the novels of D.H. Lawrence were considered to be obscene, pornographic and voluptuary since the English had not yet forsaken the Victorian prudery of the nineteenth century. However, Lawrence was not at all unnerved by such adverse criticism; rather he defended himself by claiming that he was writing about the facts of life asserting that sex was a source of life and its proper consummation was a spiritual experience leading towards the attainment of perfection. He was supported by critics like F.R. Leavis and Baker who stated that to Lawrence "not only was sex the way the woman fulfills her being and man of his chief creative functions, a reason for which he extolled marriage, but the sexual experience was the access to new realms of consciousness, an initiation into divine mysteries, the mystery of the other world that is close behind us".

The theme of sex as expounded in the novels of Lawrence received a proper recognition thirty years after his death. He was no longer regarded as a 'sex mad and homosexual fascist, a mindless and misguided genius scarcely worth the attention'. His novels were read and began to be appreciated in the light of the theories propounded by Sigmund Freud. Simultaneously, greater impetus became prominent for studying his novels due to extension of Freudian model by the doctrines postulated by Jung stating that the sexual experience strengthens human relationship, if the partners are compatible whether the experience is hetero or homo or marital or extramarital. In the Jungian principle, sex was neither immoral nor obscene; it was just a biological urge leading to closer affinities among human beings. In the works of Lawrence in addition to the influence of Freud and Jung, we can also locate a powerful impact of Marxian system as the novelist tends invariably to endeavour for establishing social equality.

A serious perusal of the novels of Lawrence reiterates the notion that he was much concerned about the issues pertaining to the interrelationships and interactions between human beings. Lawrence's first novel *The White Peacock* (1911) is autobiographical because Cyril Beardsall, the narrator is similar to Lawrence in his lifestyle and his view of life. Interestingly enough his mother was a Beardsall before marriage and the setting of the novel is Eastwood, Lawrence's own region. The unhappy relationship between men and women is highlighted in the novel. Cyril's close friend, George Saxton, son of a farmer falls in love with Cyril's sister, Lettie Beardsall. However, Lettie's marriage to Leslie Tempest, the heir of a mine owner emotionally upsets George culminating in his recoursing to drinking in order to drown his sorrow and his subsequent marriage to a common place girl fails adding to his physical and emotional ruin. On the other hand, Lettie's marriage with the rich man is also marked with unhappiness and frustration. Another love relationship portrayed in the novel is that of Emily, George's sister and Cyril though the marriage does not materialize.

Critics indicate certain unavoidable lapses in *The White Peacock*, for example, the major action of the novel concerns intimate exchanges between characters of which the narrator is not one. Cyril, the narrator appears to be a peeping Tom and an eavesdropper and though projected as the protagonist he does not participate directly in the action. Another flaw of the novel is that Lawrence chose the theme about a social setting of which he did not have any firsthand experience thereby the interrelationships of different groups appear to be artificial as well as unconvincing. Lawrence was better acquainted with the rural world hence the character of George Saxton has been properly sketched. Nevertheless, *The White Peacock* prepared the foundation of and paved the way for the later novels of Lawrence polarizing around humanistic themes.

The Trespasser (1912) concentrates upon the theme of extreme sensual preoccupation entangled with intense sexual frustration. It is not entirely an original novel but is an adaptation of a work by Helen Corke, his friend from London school teaching days. Lawrence describes the unhappy love affair between Sigmund, a violinist and Helena, a school teacher whom he teaches music though he is a married man. Sigmund celebrates a holiday with Helena in the Isle of Wight for five days during which this intimacy made him aware of Helena's sexual coldness. The propinquity comes to an end; Sigmund leaves her and commits suicide on returning home. The novel, in spite of its simple and weak plot was appreciated due to its poetic prose.

The fundamentally autobiographical *Sons and Lovers* (1913) was originally published under the title of *Paul Morel*. The life of Lawrence supplies the main nucleus to the novel in the sense that it deals with Oedipus complex which existed between him and his mother. Some critics allege that the theme of sex hovers around the author's association with Jessie Chambers as well. Paul, the protagonist is the son of coal mine Mr. Morel; incidentally Lawrence's father was also a coal miner. Like Lawrence Paul is portrayed to be attached more to the mother rather than to the father. The novelist has dealt with only those aspects of life in this novel which bring out the psychic elements of his personality and the conflicts he experienced in his personal life.

Sons and Lovers comprises of a well-knit plot. Mrs. Morel, a lady of cultivated and refined taste faces an unhappy and troubled marital life with her husband Walter Morel, a coal miner thereby turning to her sons for love and affection which was denied by her husband. After the death of her elder son, William she became more attached to Paul though this closeness had an adverse effect on Paul as such he falters to have a satisfactory relationship with any other woman. He develops an affair with Miriam, a young girl from the neighbourhood farm who awakens the artist in Paul. So far as man-woman alliance is concerned it tended to be unsuccessful due to Paul's greater attachment to his mother and his inclination not to be subordinated to another woman. Miriam was romantic, religious, possessive having several sexual inhibitions and these resulted in an impediment to the natural flow of her emotions creating psychic problems for her and influencing her relationship with other men. She never cherished love to be a natural emotion or a biological need but for her it was a 'religious obligation' to be looked upon with great sanctity. To quote from *Sons and Lovers*:

> Oh Lord, let me not love Paul Morel. Keep me from loving him, if I ought not to love him, make me love him.... But, Lord if it is Thy will that I should love him, make me love him,—as Christ would, who died for the souls of men. Make me love him splendidly because he is Thy son. (208)

Her inhibitions had rendered Miriam almost frigid. Snapping his relationship with her in the beginning Paul soon reverts to her attempting to initiate her into sexual life. He lives with her for a week but within this short span of time his passion is worn out and he suffers from a sense of failure. Ultimately, he severs his association with Miriam. Paul is equally responsible for the disruption of his alliance with Miriam caused by an internal conflict which makes it difficult for him to achieve sexual harmony.

Paul, then, meets Clara, a lady differing from Miriam in several ways. She is a married woman of thirty while Paul is only twenty-three. Their friendship soon develops into an intimate relationship though the intensity of their passion does not continue for long, hence Clara decides to return to her husband, Baxter Dawel. Paul found in Clara a woman who was too demanding physically yet he felt attached to her for comfort after his mother's death as Clara is considered by him a mother-figure who surrenders her body to Paul merely to satisfy her own physical needs. During intimate moments, she consciously compared Paul to her husband eventually discovering that Baxter had loved her 'a thousand times better' than Paul. Realizing

Clara's eagerness to reunite with Baxter, Paul helps her in that. Thus the relationship between Paul and Miriam was marred by the woman's extreme religiosity while that of Paul and Clara suffered as the consequence of her extreme passion.

After the departure of Clara with Baxter Paul suffers from a vacuum in life. The death of his mother made things worse. In his loneliness Paul once again thought of Miriam. One Sunday he met her at church, inviting her to his apartment he proposed to marry her which did not materialize. Paul is a lost man without the support of his mother unable to cope up with the harsh realities of life and happiness seems to evade him. Clearly enough the main theme of *Sons and Lovers* is personal relationship though the novel has an organic unified structure recording the lives of people in contact with each other. Regarding the theme of the novel David Daiches comments rightly:

> *Sons and Lovers* is a book about modern civilization as well as about forms and perversions of love. Indeed all Lawrence's novels are about modern civilization (and of course about other things as well). But for Lawrence problems of civilization must always be focused through problems of personal relationships, for civilization is just by the kind and qualities of human relationships it makes possible. (145-46)

The progress of the novel is chronological recording the ending of old relationships and the beginning of new ones thereby focusing attention on personal experiences as well as on the interaction among various human beings.

Carefully woven into the narrative are significant symbols. However, the use of symbols does not obstruct the smooth rendering of the novel. In fact a casual reader is unaware of the symbols. For instance, the coal pits mentioned in *Sons and Lovers* stand out as a concrete reality the entire community life depending upon them. At the same time they symbolize a particular way of life or even a specific attitude towards life. The coal pits have a close association with the life of Walter Morel. The unified life of miners reveals the novelist's conjecture that finer human ethics like unselfishness, compassion and togetherness exist in the lower section of society and among uneducated labour class, and the bonds of human relationship is their paramount virtue as against the selfish behaviour of the affluent classes.

Nature plays a vital role in the development of the novel being an active participant in the lives of the people having the power to arouse them emotionally. For example, when Paul and Miriam are together the orange moon incites erotic craving in Paul. Similarly when Paul and Clara are together on the bank of the river Trenton, the turbulent water enhances their infatuation. Thus objects of nature symbolize human passions. At other moments the rose bush witnesses the warm relationship between Paul and Miriam. The picking of flowers by Paul, Miriam and Clara signifies each one's attitude towards life. Paul plucks the flowers scientifically and puts them in a lively bunch; Miriam picks flowers lovingly but her bunch seems lifeless. Clara is opposed to the plucking of flowers as it destroys the life in them indicating that she has no desire to be 'picked' by any man.

Sons and Lovers a landmark in Lawrence's career as a novelist contains a successful fusion of the modern and the traditional elements. Beginning as a traditional novel it ends as a modern one. In the first part of *Sons and Lovers* the novel has a straight forward narrative with a well-knit plot and suitable characters. With the gradual progression of the story, the novelist probes deep into the minds of the characters. The modern element begins to show up prominently especially in the use of symbols, the emphasis on the psyche, the technique of impressionism and the glorification of sex. The sequence of events is chronological, no doubt, but simultaneously the narrative moves backwards and forwards as in a psychological novel. It would be quite appropriate to identify *Sons and Lovers* as a transitional novel, having elements of the traditional novel giving ample scope to the new impressionistic and psychological one.

In *The Rainbow* (1915) Lawrence overtly emphasizes the impact of industrialization on the human psyche flaunting its dehumanizing and destructive influence as well as its responsibility in the breakdown not only of the community but also of the degradation of the individual. Industrialization induced a gradual disintegration of healthy human relationships leading to the absence of unwavering rudiments to which the individual looked for sustenance. Before the rise of the age of mechanization a sort of communion existed between farmers and miners but soon workers became slaves of machines surrendering the finer aspects of human togetherness.

Located in the post industrial era, *The Rainbow* gyrates around the theme of matrimony stipulating as to how an individual can get fulfillment through marriage. Lawrence traces the history of three generations of Brangwens, all yeoman farmers living on the Marsh farm in harmony with nature. The men preferred the old way of life while the women of the family were different desiring change and anticipating the industrial growth to provide them with better alternatives of life. To quote from the novel:

> The women looked out from the heated, blind intercourse of farm life, to the spoken word beyond. They were aware of the lips and the mind of the world speaking and giving utterance, they heard the sound in the distance, and they strained to listen. It was enough for the men that the earth heaved and opened its furrows to them, that the wind blew to dry and wet wheat, and set the young ears of corn wheeling freshly round about.... But the woman wanted another form of life than this, something that was not blood-intimacy. Her house faced out from the farm-buildings and fields, looked out of the road and the village with the church and Hall and the world beyond. She stood to see the far off world of cities and governments and the active scope of the man, the magic land to her, where secrets were made known and desires fulfilled. (4)

The first part of the novel concentrates upon the subject of Brangwen women's anticipation of modernization then describing the changes produced by the opening of new collieries and the construction of a canal. Thus Lawrence tends to show the impact of the changing social scenario in England upon the Brangwen family. The men in the family are instinctive while the women crave for betterment.

Tom Brangwen remains on the farm though the other members of the family transit to the city and adopt bourgeois manners. Tom meets Lydia Lensky, the widow of a Polish revolutionary who came to live in the village with her daughter Anna. Tom and Lydia fall in love and are happily married. Lydia is six years older to Tom. Initially their married life is satisfactory but soon the two lost their marital compatibility becoming intolerable to each other. Anna grows up to marry Will, Tom's nephew. The second section of *The Rainbow* is devoted to the description of the conjugal life of Anna and Will. Anna finds great fulfillment in childbearing. Will too, is happy though thinks that his ambitions have been truncated owing to family commitment. On gaining maturity Ursula, their daughter disapproves of her mother's attitude to life specially her limited interests in the family. Ursula falls in love with a Polish young man, Anton Skrebensky, a kinsman of Lydia Lenski working as a subaltern in the British army.

The third section of the novel depicts the life of Ursula and Anton. Anton leaves to fight the Boers in a war and returning after six years finds Ursula a different woman who leaves him as he fails to provide her the fulfillment she requires, that is emotional stability as against his extreme infatuation. Ursula discovers that she is in the family way but her desire to get married to Anton does not materialize because he is already married to his colonel's daughter. Though Ursula miscarries the child she continues to be hopeful that someday her lover will return to her. This is when she sees a rainbow which becomes a symbol of hope and promise of a bright future as described in the end of chapter sixteen of the novel:

> And the rainbow stood on the earth. She knew that the sordid people who crept hard-scaled and separate on the face of the world's corruption were living still, that the rainbow was arched in their blood and would

> quiver to life in their spirit, that they would cast off their horny covering of disintegration, that new, clean, naked bodies would issue to a new germination, to a new growth, rising to the light and the wind and the clean rain of heaven. She saw in the rainbow the earth's new architecture, the old, brittle corruption of houses and factories swept away, the world built up in a living fabric of Truth, fitting to the over-arching heaven.

Lawrence believed that the root cause of the unhappiness and the suffering in modern life was primarily an offshoot of the maladjustments in human relationships more so because people were cut off from each other. *The Rainbow* as also his other novels does not offer sex as the solution to the vital problems of modern man, contrarily affirming that sex certainly cannot be the resolution to the issues brought forward by the complexities of modern life and civilization. *The Rainbow* naively suggests that men and women must rise above the level of physicality concentrating upon mutual understanding and fulfillment of the whole being that is both the flesh and the spirit together. Though *The Rainbow* typifies the novelist's entire concept of human relationships when he infers that sex relationship stands at the very core of man-woman relationship, yet sensuality is not the final explication of balanced and permanent human relationships. However, Lawrence is strongly against the idea that either partner should in any way be subordinated to the other for the sake of adjustment. Ursula Brangwen in the novel represents the individualistic spirit of the age. She defies the conventional idea of a woman's dependence and the consequent marital thralldom preferring to become a school teacher and leading an independent life.

Regarding the duality of theme, the following excerpt from W.W. Robson's essay in *The Pelican Guide to English Literature* is meaningful where he compares *Women in Love* with *The Rainbow:*

> But above all *Women in Love* is the more 'modern' of the two, the one in which Lawrence is more concerned with what we recognize as contemporary life. There is

> something of a pastoral, idealizing, idyllic quality about *The Rainbow*—at any rate, in the earlier part, before the advent of 'modern' life in the story of the childhood and the youth of the girl Ursula. That earlier part has a certain epic spaciousness which is unlike anything else in Lawrence. *The Rainbow* compares with *Women in Love*, in this respect, as *War and Peace* does with *Anna Karenina*. (288)

Women in Love discusses the life of Ursula Brangwen and her sister Gudrun. Ursula falls in love with Rupert Birkin while Gudrun with Gerald Crich. In the character of Birkin one finds much similarity with his creator Lawrence. Ursula had been searching for a man like Birkin and they appear to be happy together. In this relationship Lawrence's belief finds expression that the sexes must fulfill each other but when the woman begins to dominate, the conjugal happiness is lost. Birkin is critical of modern civilization upholding the traditional principle of male domination. Similarly, the relationship between Gudrun and Gerald is dissatisfying as the woman has a tendency to dominate over man. Gerald's parents had an unhappy married life because his mother contained an aggressive temperament whereas the father had a benevolent frame of mind. Inheriting his mother's ruthlessness Gerald suffers from an inner uncertainty, his nature is divided which is amply manifested in the manner he conducts his life revealing a tendency of desperate assertion of will. Gudrun resolves to resist Gerald's attitude and to set right their lives for which she confides in Ursula. Ursula is not sympathetic knowing that Gudrun suffers not being able to comprehend what love really is. Thus Gudrun and Gerald live a life of conflict throughout.

Incidentally, Gudrun meets Loerke, an Austrian sculptor while camping in a snow-bound Alpine valley. Loerke is portrayed as a highly symbolic intruder deeming that art and the world have nothing to do with each other. Gudrun also agrees with him though Ursula feels that 'the world of art is the only truth about the real world' but the two disagree on this point. Gerald feels isolated because of this new alliance between Gudrun and Loerke. During an argument Loerke gets annoyed knocking Gerald down. In his exasperation and frustration, Gerald attacks Gudrun just refraining himself from killing her and walking away in the snow. His dead body is discovered next morning; meanwhile Birkin and Ursula return to England. The Gerald theme appears to be both a continuation as well as contrasting to the Birkin theme. Gerald and Birkin betray a kind of disparity so common in the stories of D.H. Lawrence. Integrity manifests itself in personal, particularly sexual relationships. Its presence signifies creativeness while its absence, disintegration. Birkin and Ursula move forward towards distinctiveness. Gerald and Gudrun resolve back towards inanimate matter which is symbolized in the novel by ice and snow. The life theme is presented though Birkin and Ursula whereas the death theme constitutes the fabric of the relationship between Gerald and Gudrun.

Some interpretations consider *Women in Love* as a sequel to *The Rainbow*, probably due to two facts. The primary reason may focus on a coincidental factor that Ursula Brangwen appears in both the novels whereas the lady in the later novel is not a continuation of Ursula of the former story; repetition of a name does not necessarily correlate the two novels. At the same time, Lawrence mentioned in one of his letters that *Women in Love* was complementary to *The Rainbow*. This statement has been completely misunderstood. Hena Maes-Jelinek offers an impartial view when she writes:

> If *The Rainbow* is the chronicle of a civilization, *Women in Love* (1920) draws a picture of society at a definite point in the course of its development. Whereas *The Rainbow* was the story of a world in revolution, *Women in Love* records the consequences of the change, describes what society has become, and seeks a way out of its sterilizing grip. It renders the individual's lonely struggle towards salvation as an effort to infuse a new meaning into personal and social relationships. (81)

The only similarity between these two novels (barring the repetition of a particular name) lies in the theme of unfulfilled love. However, in *The Rainbow* the discontentment of love is not depressing for the female character because she visualizes hope for a better future in the symbol of *The Rainbow*. On the other hand, in *Women in Love* we have one fulfilled love no doubt, but the other unsuccessful love results in depression and psychological frustration. It should also be remembered that so far as the theme of love is concerned, all the novels of D.H. Lawrence are interconnected as the same type of denouement of male-female syndrome is developed as the central theme of all the novels.

Begun in 1912 and published in 1920, *The Lost Girl* was considered and regarded initially as a minor and the least interesting of his works yet its heroine, Alvina Houghton is one of the most humanely appealing of all Lawrence's heroines. The life of Alvina is sketched from childhood to marriage convincingly in the pattern of a social comedy. The descriptions of nature are intense and pictorial. Alvina Houghton is the daughter of an early twentieth century British theater owner, James Houghton whose death frees her from the constraints of pleasing her father but being in debt she sells the theater though continues to manage it when traveling minstrels come to perform. Alvina gets attracted to the quiet natured Ciccio, an actor/singer in the group. When Alvina joins the troupe as its piano player she and Ciccio grow closer. This relationship is doomed to failure right from its inception because Alvina is conscious that Ciccio belongs to a lower social status. Alvina begins to tire of traveling also realizing that Ciccio's was only desirous of developing physical relationship with her. Alvina accepts a nursing position and leaves the troupe. She treats patients and enjoys life as a nurse with her own money and duties, but she is lonely. A bachelor doctor becomes enamored with Alvina and offers marriage. She is hesitant because she doesn't love him and requests a month to decide whether to accept his offer of marriage. By chance, she sees Ciccio on the street. She tries to avoid him, but he follows. He serenades her as she tends to a woman giving birth. Alvina soon concludes that she can't accept the doctor's proposal. Alvina and Ciccio marry and go to Naples, Italy though he is hesitant to return there fearing that Alvina will not like life as the wife of an Italian farmer. Alvina finds happiness with Ciccio though life is much more tough than it was in England. Alvina is expecting a child when Ciccio is called up to fight for Italy during the World War I. Alvina must decide whether to stay in Italy or return to England. Ciccio must decide whether to return to Alvina after the war. This novel brings out the truth that sex is not the only criterion for a happy and stable married life for which a proper human bonding is necessary.

In *Aaron's Rod* (1922), the next novel by Lawrence action begins in industrial England and just like in *The Lost Girl* transits to Italy later. Aaron Sisson is a school teacher who relinquishes the profession after three years for becoming a prosperous collier. When the story begins he is married having three daughters. One day he leaves home and with his musical talent obtains employment as a flautist at Covent Garden, subsequently meeting an American lady on his visit to Italy, has a brief affair with her and then deserts her. While staying in London he had met Rowdon Lilly, a writer with small income who accompanies Aaron to Italy where they have a sort of homosexual relationship which is soon abandoned. Aaron clings to his flute which is like a rod (hence the title *Aaron's Rod*) and is a symbol of creative life. Meeting his wife Lottie after sometime he responds to her sexual and emotional appeal but sternly resents her dominating attitude eventually leaving her for good.

Kangaroo (1923), set in Australia was composed in just six weeks during the sojourn of Lawrence in New South Wales. The theme of marriage as well as the idea of relationship between man and man finds expression once again. Richard Lovat Somers, a writer visits Australia with his wife Harriet. Being discontented with writing he desires searching other alternatives of livelihood while his wife is contented with his present profession. They meet Jack and Victoria Calkottz in Australia. Jack, a motor mechanic is involved in a political movement headed by Ben Cooley, a Jewish lawyer popularly addressed as Kangaroo. Jack attempts to involve Somers in the movement who resists this invitation. A large part of the novel is devoted to describing the love-hate relationship between Somers and Ben Cooley. Ultimately Ben threatens Somers to leave Australia if he doesn't join his group. Incidentally, Cooley is killed in a clash with a labour leader, Struthers while Somers and Harriet leave Australia. The marital life of Somers is unhappy because Harriet has a tendency to dominate her husband. Somers is a frustrated man as his interaction with other men proves largely unsatisfactory and he feels a lack of emotional response in such relationships as well as in the company of the wife.

In *Kangaroo,* Lawrence discusses the topic of religion in addition to his recurrent theme of human relationships which is a diversion of subject matter though he has failed to exploit this idea fully. He writes about the 'dark gods' identified with the primitive pagan gods of Mexico. In his frustration due to the failure of human relationships Somers quests for alternatives which lead him to primitive customs. He searches for a radically new source of power referring to it as the Dark God. On the other hand, he puts forward a significant statement about this notion in one of his discussions with Kangaroo (Ben Cooley):

> 'It means an end of us and what we are, in the first place. And then a re-entry into us of the great God, who enters us from below, not from above'....
>
> 'Not through the spirit. Enters us from the lower self, the dark self, the phallic self, if you like.' 'Enters us from the phallic self?' snapped Kangaroo sharply. 'Sacredly. The God you can never see or visualse, who stands dark on the threshold of the phallic me.' 'The phallic you, my, dear friend, what is that but love.' Richard shook his head in silence. 'No', he said, in a slow, remote voice. 'I know your love, Kangaroo. Working everything from the spirit, from the head. You work the lower self as an instrument of the spirit. Now it is time for the spirit to leave us again; it is time for the Son of Man to depart, and leave us in dark, in front of the unspoken God; who is just beyond the dark threshold of the lower self, my lower self'. (135)

The idea expressed in the above passage appears incoherent and inconsistent if considered in isolation but in the context of the next novel by Lawrence it becomes important and meaningful when the novelist shifts his theme to Mexico.

Lawrence had spent some time in Mexico in 1923 and 1924 before embarking on *The Plumed Serpent* (1926). In this novel Lawrence maintains that the regeneration of Europe's crumbling postwar society must come from a religious root, and if Christianity is dead, each region must return to its own indigenous religion. The novel proclaims a serious attempt to assess the nature of religion. The novel expresses Lawrence's dissatisfaction with Christianity, on the one hand, and his effort at the glorification of the primitive religion of Mexico on the other. Kate Leslie, a forty-year-old Irish divorcee visits Mexico. Her demised second husband was a distinguished Irish rebel. Kate finds Mexico in a state of chaos and degeneration. She witnesses a bull fight in the company of two American male companions and finding the whole thing disgusting leaves the place in despair after which she encounters two Spaniards, Ramon and Cipriano with whom she goes to the lake of Sayula where people are preparing to receive and worship the pagan gods of Mexico. The chief God of the pantheon is Quetzalcoatl, the Plumed Serpent. In the scene which is enacted the death of Christ is shown, symbolizing the rejection of Christianity and announcing the arrival of Quetzalcoatl. Later Kate marries Cipriano in an unusual mystical ceremony and in spite of a satisfactory physical relationship she craves for her lost freedom to travel around the world. Kate plans to return to Europe in order to visit her mother and children but unable to displease Cipriano and Ramon the plan does not materialize. The novel ends on this note.

Lawrence reiterated the fact that industrialization had left man "a creature of mechanism and automatic reaction" (77). When Kate visited Sayula, she rapidly concluded that

> Wherever the iron rails run, and passengers are hauled back and forth in railway coaches, there the spirit of rootlessness, of transitoriness, of first and second class in separate compartments, of envy and malice, and of iron and demonish panting engines, seems to bring forth the logical children of materialism, the bolshevists. (112)

This passage explicitly voices concerns about the disintegrating effects of capitalism on culture. Truly enough the contrivances of a materialistic and mechanistic civilization uproot the people, severing their organic connection not only with the landscape, but also disrupting and even going to the extent of destroying the "genuine" cultural traditions that grew from it. In addition, the cited passage implicates that capitalism basically acts by dividing society into a class hierarchy, thus enhancing the possibility of further social fragmentation. Consequently such a system tends to mar human relationships at large. Through the thoughts of Kate Lawrence exemplifies that the ordinary people who still maintain an organic connection with nature—are the true carriers of the primordial impulse thereby providing a significant link between human consciousness and the "higher" reality of the cosmic awareness.

In his final major work *Lady Chatterley's Lover* (1928) D.H. Lawrence returns to the industrial Midlands of England reminding us of the themes taken up in *The Rainbow* and *Women in Love*. Connie Reid marries Sir Clifford Chatterley, a mine owner. After a month of togetherness he has to return to the front where he is seriously wounded, crippled and rendered impotent. Clifford resorts to story writing as a diversion. Connie helps him in the beginning but soon gets attracted towards Mellors, Clifford's gamekeeper. Experiencing a unique sexual contentment she ultimately marries Mellors whereas being hurt that his wife had associated with a man of lower social status, Clifford gets emotionally closer to a middle aged village woman hired to tend him.

Lady Chatterley's Lover was subjected to bitter criticism for its frank description of sexual experience getting proscribed for almost three decades encountering undeserving rejection by the critics. Initially declared scandalous, it was later assessed as an essentially traditional novel, belonging to the second rank of significant English novels which are both didactic as well as catering to imaginative pleasures. Critics have aptly justified the theme handled by Lawrence because it is now accepted that in this novel the degeneration of the post-war society has been bared. At the same time it is evident that the work contains a suggestion how man can lead a richer and fuller life by abandoning intellect and by laying more emphasis on instinct. This idea reiterates that Lawrence was inclined towards a psychoanalytical evaluation of his characters. The novel also reveals that social equality essentially leads to better human relationships. In the intimacy between Connie and Mellors Marxian faith is substantiated that intuitively man desires equality but social taboos result in class division.

When *Lady Chatterley's Lover* invited strong condemnation and bitter censor Lawrence shielded it in simple but emphatic words in a letter to Harriet Munroe dated March 15, 1928:

> It is a nice and tender phallic novel, not a sex novel in the ordinary sense of the word.... I sincerely believe in restoring the other, the phallic consciousness, because it is the source of all real beauty and all real gentleness.

Indeed, the novel is Lawrence's final attack on the conventional ideas of sex which he regarded as trivial claiming the work to be wholly moral and asserting that it was his sincere attempt to make sex relationships valid and precious instead of reprehensible.

D.H. Lawrence was not only a creative genius but was also a man gifted with prophetic vision of life who desiderated employing his novels as vehicles for communication. In most of his major novels fiction and doctrine co-exist but many a time philosophy gets the better of him undermining the aesthetic worth of his novels. *Aaron's Rod, Kangaroo, The Plumed Serpent* and *Lady Chatterley's Lover* are novels of this category. On the other hand, novels like *Sons and Lovers, The Rainbow* and *Women in Love* have been admired for their aesthetic worth. Lawrence entertained predetermined ideas about life which he could not separate from his creativity. He believed that man can achieve happiness if in his quest for reality he relies more on his impulses and instincts rather than on reason. Abstract intellectualism was fatal to life and deprived man of the simple pleasures. In a letter to Ernest Collins dated January 17, 1913 Lawrence had written:

> My great religion is a belief in the blood, the flesh, as being wiser than the intellect. We can go wrong in our minds. But what our blood feels and believes and says is

> always true. The intellect is only a bit and bridle. What do I care about knowledge. All I want is answer to my blood, direct, without fribbling intervention of mind, or moral, or what not.

Lawrence drifted away from Christianity because the religion emphasized on the denial of the flesh as something unholy. He was inclined to believe more in the 'dark mysterious gods' because they could be realized and worshipped through the flesh. Lawrence's exaltation of sex has been, therefore, largely misunderstood. For him sex was holistic, capable of giving infinite pleasure and he insisted time and again that man-woman relationship in particular and all round human relationships in general can be successful only when people meet on equal terms.

Lawrence has been frequently described as a barbarian with a streak of genius. He is a genius, no doubt, but to call him a barbarian is sheer outrage. One who lives by law and worships instincts is certainly not barbaric. Diana Neill recognized his greatness and located in him something of an authentic visionary asserting that the future may be in a better position to interpret his dreams. The critic perhaps expounds that the later fiction would continue his experimentation with the theme as well as the technique. The conjecture in a way has come to be true. In the novels of Lawrence there is a fine amalgamation of the narrative and the stream of consciousness technique. His character portrayal and the plot construction are of a very high order and when necessitated by the situation, Lawrence recourses to analyzing the mind of his characters as well.

So deeply engrossed was the novelist in propagating the themes of primitiveness and the worship of instincts in his novels that he seldom bothered about the technique that was employed in his writings. The general criticism launched against him is that his novels are formless. Truthfully enough in the novels of Lawrence one does not find plot or character in the conventional sense; his situations are merely maladjustments and counter-balance of the life impulse personified as the different characters of his novels. The novel becomes something new in his hands. David Daiches observed that Lawrence was a great innovator who put the novel form to new usage liberating it from the limits of simple narrative which existed for the past two centuries dominating the prose fiction. Middleton Murry also maintained that art was not the ultimate aim of the novelist. He did not want to be restricted by the shackles of traditional novelistic form and consequently his writings were purely impressionistic. The stories of Lawrence progress chronologically, no doubt, but he desired the real links between incidents to be emotional and not logical or chronological. The narrative moves from the past to the present, from the external to the internal and vice versa.

What Lawrence attempted or dared to experiment within the matter of theme launched a new pattern for the later novelists. The sexual theme existed in the English novel but it was expressed in an inhibited and restricted manner. Lawrence for the first time used the physical relationship between men and women as an overt theme in his novels not hesitating to use certain tabooed words and not feeling embarrassed in developing in words situations of intimacy between the sexes. The Post-World War II fiction in England also divulges this type of boldness. A vast number of novels employ the man-woman relationship as their fundamental theme not only on the social, economic, political or psychological level but also by boldly describing the biological urge and its fulfillment between men and women.

D.H. Lawrence's conception of novel is inextricably associated with life. For him, novel was a powerful medium for interpreting life and for explaining human relationships. In his literary essay "Why the novel matters" he professed that a novel gets animated when it deals with life as there is a sort of unity in all living creatures in the world. The purpose of art must be to identify the relationships between man and the cosmos as well as among all human beings. Ironically sex finds an ample place in all his novels which were instantly acknowledged as obscene and pornographic. Nevertheless, speaking out in self-defence, he alleged that sex was an undeniable fact of life, a source of life and its consummation may be equated with a spiritual experience. The inter-relation between man and woman, man and man and between human beings and the universe is the main basis of Lawrence's works. By doing so the novelist was able to give an exhaustive picture of life. In this sense his novels do not remain merely a fictitious chronicle of life for the novelist probed beneath the surface as well and assumed that there was much more beyond 'the boundaries of a man's conscious mind'.

D.H. Lawrence provided some fresh directions to the twentieth century English fiction, his foremost contribution being the highlighting of the thematic significance of projecting the psycho-sexual inclination of human beings. His novels have employed the Freudian concept in order to illustrate veraciously a foremost involvement of the twentieth century men and women. The European life perceived a transformation of values in which religious norms were crumbling leading to uninhibited sexual indulgence so out of defiance and as a reaction, to what they verbosized as the collapsing social system, the younger generation began declining the so-called traditional antiquated way of life. In spite of being cognizant of a possible ostracization, Lawrence has presented this aspect of intensifying sexuality rationally through his novels. Lawrence thus initiated another trend pertaining to the theme of the working class dilemma in a social set up which was marred by economic insecurity, political intrigues and several other socio-familial uncertainties.

Works Cited

Aldington, Richard (ed.). *Selected Letters of D.H. Lawrence.* Penguin Books, 1954.

Crossland, Rachel. "What D.H. Lawrence Understood of the 'Einstein Theory'" published by Modern Humanities Research Association, January 2013.

Daiches, David. *The Novel and the Modern World.* University of Chicago Press, 1960.

Ford, Boris (ed.). *The Pelican Guide to English Literature: The Modern Age,* England: Penguin Books, 1970 edn.

Fraser, G.S. *The Modern Writer and His World.* England: Penguin Books, 1964.

Holton, Gerald. *Einstein, History, and Other Passions: The Rebellion against Science and the End of the Twentieth Century.* Cambridge, MA: Harvard University Press, 2000.

Hough, Graham. *The Dark Sun: A Study of D.H. Lawrence* (1956). New York, Macmillan, 1957.

Maes-Jelinek, Hena. *Criticism of Society in the English Novel Between the Wars* [online]. Liége: Presses universitaires de Liége, 1970 (generated 17 August 2014). Available on the Internet: <http://books.openedition.org/pulg/876>.

Lawrence, D.H. *Fantasia of the Unconscious.* Rockville, Maryland: Serenity Publishers, reprint 2008.

———. *The White Peacock.* Cambridge: Cambridge University Press, Reprint edition, 1981.

———. *The Trespasser.* Cambridge: Cambridge University Press, Reprint edition, 1984.

———. *Sons and Lovers.* New York: Chelsea House, Reprint edition, 1988.

———. *The Rainbow.* Vintage Classics, Random House UK; Reprint edition, 2011.

———. *Women in Love.* Cambridge: Cambridge University Press, Reprint edition, 1987.

———. *The Lost Girl.* Cambridge: Cambridge University Press, Reprint edition, 1981.

———. *Aaron's Rod.* Penguin Twentieth-Century Classics Paperback, Reprint edition, 1996.

———. *Kangaroo.* Penguin Twentieth-Century Classics Paperback, Reprint edition, 1997.

———. *The Plumed Serpent.* Cambridge: Cambridge University Press, Reprint edition, 1987.

———. *Lady Chatterley's Lover.* Bantam Books, Reprint edition, 1983.

Leavis, F.R. *D.H. Lawrence: Novelist.* London: Chatto and Windus, 1967.

Neill, S. Diana. *A Short History of the English Novel* (1971). London, New York, New Delhi: Jarrolds; Kalyani Publishers, 1971 [reprinted 1979].

5

The Lonely Pastoral

Carole Rozzonelli

Lady Chatterley's Lover[1] by David Herbert Lawrence is a novel against modernity, Western casteism in English social life and their uncouth and destroying ways. But it also puts a final seal on the possibility of representing pastoral in literature as an ultimate way of escape from the ugliness of contemporary world and its "satanic mills".

However, the novel does not stand at all for tradition (albeit a touch of ambiguous nostalgy for a past "merry England") and established social order. It would be proficient to speak of a double antithetic vision: of nature as a haven teeming with uncorrupted energy and life, in juxtaposition with the intruding presence of man and his looting of "her" riches and beautiful heritage.

It is seminal to this discourse the location of this novel: among the coal pits of the Midlands and around what is left of the mythical forest of Sherwood, the very kernel of English folklore and the acknowledged right to rebellion. Now the coal pits and the steel works have laid a thick lager of grey dust upon the stately oaks, the lawns and the flowers.

Even the starry darkness is ravished by the fires and the electric light of the night shifts, in a hellish figuration of the greed and social injustice that is corrupting the beauty of nature and the harmony of human relationships, both personal and public.

Behind this double failure lurks darkly the split, and no more human, society depicted in *The Time Machine* (H.G. Wells 1895), with its degenerated and lemur-like race of machine-tenders, the Morlocks, and its underground factories. A reader can easily detect in the thoughts of Connie, who goes by car through the Midlands, the echo of the provoked gap that in H.G. Wells has destroyed once for all human civilisation,

> Tevershall! That was Tevershall! Merrie England! Shakespeare's England! No, but the England of today, as Connie had realised since she had come to live in it. It was producing a new race of mankind, over-conscious in the money and social and political side, on the spontaneous intuitive side dead, but dead. Half-corpses, all of them: but with a terrible insistent consciousness in the other half. There was something uncanny and underground about it all. It was an under-world. And quite incalculable. How shall we understand the reactions in half-corpses? When Connie saw the great lorries full of steel-workers from Sheffield, weird distorted smallish beings like men, off for an excursion to Matlock, her bowels fainted, and she thought: Ah God, what has man done to man? What have the leaders of men been doing to their fellow men? They have reduced them to less than humanness, and now there can be no fellowship any more! It is just a nightmare. (153)

Instead of focusing on social strife and the consequent collapse, Lawrence introduces the theme of physiological bareness. Connie would have a son (not a daughter, anyway), to keep alive the faint hope for a sanitized future,

> She felt again in a wave of terror the grey, gritty hopelessness of it all. With such creatures for the industrial masses, and the upper classes as she knew them, there was no hope, no hope any more. Yet she was wanting a baby, and an heir to Wragby! An heir to Wragby! She shuddered with dread. (153)

However, the stunted and distorted figures of the workers seem to give the lie to the material feelings nurtured by Connie. They foreground instead her high-class fright in front of all this ugliness and malevolence,

> The common people were so many, and really, so terrible. So the thought as she was going home, and saw the colliers trailing from the pits, grey-black, distorted, one shoulder higher than the other, slurring their heavy ironshod boots. Underground grey faces, whites of eyes rolling, necks cringing from the pit roof, shoulders out of shape. Men! Men! Alas, in some ways patient and good men. In other ways, non-existent. Something that men *should* have was bred and killed out of them. Yet they were men. They begot children. One might bear a child to them. Terrible, terrible thought! They were good and kindly. But they were only half, only the grey half of a human being. As yet, they were "good". But even that was the goodness of their halfness. Supposing the dead in them ever rose up! But no, it was too terrible to think of. Connie was absolutely afraid of the industrial masses. They seemed so weird to her. A life with utterly no beauty in it, no intuition, always "in the pit". (159)

In *The Time Machine* the abyss of human retrogression was born out of the pastoral dream turned sour with a revenge. The ruling class has destroyed its hegemonic power through idleness and the giving away of the struggle for survival. A similar coming doom hangs over the lives of the landed industrialists in *Lady Chatterley's Lover*. They are viewed as a sorry and ageing lot, whose family mansions are progressively pulled down to build rows of bleak residential semidetached villa. This process of "uglification" parallels the physical disablement (from the waist downwards) that haunts Clifford. His halved virility (dead legs and maimed reproductive capacity set upon ruddy features and broad shoulders) stand as a desolate counterpart to the felled down old oaks in his landed property, to make timber for the First World War trenches.

Both trees and man have been sacrificed to the gods of modern warfare, after being desecrated and polluted in the name of mammon. A further ironical twist equates the lame Clifford to the modernized coal-pits: both of them have been hybridized. He is partly flesh partly machine, that is a machine-tended human being, whereas the entrails of Mother Earth clatter and pulse and beat as their breath were replaced and stifled by some artificial motion.

This wasted landscape might introduce us to a series of denied functions. First of all, the substitution of the natural ways and law with impersonal mechanics leads fatefully to an exchange in fatherhood. An heir becomes for Clifford an asset for his future (that is, the permanence of his family tree), whatever his natural father might be.

The mother is viewed as a mere container for male seed, in an extreme stand of ruling patriarchy against decline and fall. Such a functional reduction of womanhood to an impersonal agency of subaltern reproduction, not of the species but of a hegemonic ruling class on the wave, dominates man-woman relationship. The individual note is however struck by equating the maternal drive to a fulfilled wish that harmonizes the woman with the cycles of nature: the empathy in this impulsive thrust is underlined more than once in the novel.

For instance, an imagined "reverderie" gives new life, colour and force to a previously dying landscape,[2] in a way that seems to disrupt for a while the deadly synchrony between "art" and nature that makes an excatia (a wasteland) of the proud English park. The empty stillness of the winter wood echoes through its silence, only broken by a faint tearful dripping, the emptiness of Connie's womb, in a double representation of death in life, "In the wood, all was utterly inert and motionless. Only great drops fell from the bare boughs, with a hollow little crash. For the rest, among the old trees was depth within depth of grey hopeless inertia, silence, nothingness" (65).

This utter sense of void is both metaphorical (*néant*) and at the same time biological (the bareness of the married couple), in the darkening synthesis that transfers the condition of psychic uneasiness from man to nature. This paradoxical encounter brings to the front the alienated condition from which suffers the human being, who is reduced to a mere biological (or elemental, according to Lawrence) entity.

Such a process concerns, and makes alike although in different ways, the lower and upper classes. Regarding the former, they are considered to be not fully human, since they have become all one with the coal and the steel,

> Perhaps with the passing of the coal they would disappear again, off the face of the earth. They had appeared out of nowhere in their thousands, when the coal had called for them. Perhaps they were only weird fauna of the coal-seams. Creatures of another reality, they were elementals, serving the element of coal, as the metalworkers were elementals, serving the element of iron. Men not men, but animas of coal and iron and clay. Fauna of the elements, carbon/iron, silicon: elementals. They had perhaps some of the weird inhuman beauty of minerals, the lustre of coal, the weight and blueness and resistance of iron, the transparency of glass. Elemental creatures, weird and distorted, of the mineral world! They belonged to the coal, the iron, the clay, as fish belong to the sea and worms to dead wood. The anima of mineral disintegration! (159-60)

In a similar way the development of romance between the lady and the keeper follows a seasonal rhythm, in accordance with the progress of nature ("reverderie"),

> Connie went to the wood directly after lunch. It was really a lovely day, the first dandelions making suns, the first daisies so white. The hazel-thicket was a lace-work of half-open leaves, and the last dusty perpendicular of the catkins. Yellow celandines now were in crowds, flat open, pressed back in urgency and the yellow glitter of themselves. It was the yellow, the triumphant powerful yellow of early summer. And primroses were broad and full of pale abandon, thick-clustered primroses no longer shy. The lush dark green of hyacinths was a sea, with buds rising like pale corn, while in the riding the forget-me-nots were fluffing up, and columbines were unfolding their ink-purple ruches, and there were bits of blue bird's-egg shell under a bush. Everywhere the bud-knots and the leap of life! (165)

The return (or "leap") of life also means the submissive role of the individual to the blind instinctual impulse embodied by the forces of nature: the maternal wish is something analogous to the sap pushing its way upwards in the born again greenery. Its energy transcends the mere individual. This is made clear in the functional theory expressed by Clifford,

> Aristocracy is a function, a part of fate. And the masses are a functioning of another part of fate. The individual hardly matters. It is a question of which function you are brought up to and adapted to. It is not the individuals that make an aristocracy: it is the functioning of the aristocratic whole. And it is the functioning of the whole mass that makes the common man what he is.
>
> Then there is no common humanity between us all! (183)

These words lead us back again to *The Time Machine*, and to its deterministic environmental influence on human beings. Here function originates two different and split races, the Eloi and the Morlocks, both of them devoid to a major extent of their original human features. This happens either because of an excess of beautification and simplifying refinement or because of an excess of alienating obedience to function. The latter procedure is further theorized by Clifford, when he speaks of the necessity that people must be brought up to specific function and fully adapted to them.

The next step to the functional process will be the artificially induced division operated in *Brave New World* (Aldous Huxley 1932) between the stunted and half-moronic workers and the hegemonic alpha class. In Lawrence both workers and women (whatever their social position might be) share the strong imprint of a deterministic upbringing. It is not casual then that Connie should evoke scenes turning around motherhood and the care of the little ones. Not only when she visits a farm in the neighbourhood where she meets a baby girl. Afterwards she makes love with the keeper and a new harmony arises between them, in a simultaneously shared pleasure.

Connie goes home alone, and her body seems to have acquired a new fullness, as if the mother was at last fully awakened in her, or rather into her.

Connie went slowly home, realising the depth of the other thing in her. Another self was alive in her, burning molten and soft and sensitive in her womb and bowels. And with this self, she adored him, she adored him till her knees were weak as she walked. In her womb and bowels she was flowing and alive now, and vulnerable, and helpless in adoration of him as the most naïve woman.

"It feels like a child!" she said to herself. "It feels like a child in me."

So it did. As if her womb, that had always been shut, had opened and filled with a new life, almost a burden, yet lovely.

"If I had a child!" she thought to herself. "If I had him inside me, in a child!"

And her limbs turned molten at the thought. And she realised the immense difference between having a child to oneself, and having a child to a man whom one's bowels yearned towards. The former seemed, in a sense, ordinary. But to have a child to a man whom one adored in one's bowels and one's womb! It made her feel she was very different from her old self, and as if she was sinking deep, deep to the centre of all womanhood, and the sleep of creation (135).

Also her clandestine love encounters at the hut in the wood are imbued with references to the instinctual essence of motherhood, here represented by the overanxious hen quails hatching their eggs and then taking care of their little ones. She watches the birds and a feeling of emptiness overcomes her body, "She herself was so forlorn and unused, not a female at all, just a mere thing of terrors" (113).

Her words may seem inappropriately gendered to us, if they mean that motherhood is the only use of the body a woman has. It is the functional theory again. So the fussing hens teach a pedagogy of performative maternal care, they are a "mirror" for married women. The answer to this missed harmony between female body and function lies provisionally in copulation with joint simultaneous pleasure.

This implies the passive cooperation of the woman ("She could strive for herself no more", 116), and the crying inner turmoil of achieved pleasure is substituted by "a sort of sleep, in a sort of dream [...]. She lay still, in a kind of sleep, always in a kind of sleep. The activity, the orgasm was his, all his: she could strive for herself no more" (116).

Such lines are reminiscent of what Herbert Spencer had written concerning the biological identities and the respective functions of man and woman: he the active cell that coordinating cell (the "sperm-cell", according to him) that infuses the germ (or seed) of life into the receiving body of the woman ("the germ-cell"), a mere container. In Spencer brain and flesh indicate respectively the leading and subaltern functions pertaining to men and women, in a sharp division of tasks and ranks in the hierarchies staged by evolution.[3]

But an inner struggle makes Connie restless: her mnestic or ancestral heritage is set against her "modern" brain,

> Her tormented modern woman's brain still had no rest. Was it real?—And she knew, if she gave herself to the man, it was real. But if she kept herself for herself, it was nothing. She was old: millions of years old, she felt. And at last, she could bear the burden of herself no more. She was to be had for the taking. To be had for the taking. (117)

These throes give birth to a new gendered identity now—she accepts to be taken instead of taking. It would perhaps be possible to comment on this passage in Hindu terms of transition from a *viparita* attitude on the part of the woman (roughly, and too sketchily, the superior and active female position of the woman in the sexual intercourse) to her *stridharmic* duties as wife and mother.

In the first part of the novel Connie has an intimate relationship with an Irish-born playwright. He comes off almost at once and she takes successively and alone her pleasure,

> He roused in the woman a wild sort of compassion and yearning, and a wild, craving physical desire. This physical desire he did not satisfy in her: he was always come, and finished, so quickly: then shrinking down

on her breast, and recovering somewhat his effrontery, while she lay dazed, disappointed, lost.

But then she learnt soon to hold him, to keep him there inside her when his crisis was over. And there he was generous and curiously potent: he stayed firm inside her, given to her, while she was active, wildly, passionately active, coming to her own crisis. And as he felt the frenzy of her achieving her own orgiastic satisfaction from his hard, erect passivity, he had a curious sense of pride and satisfaction.

"Ah, how good!" she whispered tremulously: and she became quite still, clinging to him. And he lay there in his own isolation, but somehow, proud (29).

Her cool "viparita" behaviour has nothing to do with passion ("But occasional love, as a comfort and soothing, was also a good thing, […].", 28), it is a mild merely sexual satisfaction, or need to be fulfilled unproblematically. This implies a sort of contempt for the invirile man of the modern era, either the working-class drudge or the slightly amorphous "smart" intellectual.

True passion is to be found in the wood and in the hut, both not merely rusticated havens for a clandestine couple, but natural temples teeming with sap and young life. This is the place in which "rati", the unbound frenzy of passion, lives beyond the fetters of society.[4] As a site devoid of whatever limiting and crippling social convention, pastoral strips power and authority down to their elemental and essential quality.

Too complex human relationships are reduced, if not simplified, to the face to face ties between the two of the couple, in a game of possession whose aim is to lay bare the inner self. This happens in particular with Connie, who meets in the keeper a man in which male and feminine sensibility are melted together.

His thin body, that suggests an apparent female-like frailty, becomes the mirror into which Connie may reflect herself. But her somewhat *tat-shabav* (the man within the woman) nature is subdued by the domineering virility of the man. She discovers her body through his intimacy: their encounters have a double edge to identity, in a mixture of internal frailty and loneliness. They are sometimes shadows each other, but their meeting bodies constitute a shared identity of their own. Not one in two, but two approaching through the body each other.

Notes

1. D.H. Lawrence, *Lady Chatterley's Lover*, London: Penguin Classics, 2006 (1928). This edition is based on the third version of the novel (1927-28). Following indications of pages in the text.
2. "The air was soft and dead, as if all the world were slowly dying. Grey and clammy, and silent even of the shuffling of the collieries, for the pits were working short time, today they were stopped altogether. The end of all things!" (65).
3. Herbert Spencer, "A Theory of Population, Deduced from the General Law of Animal Fertility", *The Westminster Review 57* (1852 [New Series, Vol. I, No. II]): 468-501. Herbert Spencer distinguishes in this article sperm-cell and germ-cell: "The sperm-cell, which is supplied by the male, contains co-ordinating matter, and the germ-cell which is supplied by the female, contains matter to be co-ordinated. From the same evidence as well as from the greater abundance of the cellular and adipose tissues in women, we may infer that the nutritive system predominates in the female." This view may account for a material pulsion that is so strong in Connie.
4. The spiteful gossip (*gup-gup*) of the village in the last chapters against the sexual practices of the keeper and the scandalized reaction at his illicite, and hypergamic, relation are one with the hysterical and savage reaction of Clifford. Both lower and higher class share what seems to be a revengeful moral attitude. Paradoxically enough, punishment against the original scandalmonger (the keeper's wife) would meted out to protect the good name of the Cliffords.

6

Our Modern Marlowe: Lawrence as English Outsider and Cultural Insider to America's Literary Re-birth

Jeffery Moser

Whether rejection, legal confrontations, innate restlessness, illness or sexual desire and frustration most spurred the spontaneous travels and periodic residences away from his native England, the writings of D(avid) H(erbert) Lawrence (September 11, 1885-March 2, 1930) left an indelible mark upon modern literature. Lawrence's work offers a monumental record of aesthetic concern and observation of the disruptions in social life after the stiff propriety and conservatism of the Victorian Age gave way to the mental posture of the Edwardians who questioned and criticized authority in religion, morality, art, and virtues. Especially after World War I, distrust and discomfort with tradition birthed new attitudes about beginnings and endings and any gap between both should be brief. Lawrence is why Fiona Becket aptly stated that, as a poet, Lawrence thought "metaphorically" and best wrote the "unconscious" (1).

Hence, the writings of D.H. Lawrence represent a certain elegance and brilliance in thought, conduct, and art we now identify as modernism. His work offers the critical examination of institutions and show a perceptive and doubting mind in conflict with public and private matters. As the Twentieth Century unfolded conflict and distrust were unavoidable and Lawrence reveals the fear and frustration with society's ills, its rapid changes by technology and cultural discord from interaction and unflinching custom. Most of all, Lawrence's work shows an inquisitive and intellectual man with a conflicted spirit. In a letter addressed to D.H. and Freida Lawrence and dated 12 February 1915, E(dward) M(organ) Forster wrote, "I like the Lawrence who talks to Hilda [Doolittle] and sees birds and is physically restful and wrote *The White Peacock*, he doesn't know why...he sometimes interest and sometimes frightens and angers me, but in the end he[I] will bore him merely, I know... I will forward the Woolf novel to you tomorrow, and read & return *The Rainbow* quickly if it is lent to me" (Lago and Furbank 219).

Four months later, Lawrence responded to Forster with a note and copy of his latest novel, *The Rainbow*: "According to my promise, I send you as much as is done of my philosophy—about one/fourth. I can trust you to take me seriously, and really to read. Because whatever I may be, you do listen" (Lago and Furbank 219).

As a man who was even skeptical about himself, about who he was and who he should be, this helps to explain, in part, why foreign places became Lawrence's literary escapes, and even his muse for writing in spite of, rather than because of, his life-long poor health. These new places allowed him to relax, even laugh—be human. In his series of short stories in Mornings in Mexico (published 1934), although he was describing parrots, one cannot help but think the writer was using the birds to describe Frieda and himself in their new and tantalizing surroundings: "They make my diaphragm convulse with little laughs, almost mechanically. They are quite a commonplace pair of green birds…they listen intently. And they reproduce" (5). Lawrence never seemed to dispel from his works a sort-of Wordsworthian quality of "looking back" to his home country, especially his childhood and coming-of age-years after high school and when he became a pupil-teacher at the British schools of Eastwood and then, at Ikeston, between 1901 and 1905. There he met and befriended Jessie Chambers who would become a critical intellectual companion. She inspired Lawrence to write and publish poetry and his first novel after he matriculated at the age of 22 from teacher's training at the University College in Nottingham. Lawrence joined the staff of Davidson Road

School in Croydon. His friendship with Chambers followed by his move to Davidson worked wonders on Lawrence's emotions and gave him some financial independence, mutually ushering in his literary career.

Many years later, Lawrence's numerous occasions away from England permitted the influential writer to seek unfamiliar and exotic places, explore different literary horizons, experience newfound friendships, and likely, even intimacy. While he traveled and lived in Italy, Germany, France, Australia, and elsewhere, Lawrence's time spent in Mexico and the southwestern United States proved to be especially fortuitous, at the least, and well-timed, at best. It was as if America's Southwest strengthened him, making him a far different character than the Army that once humiliated him when he registered and then rejected him from serving in World War I (Bachrach 1-2). Lawrence would recall that sense of alienation and feeling of dejection in his semi-autobiographical novel *Kangaroo* (1923), which is set in Australia where Lawrence and his wife Frieda (six years older than Lawrence) spent four months in 1922 in order to circumvent European politics and post-WWI life.

Never a strong man and with his boyhood not immune to bullying at school, his altogether life of personal loneliness and illness made living in New Mexico an antidote. There he had the license to write, separated from his native country and all that it reminded him of his past. He wrote more freely, transparently, and about passion and the human spirit, powerfully expressing his evolving ideas about the essential duality of our lives. No longer suffocated by English sensibility, Lawrence's bouts of serious illness and brushes with death, together with the horrors of World War I, removed from him all illusions about anything permanent in life. He exhibited a heightened awareness of mortality and this motivated his writing and in his publicly-displayed constancy for Frieda Weekley, the apparent, prevailing love of his life. Her maiden name was von Richthofen, and she first married Lawrence's modern language professor, Ernest Weekley, when the three first met at Nottingham. Even though Ernest and Frieda had three young children, Lawrence and

Frieda stole away to her parent's home in Metz, Germany, in 1912.

Lawrence's instant charm and brash love with Frieda was at odds with his conflicting romance-turned-disenchantment with England. However, his quickness in spirit and passion allowed Lawrence to develop close friendships with many leading English literary luminaries. Between 1912 and 1914, on short visits back to England from Germany, he met and associated with David Garnett (already known from childhood), Bertrand Russell, Lady Ottoline Morrell, John Middelton Murry, Richard Aldington, and Aldous Huxley. Lawrence also connected with other famous writers, like M(ary) L(ouisa) "Mollie" Skinner from Australia and short-story writer and New Zealander-born Katherine Mansfield. Mansfield introduced Lawrence to the Welsh poet W.H. Davies, a close friend of Forster's. Although there is no further information for the record to explain why, beyond a fondness between the two for each man's writing, Lawrence invited Davies to come live with Frieda and him in Germany. Too, Lawrence's relationship with the young Jewish artist Mark Gertler in 1913-14 may have involved more than the two becoming good friends. As a result of these associations, plus literary networks with leading British publishers and editors, Lawrence's opinions and readings of the great writers of his time, and then, some of them in return reading and commenting about Lawrence's work, such as Forster and Davies, helped to establish Lawrence's considerable reputation as one of the most influential writers of the Twentieth Century.

Specifically, Lawrence's writing from abroad, including in North America, portrays his life-long yearning for new experiences and innovative literature that he then incorporated into his short stories, novels, poems, essays, and plays in order to provoke and interest readers and audiences as much as they could the writer himself. Lawrence also tested the love or rather patience, even "marbles" if you will, of the more liberal and bravest editors and publishers during his lifetime, including Ford Maddox Ford and William Heinemann, the latter whom however, censored and removed parts from Lawrence's draft of his first novel, *The White Peacock* (1911).

In 1912 followed Lawrence's second novel, *The Trespasser*. His third novel, *Sons and Lovers* (1913), is a semi-autobiographical novel that explores the emotional conflicts through the protagonist, Paul Morel, and the suffocating relationships with a demanding mother and two very different lovers. It is a pre-Freudian exploration of love and possessiveness. Lawrence was also one of the great short story writers of his time. His stories show the variety of his achievement and these works develop from early realism towards myth and fairy tale, murder, ghost stories, and altered nostalgia. Of note, "Love among the Haystacks" (1930), a short story written and heavily revised between the years 1907 and 1914 and not finally published until the year that Lawrence died, centers around a love story involving two brothers. Geoffrey and Maurice work for their father on a farm making hay. However, the two brothers are contrary men, and, as Lawrence devised his plot, they meet two very contrary women. The story builds up themes of fear, isolation, rejection, and unfulfilled desire infused with the ideals of nature, family, community and hetero-normative relationships.

Set in the rural midlands of England, *The Rainbow* (1915), was Lawrence's fourth novel and the work which Forster reviewed. It is perhaps Lawrence's best constructed fiction, aside from the fact that, in spite of his reputation as one of the major writers of the Twentieth Century, he remains an author for whom scholars and critics continually make apologies (Kiley 91-107). *The Rainbow* revolves around three generations of the Brangwen family over a period of more than sixty years, setting them against the emergence of modern England. When Tom Brangwen marries a Polish widow and adopts her daughter as his own, he is unprepared for the conflict and passion that erupt. Suffused with biblical images and references to perceived Christian absolutes, *The Rainbow* addresses searching human issues and moral philosophy within a setting of precise and vivid detail. A sequel to Lawrence's *The Rainbow* was the novel *Women in Love*, completed in 1917 (multiple versions were written, revised and published in both England and New York between 1913 and 1921). It continues the story of the Brangwen sisters in the coal-mining town of Beldover. Based in part on Lawrence's own stormy marriage to Frieda, complicated by her German aristocracy and made more difficult during and after WW I, the narrative is charged with intense feelings, psychological insights, and descriptions of divergent sexual desires and gender issues.

For example, in this fifth novel, coal-mine heir Gerald Crich begins a passionate relationship with a young female artist from the English Midlands named Gudrun Brangwen. However, Gudrun falls in love with a puny Jewish painter named Loerke that enrages Gerald. Perhaps his most controversial and court-challenged works, second only to *The Rainbow* (1915), which was prosecuted by the authorities and banned on grounds of obscenity, is unfailing in its fresh perspectives about the times and pushes the boundaries for fiction exploring whether there can ever be a perfect relationship between men and women, women and women, or men and men. The novel climaxes with Gerald's death, frozen on a mountain where he has exiled himself over Gudrun and his stormy affair.

However, the novel concludes around Rupert Birkin, who is married to Gudrun's sister, Ursula. The couple are pining for Gerald. The two men had met and become life-long companions when Rupert was a young school inspector and visited a school near Gerald's coal-mine. Not lost upon readers or critics is the biographical comparison to Lawrence's life, a former school teacher and son of a coal miner, growing up in a home that was surrounded by mines that dotted the English countryside and in a rural/small-town community besought with the genteel life just like his birthplace of Eastwood. The last pages of the book take place about three weeks after Gerald's passing and with Rupert consoling Ursula and himself, explaining how he misses Gerald, and for all of the reasons Ursula does. It is reference to Birkin and Gerald's undeniable homo-socialness as well as the two men's shared queer desires and relationship. Lawrence's overt manifestation with the subject of homosexuality in this novel parallels a strong relationship he developed with a young farmer named William Hocking while Lawrence was writing the novel and when he was living with Frieda on the peninsula of Cornwall between April and October of 1916. Many years later, Frieda acknowledged that her husband's relationship with Hocking was sexual, at least it was what she suspected (Spalding 169-70).

Truly, Lawrence's writing and art challenged conventional expectations and angered authorities. His literary subjects, unstable characters, and erratic and conflicting friendships in fiction and real-life were the reduced and aesthetic observations of the changing cultural attitudes Lawrence was witnessing as a "separatist" from England and an emotional man deeply focused on questions about society, politics, and relationships between men and women. If Lawrence was indeed the deepest of deepest, closeted homosexuals, neither literary acquaintances nor his closest friends outed him. Certainly the writer would have denied it if they had, although the entire matter would have been a bit unbelievable as Lawrence's novels, notwithstanding the example of Rupert above, are designed with characters and plots to favor men/heroes who portray and champion traditional masculinity, are supported by female counterparts, and carry out lives that mostly settle questions of identity and trump any male's faults and weaknesses.

Rejection in 1917 by publishers of *Women in Love* substantially spurred Lawrence's desire to go to America. However, that want would not be met until 1922, and not until after Lawrence and Frieda visited and lived in Italy and Australia and on the Mediterranean island of Sardinia. Following a torrid love affair with Rosalind Baynes in 1920, when Frieda returned alone to Germany to visit family in 1920, and then, writing a series of poems which eventually were published as *Birds, Beasts and Flowers* (1923), in August of 1922 Lawrence traveled to California with Frieda via the South Sea Islands. In September they traveled to Santa Fe where Lawrence met American poet and scholar of Chinese Literature Witter Bynner, a graduate of Harvard. At the time, accompanying Bynner and living with him in an adobe-style house in Santa Fe was ex-Berkeley journalism student Walter Willard "Spud" Johnson. Prior to their meeting, Lawrence had read some of Bynner's published poetry and become greatly fond of, what he termed was, Bynner's ability to hint and praise, but not vilify, sexual awakening. Obviously, Lawrence incorporated Bynner's "hint[s]" into his own prose.

Lawrence and Frieda settled comfortably into Taos, New Mexico, at the invitation of Mabel Dodge Sterne (later Luhan). She was the unchallenged patroness of arts and culture in Taos. The Lawrenc' and Luhan's meeting was the beginning of an intense, sometimes strained, relationship. She called Lawrence "Lorenzo." The daughter of a well-to-do Buffalo, New York family, Mabel had a long history of cultivating arts and letters, surrounding herself with famous artists and writers in her salons in Florence, Italy, and New York City. She continued her support of literature and the arts at Taos.

Lawrence encouraged Mabel to write about her own exciting life and, while back in Italy in 1925, continued corresponding with Mabel and edited manuscripts she sent to him. Her book, *Lorenzo in Taos* (published 1932) is written loosely in the form of letters to and from D.H. Lawrence, Frieda Lawrence, and Robinson Jeffers, the celebrated poet who had been a guest of Mabel's in Taos, with references to Dorothy Brett and also to Spud Johnson, who was the romantic intrigue of Bynner, among others. Luhan considered her residence in New Mexico an escape to reality. Eventually Lawrence would see his time in New Mexico to prove the same: escape and also comfort and cures to his career and health.

In December of 1922 the Lawrences moved up to Del Monte Ranch, north of Taos. There, Lawrence rewrote his prose non-fiction Studies in Classic American Literature. Studies is specially significant in that the work, entirely devised and written while Lawrence was residing in Mexico and New Mexico, provides a foundation for modern literature and consciousness—essentially of a new American critical literature and attitude. The piece succinctly assesses America's literary experience, cultural motives and nationhood development during the seventeenth, eighteenth and nineteenth centuries.

In Studies Lawrence pointedly asks, "What did the Pilgrim Fathers come for," and he questions the United States' "revulsion" from "the old authority of Europe", criticizing the "glory" of democracy. Lawrence deduces "Americans have always been [and likely always will be] at a certain tension" as they are, as he wrote down, "the masterless" of liberty and literature. In Lawrence's view, what American writers had produced over a little less than three centuries could best be summed up as mere extensions and less-than-resounding cries of freedom by the Bald Eagle. Lawrence wrote that America's national emblem "shriek(ed)" and was really just a "Hen-Eagle" (11). He concludes nothing had changed between Benjamin Franklin and Herman Melville, except that Hawthorne, if also no less clinging to the same beliefs as Lawrence's two illustrious bookends to America's greatest writers and thinkers, at least showed he was more cunning. Likewise, Lawrence believed Poe had artfully demonstrated how "love" is truly a "mysterious vital attraction" yet not even Hawthorne or Poe had shown themselves to be any less susceptible than any other American writer before and up to Lawrence's time of "subscribing to the whole spiritual life of society" (98). Lawrence felt that America's writers could do better by admitting "God won't save us" and giving up on "surgery," too (99).

With Studies, Lawrence set down essential insights about, and even a guide to writing modernism: that American literature must mirror cultural changes underway and embrace the hard facts that faith and love have limits. Lawrence espoused that, unless there were a "mixing and confusion" of the two, spirit and sensuality, death came too quickly. If life was lived with no experiences involving "ecstasies of extreme love" then, as Lawrence surmised (lived), every individual will have lived their life as "an arrogant man, and a fool" (75). At this time, finally arriving and thriving in America, for Lawrence there was no turning back or repeating the past in literature. As he contemplated and then envisioned America's literary and national future, Lawrence surmised that the choice for writers was either "Paradise" or as he coined it, what would lead to the "bottomless" "destiny" of "Purgatory" (146-47). In prefiguring readers' natural "Why?" to his essay, Lawrence advanced the following: "Heaven knows. But we've got to grind down our old forms, our old selves, grind them very small, to nothingness.

Whether a new somethingness will ever start, who knows?" (147).

Lawrence finished Studies at Taos in September of 1922 but it was not published in the USA until August of 1923. The work reveals Lawrence at his best, in his literary prime and maintaining the integrity of his working-class Nottinghamshire heritage. He was telling the truth of the day while also sharing his learning, passion, and the judicious care for his friends and self. Once, Lawrence remarked to Mabel Dodge Luhan, "We are always moving on—but we take ourselves along! Shall we try awhile longer?" (Luhan 91).

During the summer of 1923, D.H. Lawrence and Frieda traveled to Mexico. There, Lawrence wrote "Quetzalcoatl", an early version of his novel *The Plumed Serpent*, another work telling much about the cultural and political divisions and discomforts of Lawrence's era. While laden with pagan imaginings, Serpent continues to display Lawrence's capacity for communicating and translating prose into drama. The novel is a notorious late work that Cedric Watts has appropriately labeled is abounding in "the politically incorrect" (v-xxiv). Watts's recent interrogation of Lawrence's narrative force identifies his phallic power and rhapsodic excess (v-xxiv). True to a vein running through all of Lawrence's work, the novel (his ninth if we count the incomplete Mr. Noon, written between 1920-21) expressly shows the author as "neither one thing nor another" but "divided against himself", an echo from his letter to Forster eight years earlier and a work repeating themes of social prejudice, of class against class, of man versus nature, and of men who "lack the spark of divinity" yet are attracted to competing "cult[s]" of brutality and sensuality (Sagar 25).

Lawrence would revise the manuscript of *The Plumed Serpent* and finish it at Oaxaca in 1925. Between 1923 and 1925, Frieda and Lawrence would travel to England, France, Germany, Mexico and then return to New Mexico, at times traveling separately and together. When he revised *The Boy in the Bush* from Mollie Skinner's manuscript, Lawrence has apparently dismissed, even deeply suppressed, his earlier and intense views of homosexuality which he made blatant in *The Plumed Serpent*. Still, his collaborative work with Skinner, *The Boy in the Bush*, was worked on by Lawrence while he stayed in Mexico in 1924. That stay would also inspire Lawrence's last novel, *Lady Chatterley's Lover* (published in Florence in 1928). *The Boy in the Bush*, however, a much forgotten novel by critics, tells the adventures and vaulted thoughts of Jack, a newly-arrived young Englishman and his reactions to Perth and the Australian outback. Jack befriends Tom and the two young men's friendship and experiences in the novel are so complete and realistic that they hearken to Lawrence's real friendships, especially his close friendship with Aldous Huxley in the 1920s when the two, for a brief while, lived near one another in Italy. Even though Huxley had a wife and young son, he would often visit Lawrence and the two writers would spend time, even days, alone together: Lawrence away from Frieda and Huxley absent his home and family, his young son and wife Maria (Nys) Huxley. Before coming to Italy, Huxley had associated with the circle of intellectual and artistic members of the Bloomsbury Group including Bertrand Russell, Lady Morrell, Lytton Strachey, Duncan Grant, Clive Bell and his wife, Vanessa, Virginia Woolf's sister. By networking among the Bloomsbury Set and their unconventional views about aesthetics, literature, criticism, and economics, Huxley, then, was already enabled to become an effective translator and persuasive companion to the dislocated Lawrence about modern ideals including pacifism, feminism and sexuality. Ambitious and powerful, both *The Plumed Serpent* and *A Boy in the Bush* resonate with Lawrence's new thoughts, in tune with the changing attitudes about art and literature in the Western Hemisphere, and also about the relationships that unfolded at Lawrence and Frieda's ranch during their various stays in New Mexico.

In many literary respects, notwithstanding some intriguing biographical similarities, Lawrence is a lot like the Elizabethan dramatist, poet, and translator Christopher Marlowe (1564-1593). Both writers possessed shared gifts for the original, passion, a want to write at the extremes, and a hands-on sensibility of how the literature of old (in their respective times) was giving way to variation, that is, that discomfort with historical dimensions and traditional expectations meant genres needed to be altered and replaced—they just had to be. Marlowe and Lawrence, each, stood at the crossroads of religion, literature, art, and politics when society was being reconfigured by a new generation of thinkers, writers, artists and statesmen who found themselves in the business of "self-fashioning", a concept that Stephen Greenblatt has illustrated to evaluate Marlowe's era and the Renaissance in England as it unfolded: that a conscious effort was made to imitate praised models in society.

Stephen Greenblatt expounded on this concept in 1980: "... that in sixteenth-century England there were both selves and a sense that they could be fashioned" and, further, "that there is in the early modern period a change in the intellectual, social, psychological, and aesthetic structures that govern the generation of identities" (Greenblatt 1). Hence, along Greenblatt's notion that sixteenth-century writers, including Marlowe, began to articulate how selves could be molded, and by themselves first and foremost, at the beginning of the twentieth century and in a post-WW I and pre-WW II era, this same kind of "self-fashioning" urge among writers (and others) to "mold" themselves a little differently than their elders and against the all-too rigid past that had institutionalized politics, religion, literature, art, and human behavior began to emerge. Lawrence was attune to this new movement.

Further, both writers were censored, and, for all practical purposes, during their era Marlowe and Lawrence wrote truths about their respective society, and when readers and authorities least expected that and more dangerously, wanted them to be kept unknown. Also, each writer died young. When he was only 29, the year 1593 marks the death of Marlowe, and it is only here that his documentary record, as Lukas Erne has stated so well, "gets fuller, owing to the circumstances surrounding his death" (32). Marlowe was fatally wounded by Ingram Frizer, whom, in apparent self-defense, used a dagger to mortally stab the poet-playwright above his right eye. Apparently, the dispute was over the issue of some bill at the Eleanor Bull, perhaps over an unpaid bar tab as the Bull was allegedly a licensed tavern. Lawrence succumbed to tuberculosis and died at the age of 44 at Vence, Alp Maritimes, France, in March 1930. In the 1590s, Marlowe was surrounded by plague-affected London, and while he spent the last months before his murder writing the narrative poem "Hero and Leander" (published in 1598, although the manuscript had been circulating for years before, at least reaching Shakespeare in 1592 and serving as a model for the latter's first long-poem Venus and Adonis).

Marlowe's last poem is erotic. Ovidian in tone, along with the manners found in the digressive story about Mercury and the country maid, Marlowe translated and innovated upon another work by Ovid, the Amores. He translated and transposed his own masterful version to communicate the meeting, wooing, and eventual sexual consummation of the love between "Venus' nun" Hero and her male pursuer Leander. It is clear Marlowe wanted to dramatize his questions and concerns about, and even his opposition to, accepted morals and decorum. Likewise, Lawrence's prickly subjects, most of all, the subject of sexuality and its graphic description in his novels, especially disturbed latent-Victorian sensibilities (but not of the Bloomsbury writers and philosophers). Lawrence drew the ire of his critics and censors, and his use of metaphysics and sexual disruption roar throughout his early twentieth century narratives. To Lawrence's anger, Freud's commentary on sex from a scientific view was unacceptable. D.H. Lawrence wanted to create space for art and literature to offer an equally authoritative voice, if not a more accurate one. Nonetheless, like Christopher Marlowe, Lawrence, and each writer in his own way and time, proved their unique gift at communicating and giving readers something new.

More precisely, Lawrence resembles and contrasts Marlowe in other, very interesting, selected biographical, authorial, and mythological aspects. Their personal lives were as passionate as their writing, and, undeniably, both produced divergent and exceptional works in various genres, even experimenting with cross-genre. As this essay has already suggested, the chauvinism of his characters and plot returns to tradition, nature, and custom permitted Lawrence to round out his fiction and poetry while tensions of doubt and frustration underpin them. His work is juxtaposed with the very passionate personal life Lawrence's friends and himself kept so guarded. The notoriety of Marlowe's private life, which led to accusations, and even myths, of atheism, religious blasphemy against his Protestant England, subversions to the crown, and somewhat-avowed homosexuality, added spice to Marlowe's reputation while he was living and became insuppressible aspects that have continued to invigorate his interest to scholars and critics ever since.

Like Lawrence, Marlowe's first and memorable tragedy, Tamburlaine the Great (written circa 1583-86 and first performed 1587) is burdened with youthful rhetoric but shows the emerging playwright's genius at communicating powerfully, like Lawrence. Marlowe's use of high astounding terms in Tamburlaine, and its sequel, the second part of Tamburlaine (1587) set Marlowe on a course of delivering great drama. Marlowe would become immortalized onstage and subsequently in printed play texts and books of poems for bravely narrating socio-political consequences and domestic realism of overreaching heroes whose bold defiance of social, political, religious, and sexual constraints and morals invited admiration and censorship, no different than Lawrence's writings spawned. Marlowe's long-poem "Dido, Queen of Carthage" (1584) displays Marlowe's confidence and his influence upon contemporary writers, including Shakespeare, to translate narrative and then transpose their own narratives out of the classics while showing ease and familiarity with poetry and its legacy as the first genre. Thus, Lawrence's reputation as a novelist has meant that his achievements in poetry have fallen short of their comparable, deserved recognition, and even, perhaps as much as Marlowe's plays are more chosen than his poetry is chosen by college instructors for their seminar syllabi and referred to by critics and Elizabethan and Jacobean scholars.

However, Lawrence's *Collected Poems* of 1928, plus "Pansies and Nettles" and numerous poems in notebooks in which Lawrence was still writing when he died, shine with the poet's remarkable originality and distinctive achievement. David Ellis has noted the "undoubted unevenness" of Lawrence's poetic work and argued for favorite selections from his poetry (*The Complete Poems of D.H. Lawrence* xviii). Still, Ellis, along with other scholars, including Gary Watson, Elizabeth Sargent, Keith Sagar, Mara Kalnins, and Patrick Cheney, to name a few scholars, have been forced to admit Lawrence's poems are worthwhile study, and further, Ellis confirms Lawrence's poems convey "courage" and "the searching honesty" of a writer scrutinizing "both the outside world and himself" (xviii). In one short poem, from Pansies, "Desire Goes Down into the Sea," Lawrence describes that, "All day long I feel the tide rocking, rocking/ though it strikes no more/ in me" (371). Astute Lawrencean scholars and readers interpret these lines as the twentieth-century poet-novelist-essayist-critic artfully mitigating suppressed ideas and desires of his society and in himself that were bubbling up and which he so desperately wished to release, but that he chose for his writing to describe, at least to suggest and hint. These were generated from what he most hoped for: that literature, especially American literature could, should and would raise and disperse first, and then, eventually, British literature.

Hence, Lawrence, like Marlowe—both—modulated between themes of freedom and restriction, between the spiritual and the material, between England and its empire, and between one class and another in their own world. While their respective works are memorably dramatic and poetic, they present conflict, valorize freedom and dissent, and rank difference. Difference is either privileged in Marlowe's case, especially regarding sexuality, gender and class, or is favored as a force against social norms in Lawrence's case and as per the other categories listed above. Lawrence's society's preference for a dominant masculine hierarchy coincided and competed with his changing beliefs and developing sense that sexual freedom and spiritual license were fine, as long as the first, sexuality, was restricted and encouraged by heteronormative relations, anyway that is how he rounded out his narratives. Secondly, when religious fervor acknowledged the concept of a Judeo-Christian tradition and as long as it aligned with the Christian theology of supersession, Lawrence believed that essentially religion, any kind, was no less the institutionalized reaction to stories and myth, whereby the Christian covenant (or Testament) with God supersedes the Jewish one. It is not that Lawrence was anti-Semitic or that he held any disregard for other beliefs beyond Christianity and Judaism. If he were living today, I believe Lawrence would be a staunch political supporter and strong literary voice for civil rights, equal rights, and voting rights. No, Lawrence was neither 110% Christian convert or anti-Jewish; he wrestled imaginatively and emotionally throughout his entire life with the Christian creed he roundly rejected at the age of twenty-two at the University College of Nottingham where he obtained his teacher's certificate in 1908. His fiction, plays, and poetry reflect fluctuating and changing views about Christianity. These served him as a base to run away from and base to run back to in his personal life and career, just like his hard scrabble, blue-collar upbringing under a father who worked in the coal mines and a mother, while she was an avid reader and lover of literature, supplemented the family's income by working in a lace-making mill: hence, Lawrence wrote struggle. Childhood and his family's Protestant-Congregational values made a great impression on him, and never departed from his conscience. His mother encouraged him to read books and instilled within him the desire to do well in school in order to rise above the family's humble economic condition.

Consequently, in 1914 Lawrence offered the description of himself as a "passionately religious man" who writes "from the depth of my religious experience". In essence, Lawrence's views on religion, as with many of his other beliefs, grew out of experience and thus, like his permissive views on sexuality, class, and principles for living, were as Mark Kinkead-Weekes recently deduced, altogether "complicated" (379). Aside from chauvinism, and as already mentioned more than once, Lawrence's views and politics on sexuality and gender advocate license, at least a modest permissiveness. Similarly, Marlowe's most accomplished play, *The Troublesome Reign and Lamentable Death of Edward II, King of England* (1592) depicts the tragic defeat and eventual murder of a homosexual king besieged by powerful aristocrats unwavering in their efforts to bring a halt to Edward's court excesses and bold romances. Edward's open affection for his court favourite Gaveston, and later, the upwardly-mobile Hugh le Despenser, brings on the growing hatred of his queen, Isabella and the revolt by the barons who ultimately capture and murder Gaveston, execute Despenser, and then confine Edward, sexually degrading and then killing him in a revolting and tortuous murder. If Marlowe's drama lacks any grandeur and modesty, it nonetheless communicates later Lawrencean language of discord between men and women and the marked dichotomy between man's propensities for brutality and sensuality. The work is Marlowe's best constructed drama and most realistic at depicting the private lives of men and women in high places and their friends and lovers who mix and mingle around and below them, even those who move up from low beginnings and grasp onto change with ease.

Finally, in terms of canonization, each writer wrote in the shadow of other worthy contemporaries. To some degree, both Lawrence and Marlowe, became literary castabouts, thrown into the shadows of their rivals via modern critics' efforts at canonizing our literature: Marlowe's merits have been diminished by Sidney, Shakespeare, and even Milton; Lawrence by Joyce, Proust, and even Virginia Woolf. Both writers had their authorial legacies besieged by contemporary nemeses: Marlowe has been plagued by Ben Jonson's denunciation of him as an anti-masker. Similarly, Peter Quennel would often berate young writers in the 1960s, 70s and 80s when he felt they were calling up outdated tone, old manners and tradition in their writings and which Quennel deemed post-modernism, especially avant-garde poetries, should have dispensed, asking them "how well they knew D.H. Lawrence"? (Kemp 6).

There are also some other, last notable contraries in the two writers. Paradoxically, each writer was criticized during their lifetime for their bold counseling of others about sexuality. Lawrence was chastised for his heterosexual presumptions and fanatic heterosexual "strategy he deployed to enact it" (Scherr 30). The creative and well-mannered intellectual Forster, who was a homosexual, viciously attacked Lawrence for being a "deaf impercipient fanatic who has nosed over his own little [hetero] sexual round until he believes there is no other path for others to take" and that is what frightened Forster the most about Lawrence, if not also making Lawrence attractive to him (Lago and Furbank 219). While for some time yet the Eastwood, Nottinghamshire-born Lawrence will likely be best remembered for his provocative novels, his short stories, poems, criticism, plays, and essays truly deserve a fresh look, and not without their assessment in the context of continually rethinking and reworking literary criticism and modernism.

In fact, it was Lawrence's poetry that earned him his first work in print and brought him into contact with leading literary figures and emerging modernists including, initially, David Garnett and Ford Maddox Ford, and then with others. Ford published some of Lawrence's poems in the November issue of *The English Review* in 1909, and then agreed to read a manuscript of Lawrence's first novel, *The White Peacock* (1911). The book was narrated in the first person with a strong but detached and mildly romantic character named Cyril Beardsall. Cyril allowed the budding Lawrence to develop his characters, describe relationships and make account of events as plot unfolds, laying down one of Lawrence's most distinguishable characteristics he would sustain throughout his lifetime: that of a strong and confident narrative voice. Because Lawrence's characters in *The White Peacock* resembled real-life family, friends, and places surrounding his childhood home in the countryside, the novelist's ability to portray realism with accuracy, detail, and intellectual imagery, opened a path for Lawrence to express a range of emotions in future works that eventually cemented a bond with readers. Critics and readers came to expect Lawrence's writings contained first-hand accounts of the author's personal life and that, these were glimpses and mirrors into the writer's most private passions and hopes.

With his fourth novel, *The Rainbow* (1915), Lawrence experienced the harsh reality of censorship. The book was seized by authorities and banned on the grounds of obscenity life; Lawrence was prosecuted. With this misfortune, Lawrence's writing career took an inconvenient turn, and at the same time, his personal life became more complex and difficult. He was unable to find a publisher for his fifth manuscript called *Women in Love*. Its publication would not come until 1920, along with his collection of poems in 'Bay' and his next novel *The Lost Girl*. When he could not find a willing publisher for his work, whether in England or the USA, he never stopped revising. Much of his work was completed while he was living outside of his native and familiar England and his short stories and poetry promises readers immersion in the unexpected and new—i.e., modern America. As Marlowe demonstrated long before him, Lawrence wrote in order to grant readers the great opportunity to refresh their belief in literature as a dependable record of the range of human emotion and possibility.

Consequently, written during the winter of 1929-30 and his last major work, *Apocalypse* stands as Lawrence's radical criticism of the political, religious and social structures that have shaped our Western civilization. In Lawrence's view the perpetual conflict within man, in which emotion, instinct and the senses vie with the intellect and reason, had resulted in society's increasing alienation from the natural world. Yet Lawrence's belief in humanity's unharnessed power to regain the imaginative and spiritual values which alone can revitalize our world also makes Apocalypse a powerful statement of hope. Presenting his thoughts on psychology, science, sex, politics, art, God, and men and women, and even with the inclusion of a fierce protest against Christianity, Apocalypse is Lawrence's last testament, his final attempt to convey his vision of man and the cosmos. For Marlowe, we recall the native, continental, and classical influences upon his writing. The aspirations and self-fashioning of Marlowe's hero Tamburlaine reflect the unreserved passion, wit, and impatience in both Marlowe and Lawrence. Their respective creative writings did not fail to delight and refresh as well as open new paths of narrative force and cultural truth. For Tamburlaine his fictional, communicative power came with a dagger, also fictional. For Marlowe and Lawrence, through their pens, truly!

Works Cited

Bachrach, Arthur J. *D.H. Lawrence in New Mexico: "The Time is Different There."* Albuquerque: U of New Mexico P, 2006.

Becket, Fiona. *D.H. Lawrence: The Thinker as Poet*. Houndmills, Basingstoke, Hampshire: Macmillan, 1997.

Bevington, David and Eric Rasmussen, eds. *Christopher Marlowe: Doctor Faustus and Other Plays*. Oxford World Classics. Oxford: Oxford UP, 1998.

Cheney, Patrick. *Marlowe's Counterfeit Profession: Ovid, Spenser, Counter-Nationhood*. Toronto: U of Toronto P, 1997.

Cheney, Patrick and Brian J. Striar, eds. *The Complete Poems of Christopher Marlowe*. Oxford: Oxford UP, 2006.

Erne, Lukas. "Biography, Mythography, and Criticism: The Life and Works of Christopher Marlowe." *Modern Philology*. 103.1 (Aug. 2005): 28-50.

Greenblatt, Stephen. *Renaissance Self-Fashioning: From More to Shakespeare*. Chicago, IL: U of Chicago P, 1980. 1-321.

Greenblatt, Stephen, et al. *The Norton Anthology of English Literature: The Major Authors: The Middle Ages through the Restoration and the Eighteenth Century*. 8th edn. Vol. A. London: Norton, 2006.

Kemp, Peter, ed. *The Oxford Dictionary of Literary Quotations*. Oxford: Oxford UP, 1997.

Kiley, Robert. "Accident and Purpose: 'Bad Form' in Lawrence's Fiction." *D.H. Lawrence: A Centenary Consideration*. Eds. Peter Balbert and Phillip L. Marcus. Ithaca: Cornell UP, 1985.

Lago, Mary and P.N. Furbank, eds. *Selected Letters of E.M. Forster: Volume One 1879-1920*. Cambridge: Harvard UP, 1983.

Lawrence, D.H. *Apocalypse* (1931). Ed. and Intro. Mara Kalnins. London: Penguin Books, 1995.

———. *Mornings in Mexico* (1934). Amsterdam: Fredonia Books, 2003.

———. *The Complete Poems of D.H. Lawrence*. Intro. David Ellis Ware, Hertfordshire: Wordsworth Classics, 2002.

———. *The Plumed Serpent* (1926). Intro. Cedric Watts. Ware, Hertfordshire: Wordsworth Classics, 2009.

———. *The Rainbow* (1915). Ed. Mark Kinkead-Weekes. Intro. James Wood. London: Penguin Classics, 2007.

———. *Selected Stories*. Ed. Sue Wilson. Intro. Louise Welch. London: Penguin Classics, 2007.

———. *Sons and Lovers* (1913). Intro. Howard Booth. Ware, Hertfordshire: Wordsworth Classics, 1999.

———. *Studies in Classic American Literature* (1923). London: Penguin Classics, 1977.

———. *Women in Love* (1920). Ed. Mark Kinkead-Weekes. London: Penguin Classics, 1995.

Luhan, Mabel Dodge. *Lorenzo in Taos: D.H. Lawrence and Mabel Dodge Luhan*. Facsimile of 1932 Edition by Mabel Dodge Luhan. New foreword by Arthur J. Bachrach. Santa Fe: Sunstone, 2007.

Sagar, Keith, ed. *A D.H. Lawrence Handbook*. Manchester: Manchester UP, 1982.

———. *D.H. Lawrence and New Mexico*. Salt Lake City: Gibbs. M. Smith, 1982.

Scherr, Barry. *D.H. Lawrence Today: Literature, Culture, Politics*. New York: Peter Lang, 2004.

Spalding, Francis. *Duncan Grant: A Biography*. London: Chatto and Windus, 1997.

7

Atrophy in D.H. Lawrence's *Sons and Lovers*

Kenneth Usongo

D.H. Lawrence's (1885-1930) novel, *Sons and Lovers*, is set in the heyday of the Industrial Revolution in England, a period when the machine essentially replaced the hand, or work hitherto done on the subsistence or agrarian level took industrial scale. While the era of the Industrial Revolution resulted in greater productivity of goods and increased services, it has also been perceived as a mixed blessing. On the one hand, it enriched most manufacturers or business owners and, on the other, it occasioned much unrest and poverty, particularly among the working class. As Paul Delany intimates, Lawrence, in his early work, "showed preference for rural settings, a measured distaste for factories and towns" (81). By referencing the invasive presence of industrialisation on the natural habitat, Fiona Becket comments that Lawrence's work "calls us at times into an ethical relationship with the material world which has increasing resonance in this planetary moment" (148). Through his protagonists in *Sons and Lovers*, Morel, Gertrude, William and Paul, Lawrence attempts to capture the spirit of the Industrial Revolution, especially its social impact on human relationships.

Simply put, atrophy means wasting away, decline, or deterioration in health or mind. In this essay, I argue that in *Sons and Lovers* Lawrence's main characters—Morel, Gertrude, William and Paul—are initially presented as full of vitality, but as the story unfolds, the characters become less vibrant because of their failings as well as the harsh economic conditions working against their interest. In other words, while the fiery attitude of Morel and the rather controlling nature of Gertrude are considerably responsible for their volatile relationship, the collier's meagre income also stifles the joy and harmony in his domestic life. Embedded in Lawrence's narrative is the argument that the transformation of the English landscape from agrarian to industrial symbolises the emotional and physical degeneration of the protagonists. Put differently, Morel's job in the mine paradoxically impoverishes his family and accentuates his matrimonial crisis.

In Lawrence, "character and action are explored through paradoxes in behavior and through a series of antipodal images like space and closure, darkness and light, nature and the machine, or vitality and somnolence, by which an inclusiveness of insight is dramatized" (Farr 9). The contradictory attitude towards life is best exemplified in the shifting romantic feelings shown by Paul to Miriam and Clara. For example, at one moment, he declares his love to them and, at another moment, he considers their emotional connection to him oppressive and seeks to distance himself from them. Similarly, Morel, in the early years of marriage appears to be well-loved by Gertrude. However, as he loses his authority within his household, he is seen more from the perspective of Gertrude and the children as violent, brutal and a moral degenerate. It is arguably Morel's ostracism by the family that "forces him to seek spaces outside the domestic universe, to find substitute places, such as the pub, the scullery and even the garden" (Michelucci 37).

The different social standings of Morel and Gertrude are partially accountable for the friction between them: one from the working class and the other from the middle class. We are told that Gertrude's father, George Coppard, was an engineer, a position that is absent in Morel's lineage. Despite the different social backgrounds of the Morel couple, Morel's romantic air sweeps Gertrude off her feet whereas her purity of English and southern accent thrill him. This young couple is portrayed as bustling with health and enthusiasm:

> He had wavy, black hair that shone again, and a vigorous black beard that had never been shaved. His cheeks were ruddy, and his red, moist mouth was noticeable because he laughed so often and so heartily. He had that rare thing, a rich, ringing laugh. Gertrude Coppard had watched him fascinated. He was so full of colour and animation, his voice rang so easily into comic grotesque, he was so ready and so pleasant with everybody. Her own father had a rich fund of humour, but it was satiric. This man's was different: soft, non-intellectual, warm, a kind of gamboling. (17)

The above quotation not only highlights the sensuous nature of Morel as opposed to the frigidity of Gertrude but also foregrounds the difference between the country and the city that these two characters appear to symbolise. And Paul dwells on this theme in his observation to his mother: "Only from the middle classes, one gets ideas, and from the common people—life itself, warmth" (298). Nevertheless, both Gertrude and Morel appear to function uninhibitedly in nature and seem to shun the artificiality of a cosmopolitan milieu. For instance, when Gertrude feels depressed, she renews her spirit by inhaling the scent of flower (14). For his part, Morel embodies a certain sensuous flame of life that fascinates Gertrude. Thus, when he requests to dance with her, the latter experiences a certain warmth through her body which makes him irresistible to her. Even when he laughs, it has a boisterous ring to it, making him more attractive to Gertrude. It is probably this kind of animation in Morel that leads Raymond Williams to state, in *The Country and the City*, that the country has gathered the idea of a natural way of life: of peace, innocence and simple virtue; the city has contrarily represented the idea of an achieved centre: of learning, communication and light (46).

Glamorous as the relationship between Morel and Gertrude appears to be as evident in their dancing, she soon discovers that he has not paid for the furniture in the house and essentially lives on debt. Morel's precarious financial situation is primarily the result of two factors: the low wage of colliers and his propensity to spend his hard-earned income on alcohol.

Concerning Morel's financial instability, Lawrence indicts the capitalism of the industrialists who showed little regard to the working class: "But although he was very steady at work, his wages fell off" (25). Moreover, Morel hardly discloses his real income to Gertrude, preferring to retain some for himself in order to spend on drinking: "If he earned forty shillings, he kept ten; from thirty-five, he kept five; from thirty-two, he kept four" (27). The consequence is that Gertrude begins to lose interest in him and now transfers her love to her son, William. She is further disappointed that Morel is unable to deliver her the bourgeois lifestyle which she desires. In other words, he is incapable of providing her with a rent-free home, furniture and other things that make for decent living.

Gertrude's shift in emotion towards her children makes Morel jealous and his relationship with her frosty: "She made much of the child, and the father was jealous" (22). This progressively leads to the situation of the protagonists becoming atrophied. Unfortunately, as Gertrude strives to change the behaviour of Morel, the more strain she puts on their relationship: "She fought to make him undertake his own responsibilities, to make him fulfil his obligations. But he was too different from her. His nature was purely sensuous, and she strove to make him moral, religious. She tried to force him to face things. He could not endure it—it drove him out of his mind" (23). Ultimately, Morel takes refuge in drinking and escaping from home. The weekends become his main delight as he looks forward to drinking, depriving the family of quality time and money: "The week-end was his chief carouse. He sat in the Miners' Arms until turning out time every Friday, every Saturday, and every Sunday evening" (25).

Morel's drinking sprees further compound his fragmented relationship with Gertrude, turning it into a physically violent one: "He came up to her, his face red, with its blood-shot eyes, thrust forward, and gripped her arms. She cried in fear of him, struggled to be free. Coming slightly to himself, panting, he pushed her roughly to the outer door, and thrust her forth, slotting the bolt behind her with a bang" (33). At such humiliating moments, Gertrude resorts to nature for consolation as she touches big, pallid flowers by their petals while also absorbing the peace of the surrounding hills that entrances her (34). By sniffing at rose flowers, Gertrude attempts to fill the void of affection which she badly needs from Morel. For his part, when he is confronted by the rather reproachful attitude of Gertrude, Morel along with his friend, Jerry, saunter in nature by gaily climbing the hillside of the Bottoms.

Gertrude's antipathy towards Morel also emanates from the latter's friendship with Jerry, who encourages him to take a tough stance towards Gertrude whereupon Morel affirms to her that "I'll make you tremble at the sound of my footstep" (49). To match words with action, he slashes the monthly ration of money which he gives Gertrude, ironically spending more money on drinking. The consequence of Morel's delinquent behaviour is that he is increasingly detested by Gertrude as noted even in her feeling of dislike towards baby Paul, the fruit of her marriage with Morel: "She no longer loved her husband; she had not wanted this child to come" (51).

The unhealthy relationship within the Morel family, partly a result of economic hardship, leads Morel to be insulting towards everyone in his household: "If, whilst he was washing in the scullery, anyone entered or left the house: 'Shut that doo-er!' he shouted, so that he could be heard down the Bottoms" (51). He becomes violent when, in a fit of anger, he flings a drawer at Gertrude, wounding her on the brow. Even when Morel manifests some remorse for his action, this does not soften Gertrude's animosity towards him, a deep-seated hatred born of the protracted misunderstanding within them and the fact Morel hardly admits his fault or clearly states regret for his misbehaviour: "She would have felt sorry for him, if he had once said: 'Wife, I'm sorry.' But no, he insisted to himself it was her fault" (56).

Morel's craving for alcohol not only alienates him from his wife and family but also leads to him stealing money from his wife in order to spend on liquor. At times, he returns the stolen money into her purse without her notice. At other times, he does not give back the money and instead shamelessly charges Gertrude with falsely accusing him of theft. Thereafter, he will feign anger at the 'wrongful' accusation and walk out of the house pretending never to return. His behaviour makes Gertrude deeply worried about the burden of supporting the family without Morel's badly needed financial assistance given that she has no income. Fortunately, Gertrude soon becomes used to his pranks because he always returns home.

Like other colliers, Morel drugs himself in order to mitigate the pains associated with his job. Interestingly, Morel exaggerates his bodily aches in order to win the sympathy of Gertrude towards him. It is often during such brief spells of peace that the Morel children are conceived: "Meanwhile another infant was coming, fruit of this little peace and tenderness between the separating parents" (64). Immediately after a baby is born in the Morel family, Gertrude transfers her love from her husband to the baby. This results in a loving relationship between mother and son to the exclusion of the father.

Unlike Morel who does not disclose his income to Gertrude, William, the oldest son, upon starting work, hands over all the money which he earns to his mother. The trust and love between them ignite Gertrude's jealousy towards William's female friends. To this end, William allays her jealousy by telling her that he will remain unmarried until he meets a woman like her: "Don't fret, Mater, I shan't get married till I meet a woman like you" (74). Unfortunately for Gertrude, her anxiety is accentuated when William gets a job in London: "Indeed, as the days drew near for his departure, her heart began to close and grow dreary with despair. She loved him so much! Much than that, she hoped in him so much. Almost she lived by him" (79). Gertrude's anxiety is compounded when William's girlfriend, Louisa Lily Denys Western, not only queens over him, but nonchalantly moves on with her life when he dies.

Although the relationship between Gertrude and Morel is rocky, she does not tolerate her children humiliating him mainly because of her endeavour to groom them as gentlemen. At one moment, she stops William from physically confronting Morel. However, Paul prays to God to end Morel's life. For his part,

Arthur deliberately does things that he knows would hurt the feelings of his father. In fact, the Morel children discuss their daily activities to the exclusion of their father: "He was shut out from all family affairs. No one told him anything" (87).

In another domain, Gertrude's relationship with William begins to flounder when he increasingly becomes extravagant, associating with people of a higher social status than himself. He also pays much attention to his girlfriend rather than to his mother. In one particular instance, he sends a seductive picture of Louisa to Gertrude. Not only is Gertrude infuriated but she is also critical of the money that William lavishes on Louisa in terms of expensive dresses and a ring. But Louisa is a rather meretricious girl who does not care about the welfare of William.

Faced with the death of her beloved son, William, Gertrude now transfers her love to young Paul. Gertrude's action stands in the way of Paul's social life because her girlfriends soon find themselves in competition with her for his love. And Paul privileges his relationship with his mother to other relationships. This explains why he cannot develop a committed relationship with any girl. For example, he envisions Miriam as controlling whereas, according to him, his relationship with Gertrude accords him some degree of freedom. However, Paul benefits from both relationships: from Miriam, he derives his artistic impulse while he enjoys emotional or psychological balance from Gertrude: "In contact with Miriam, he gained insight, his vision went deeper. From his mother he drew the life warmth, the strength to produce; Miriam urged this warmth into intensity like a white light" (190).

Paul's relationship with Miriam appears not as grounded as the one with his mother. With Miriam, Paul seems to be under the influence of passion which Lawrence describes through symbolic imagery drawn from nature: "In bosses of ivory and in large splashed stars the roses gleamed on the darkness of foliage and stems and grass. Paul and Miriam stood close together, silent, and watched. Point after point, the steady roses shone out to them, seeming to kindle something in their souls" (195).

The relationship appears consummated as attested to by the highly suggestive imagery that Lawrence employs to describe the scene: "She looked at her roses. They were white, some incurred and holy, others expanded in an ecstasy. The tree was dark as a shadow. She lifted her hand impulsively to the flowers, she went forward and touched them in worship" (196).

No sooner do Paul and Miriam appear to be riding on the crest of passion than their relationship starts becoming icy. First, after consummating his love for Miriam, a strange feeling of aversion towards her wells up in Paul: "When he was with her, he hated her for having got him, and yet not got him" (337). Second, Gertrude's feeling of emotional isolation on the part of Paul makes him reconsider his relationship with Miriam. According to Gertrude, Miriam is regarded as possessive, "one of those who will want to suck a man's soul out till he has none of his own left" (196). Third, Paul's deep love for his mother negatively affects his relationship with Miriam. In this regard, Lawrence states, concerning Gertrude, that whenever Paul "felt he had hurt her, or wounded his love for her, he could not bear it" (257). Ultimately, Paul and Miriam soon become emotionally atrophied as seen when he watches some flowers in the moon and observes that they have eventually become stiff and their scent is distasteful (338).

Another situation that instantiates atrophy in the novel is the relationship between Paul and Clara, which recreates the passionate relationship between Morel and Gertrude. Like his parents, Paul develops immediate passion for Clara: "Clara was indeed passionately in love with him, and he with her, as far as passion went" (395). Paul feels restless in her absence and attempts to make love to her at the least opportunity and everywhere, including his workplace and in the presence of her mother.

Unfortunately, Paul's and Clara's relationship appears to take the same trajectory like that of Miriam and Paul. Paul starts feeling that Clara is, like Miriam, too possessive. He embarrasses Clara by asking her: "But what do you always want to be kissing and embracing for?" (399). To the surprise of Clara, Paul eventually reconciles her with her estranged husband, Baxter Dawes. It becomes evident that Paul cannot sustain a relationship with a woman because of the lurking presence of his mother, who is determined to have him for herself to the exclusion of other women. The consequence of Gertrude's attitude towards Paul is that not only is he wayward in a relationship, but also her relationship with Morel is problematised.

When Morel visits his sick wife in hospital, he is portrayed as dishevelled and frightened: "He was a forlorn figure, looking rather as if nobody owned him" (421). This is a completely different image of the ebullient and vibrant person at the beginning of the story. There is hardly any passion between the couple, an indication of the extent to which they have atrophied: "He sat looking at her as if she were almost a stranger to him, before whom he was awkward and humble" (421). Furthermore, even when she is released from hospital, Morel's physique has so deteriorated that he is unable to carry her indoors. For her part, Gertrude watches sunflowers wither outside, which allegorise her incipient death. At this moment, the image of Gertrude is much different from the smiling and vivacious young woman we are introduced to at a Christmas ball. Now she is sickly and sad; sickness and emotional torment have had a toll on her.

Given that the relationship between Morel and Gertrude wanes mainly as a result of their individual failings and the morose economic environment, there is no denying the fact that Paul also precipitates the decline in his parents' relationship because of his emotional connection to Gertrude. In fact, in her sick days, Paul and Gertrude become much closer emotionally, bordering almost on incest: "His face was near hers. Her blue eyes smiled straight into his, like a girl's, warm, laughing with tender love. It made him pant, with terror, agony and love" (429). Indeed, as Gertrude agonises in pain, Paul feels as though his life is being systematically destroyed. He is also unable to produce any artistic work. Even when his estranged girlfriend, Miriam, comforts him with a kiss, Paul finds her gesture torturing because she cannot kiss away his pain, which is rooted in the pain experienced by his mother.

Lawrence describes Gertrude's pain by clothing it in an image drawn from nature: "The whole country was bleak and pallid, under the snow" (436). Gertrude's health situation prompts Paul to euthanise her. Paul's decision to end the life of his mother is mainly predicated on the point that he cannot bear to see his beloved mother suffer in pain. With her passing away, Paul becomes emotionally troubled; there is hardly indication that he can get emotional stability: "Often, he lost himself for an hour at a time, could not remember what he had done" (455).

Paul's troubled mind is the opposite of the feelings shown by Morel. Upon being informed of the demise of his wife, Morel manifests little or no emotion. He receives the news with astonishing calm, which underscores the absence of emotional depth in the marriage: "The miner sat still for a moment, then began his dinner. It was as if nothing had happened. He ate his turnips in silence. Afterwards he washed and went upstairs to dress" (442). The appetite for food still nursed by Morel shows the extent to which he is estranged from Gertrude. It is Paul and not Morel who has a moment of closure with the departed Gertrude: "He bent and kissed her passionately" (443). The following morning, when Morel nerves himself and enters the room in which Gertrude's body is lying, he is bewildered, frightened and dashes out of the room (444).

Lawrence appears to sum up the total disintegration of the relationship between Morel and Gertrude by configuring the scene in images inscribed in nature. As Gertrude is buried, there is a corresponding wild storm and wind, with rain pouring into her grave and leaving the cemetery deserted. For his part, in his eulogy to Gertrude, Morel claims to have done his best by her, but he avoids dwelling on any personal thoughts of her when he addresses mourners.

In a sense, the novel, *Sons and Lovers*, clearly evidences the collapse in human relationships, or the progressive degeneration of people from a healthy state to one of affliction. Through the experiences of Morel and Gertrude, William and Louisa, Paul versus Miriam and Clara, Clara and Baxter, Lawrence interrogates relationships by depicting how these characters are atrophied in one way or the other. Indeed, with the exception of Annie's engagement, almost all other marriages or engagements in the novel crumble. After all, according to Gertrude in her warning to William, relationships with women inevitably result in "a string round your neck, that you can't pull off" (80). Although economic factors can be faulted for the emotional meltdown experienced by the Morel family, for example, the culpabilities of the characters such as assertiveness, capriciousness and egoism significantly contribute to their atrophy.

Works Cited

Becket, Fiona. "D.H. Lawrence, Language and Green Cultural Critique." *New D.H. Lawrence*. Ed. Howard J. Booth. Manchester: Manchester UP, 2009: 148-68.

Delany, Paul. "Lawrence and the Decline of the Industrial Spirit." *The Challenge of D.H. Lawrence*. Eds. Michael Squires and Keith Cushman. Madison, Wisconsin: The U of Wisconsin P, 1990: 77-88.

Farr, Judith. "Introduction." *Twentieth Century Interpretations of Sons and Lovers: A Collection of Critical Essays*. Ed. Judith Farr. Englewood Cliffs, N.J.: Prentice-Hall, Inc., 1970: 1-23.

Lawrence, D.H. *Sons and Lovers*. Cambridge: Cambridge UP, 1992.

Michelucci, Stefania. *Space and Place in the Works of D.H. Lawrence*. Jefferson, North Carolina: McFarland & Company, 2002.

Williams, Raymond. *The Country and the City*. Oxford: Oxford UP, 1973.

8

D.H. Lawrence: Nature, Red Geranium and Sensual Experience

Joyashri Choudhury

"I was born nearly forty-four years ago in Eastwood, a mining village of some three thousand souls, about eight miles from Nottingham, and one mile from the small stream, the Erewash, which divides Nottinghamshire from Derbyshire. It is hilly country, looking west to Crich and towards Mattock, sixteen miles away, and east and north-east towards Mansfield and the Sherwood Forest district....

The real tragedy of England, as I see it, is the tragedy of ugliness. The country is so lovely: the manmade England is so vile...." (Lawrence, D.H. *Late Essays and Articles*, Cambridge University Press, 2004: 287).

These are words written by D.H. Lawrence in the essay, "Nottingham and the Mining Countryside". The words reflect Lawrence's love of nature and his earnest search for beauty. According to Lawrence, it was ugliness that betrayed the spirit of man in the nineteenth century.

A great champion of the working classes, Lawrence was of the opinion that the crime that the moneyed classes and people in favour of industrialization committed in the nineteenth century was by condemning the working classes to ugliness of every conceivable degree. Even more vital than bread, is actual beauty which the human soul craves for endlessly.

The effects of modernity was felt by Lawrence in his own native Midlands. It took a turn for the worse. He becomes drawn to the life of the collieries. Many of his books and stories are set against the background of the life of the miners and the collieries. Miners were getting dehumanized day by day. Ironically, even though they were the ones most connected with the earth and thereby the natural environment, they found themselves cut off from the earth and ultimately from themselves. Lawrence's attachment to the earth and nature is apparent in these lines:

> every man is really aware of himself in apartness. Then we have these hostile groupings of men for the sake of opposition, strifes. Civil strife becomes a necessary condition of self-assertion. (*Lady Chatterley's Lover* and A Propos of *Lady Chatterley's Lover* Real Author D.H. Lawrence, ed. Michael Squires, Cambridge University Press, 2002)

True community depended upon shared blood ties, a shared history and closeness to the soil.

Giulia Pissarello writing in 'Industrialism as tragedy of ugliness' D.H. Lawrence's ecological consciousness, writes that at the beginning of the twentieth century many artists had looked for worlds untouched by industrialization. The futurists exalted Modernity. Writers like Proust, Joyce, Woolf and others did not show any enthusiasm for the machine. These writers saw the modern world as a vast panorama of futility and anarchy. By adopting the so-called 'mythical method', the Modernist were in favour of the radically old instead of the radically new. This was not something new. Writers like Dickens, Carlyle, George Eliot, Hardy had written about the harm done by the industrialization of the world. Pissarello mentions that it is only with the Modernist writers that a consciousness of the environment arose. This is today labeled as the ecological consciousness.

D.H. Lawrence always sided with nature. Lawrence condemned mechanization: he was also against the savage exploitation of resources, both humans as well as natural. His novels always reflected the struggle between nature and society. He was of the opinion that nature was 'the only possible aesthetic source of existential fulfillment of the individual.' Pissarello goes on to say that it comes as no surprise that many scholars have labeled him as a 'green novelist'. He is also been called a 'future primitive' and a 'Naturist'. His letters shows his great love for Dickens. He keeps alluding to Dickensian fiction and characters. That he was greatly influenced by the realistic fiction of Dickens, there can be no doubt. Lawrence was definitely influenced by Ruskin's inflamed anti-utilitarian, anti-materialistic preaching and of Morris' dream of returning to a pre-industrial Britain.

Lawrence's poems, according to Joyce Carol Oates, are blunt and imposes upon us his strangely delicate music. They come in fragments in tantalizing broken-off parts of a whole which is too big to be contemplated and then it withdraws again. The poems gain a kind of immortality by transcending the temporal and the intellectual.

A great lover of Nature and the environment, the 'ungovernable impulses of his soul' made him 'engrossed in the beauty of the natural flux'. Lawrence was driven by the 'madness for the unknown'. He developed a technique that would be fictional and poetic, in which the prophetic voice could be given a formal expression. Lawrence realized that the spontaneous flow of life was capable of changing everything and therefore dichotomies like perfect/imperfect always stands on slippery grounds. He therefore feels very contemporary to us. Nature was always becoming to him and he continued to write impulsively. We are always accustomed to write and hear only the good side of Nature. Lawrence did exactly the opposite. He exalted in the unbeautiful. He could take the 'snake' as a subject and craft a most beautiful poem out of it. Lawrence loves the true marriage of heaven and hell. In the poem, 'Medlars and Sorb-Apples' from his volume of poems, *Birds, Beats and Flowers* (1923), he writes:

> I love you rotten, he writes:
> Delicious rottenness.

These fruits are seen by Lawrence as "autumnal excrementa". In the poem, 'Craving for Spring', Lawrence announces that the flowers of earliest spring sickens him. He is sick of the snowdrops, the jonquil, the chill Lent lilies because they possess a "faint-bloodedness/ slow-blooded, icy-fleshed" purity. He feels like trampling them with his foot. What is interesting here is the fierce, combative and sometimes peevish relationship with birds, beasts, and flowers. He takes these things of nature seriously.

Lawrence never attempted to write poetry like Shakespeare. He wrote poetry of "pulsating, carnal self". Lawrence celebrates unusual things in his poetry. The falling away, the rotting, the transient, the sinister, his own proud isolation are subjects of his poems. Joyce Carol Oates tells us how the poem 'Fish', shows us a "Mephistophelian" sleight of hand. Here the ineffable is praised. Lawrence describes the fish as:

> Aqueous, sub-aqueous,
> Submerged
> And wave-thrilled.
> As the waters roll
> Roll you.
> The waters wash,
> You wash in oneness
> And never emerge

Lawrence does not study the relationship he has with the fish. He is neither converting them into symbols of human emotions. What he achieves is to get into the 'suchness of fish'—the fish in their 'naked element', 'sway-waves'.

> No fingers, no hands and feet, no lips;
> No tender muzzles,
> No wistful bellies,
> No loins of desire,
> None.

As the poet and reader are transformed partly into fish, the poem becomes a magical incantation.

Lawrence's opinions earned him many enemies and he endured official persecution and also misinterpretation of his creative work all through the second half of his life. In 1912, Lawrence met Frieda, with whom he was to share the rest of his life. Lawrence and Frieda returned to Britain in 1913 for a short visit. He was able to meet Welsh tramp poet W.H. Davies, whose work, much of which was inspired by nature, he greatly admired. Best known for his novels, Lawrence wrote about eight hundred poems, most of which were short. His first poems were written in 1904 and two of his poems, "Dreams of Old" and "Dreams Nascent", were among his earliest published works in *The English Review*. His early works place him in the school of Georgian poets. This was a group not only named after the reigning monarch but also to the romantic poets of the previous Georgian period whose work they were trying to emulate. What typified the entire movement, and Lawrence's poems of the time were well-worn poetic tropes and deliberately used archaic language. Many of these poems displayed what John Ruskin referred to as the poetic fallacy, the tendency to ascribe human emotions to animals and even inanimate objects. Just as World War I dramatically changed the work of many of the poets who saw service in the trenches, Lawrence's own work also saw a dramatic change, during his years in Cornwall. Influenced by Walt Whitman, he began writing in free verse. He set forth his manifesto for much of his later version the introduction to "New Poems". "We can get rid of the stereotyped movements and the old hackneyed associations of sound or sense. We can break down those artificial conduits and canals through which we do so love to force our utterance. We can break the stiff neck of habit.... But we cannot positively prescribe any motion, any rhythm."

Lawrence returned to many of his early poems when then were collected in 1928. Part of the endeavour was to fictionalize it and also at the same time to remove some of the artifice of his first works. As he himself says, "A young man is afraid of his demon and puts his hand over the demon's mouth sometimes and speaks for him." His best-known poems are probably those dealing with nature as is to be found in the collection, *Birds, Beasts and Flowers*, including the tortoise poems.

> In the deep, strange-scented shade of the great dark
>   carob tree
> I came down the steps with my pitcher
> And must wait, must stand and wait, for there
> He was at the trough before me. (Snake)

The above lines from the poem, "Snake" is another of Lawrence's most spectacular poem.

Some of his most frequent concerns are those of man's modern distance from nature and also subtle hints at religious themes.

Douglas A. Mackey in *D.H. Lawrence: The Poet Who Was Not Wrong*, says that if Lawrence had any disillusionment with society its closed system of thinking, the society of nature more than compensated for it. The contact with the great impersonal, he says, and the natural forces and with birds, beasts and flowers, he was inspired with an impetus to experience the great flow of life outside him and to try to record his experiences.

In "Bare Fig Trees", Lawrence begins the poem with a natural object. He then uses it as a point of departure for a voyage into his 'creative consciousness'. Using an inorganic image to bring a heightened sense of otherness, he has the "weird fig tress...made of sweet, untarnished silver in the southern air". A mysterious life-force that is strangely wise is represented by their "nude, healthy, half-dark", "suave" features. Sitting beneath one of the tress, the poet "laugh at Time" and laugh at dull Eternity. These are certain false absolutes that man in his "uncomfortableness" has set up. These ideals become inherently bounded by the limited nature of man's mind. Mackey tells us that everything changes in the second half of the poem. The tree, a "many-branching candlebrum" turns into a 'demon' of democracy which mocks man's pretensions towards that ideal. Every twig of the tree appears to be a "sun-socket". The fig tree is exalted for representing a democratic aristocracy, where all the members of the society are aristocrats and "met the sun". The fig tree has a perfection that man attempts to emulate in an insignificant way. Human society is not a democracy of aristocrats; men are mostly out of touch with the "sun". Nature and its reality is not far from Lawrence's poems. In "Turkey-cock", Lawrence imparted another great reality by nature. The metallic image of the wattles being "the colour of steel-slag.... Cooling to a powdery, pale oxidized sky-blue", signifies the bird's otherness. Here Lawrence is trying to convey something unusual, Mackey remarks, it is a sense of imperfection in nature. That God has been somewhat sloppy when making this bird is hinted to by the words, "something unfinished", "a raw un-smelted passion" and an assertion of "raw contradictoriness".

Douglas A. Mackey continues his study by telling us next that Lawrence rejected "static perfection", he opted for verse which would be "spontaneous and flexible as flame". Likewise he is both attracted by and repelled by the turkey cock that is deep in aboriginal blood consciousness, dripping with passion of the creator's furnace. The wattled head of the turkey signifies the darkness of the Beginning and the "sun-round tail" is of the End. Lawrence is reminded of the "somber, dead, feather-lustrous aztecs", it also seems to remind him of the modern Western man, being "will-tense" and mentally consciousness. The "smelted pure" bird will usher in the resurgence of the ancient Aztec spirit. This would herald in a "new day"—a more integrated life for man. Lawrence's favourite symbol of fulfillment, the phoenix, is what the turkey will presumably become.

Lawrence inherited his passionate imagination from Thomas Hardy, remarks Dr. Andrzej Diniejko, in his study of "Thomas Hardy and D.H. Lawrence: A Literary Kinship". Thomas Hardy was regarded by Lawrence as his spiritual father. The sensual writing of Lawrence is influenced by Hardy's description of women and landscape. In the "Study of Thomas Hardy" (1914), Lawrence gives credit to Hardy for being his master and his principal influence. The study of Dr. Andrzej Diniejko shows how Lawrence transcended the view of man in society characteristic of Victorian fiction. This was similar to Hardy. He created his characters as elemental men and women. Both possessed a cosmic mind. Lawrence evoked in his fiction mysterious bond found between human existence and the natural universe. Just as Hardy laid importance in his novels, short stories and poems an awareness of the natural, so did Lawrence in the early part of the twentieth century. John Paterson observes:

> If Hardy was dear to Lawrence, it was because he rehabilitated not only Nature as a source of mystery

> and miracle but Man himself. By restoring the ancient heavenly connection between the human creature and the natural world around it, by establishing what Lawrence called 'the true correspondence between the material cosmos and the human soul'. Hardy sought like Lawrence after him to make the human character more wondrous and surprising than traditionally realistic novelists had dreamed of in their philosophies. (462)

In quite another aspect of his study of Thomas Hardy and Lawrence, Dr. Andrzej Diniejko, remarks that the dichotomy between nature and civilization, and between "flesh and spirit" is also studied by Lawrence. These were themes held dear by Hardy. Human existence is envisaged in terms of duality. The Lawrentian natural universe is akin to that of Hardy. Human beings remain united with nature by primeval bonds which modern industrial culture keeps trying to destroy. Lawrence was quick to point as was Hardy to the evil of the rapidly expanding industrialization of England. This expansion was depriving men and women of their natural instincts and personal freedom. The spiritual father of Lawrence being Hardy, Lawrence learned a new approach from him to man and nature. Lawrence believed in the organic connection between them. Human nature was robbed of its freedom by social and religious conventions. Lawrence could discern, like Hardy, the duality between "flesh and soul". Both the writers believed that human life is split between a conscious, biological (natural) existence.

Nature is to be found in abundance in D.H. Lawrence's novels. Lawrence's lovers often make love in open space, in the lap of nature. Qamar Naheed, in his book, *D.H. Lawrence: Treatment of Nature in Early Novels*, tells us how looking for eternal joy in Nature, Lawrence makes his characters his mouthpiece when they describe the grandeur of natural objects and express their tender feeling of love in natural surroundings. Like *The White Peacock*, *The Trespasser*, is full of the description of nature. The image of the sea, the sun and the moon is used in the novel. Lawrence had a philosophical bent of mind. The following passage reflects this:

> He could always sympathize with the wistful little flowers, and trees lonely in their crowds, and wild, sad sea birds. In these things, he recognized the great yearning, the ache outwards towards something, with which he was ordinarily burdened. (*The Trespasser*, Penguin Books, 1960: 44). But with Helena, in this large sea-morning, he was whole and perfect as the day.

Within the framework of *Sons and Lovers*, Nature is given an impression and fascinating treatment. When the love life of the Morels become strained, Nature comes to them as a soothing element, capable of wiping away their sorrows and troubles. When Mrs. Morel is depressed and feels uneasy within the confines of her house, she moves into the front garden and immediately the soothing effect of various flowers acts as a balm to her troubled soul. The scent of the flowers comforts her and she finds compensation in the beauty of Nature:

> There she stood, trying to soothe herself with the scent of flowers and the fading, beautiful evening....
>
> (*Sons and Lovers*, D.H. Lawrence, Wordsworth Classics, 1992)

Mr. Morel also loves the early morning. He is fond of walking across the fields. Different objects of Nature seem to him friendly and congenial. Paul and Miriam, are great lovers of Nature. The world of Nature gives him inner satisfaction. Natural beauty has a strange fascination for him and it is for this reason also and not for Miriam alone that he goes to Willey Farm. The beauty of Nature and her changing colours stimulate him. The moon and the sun play their effects on him. Flowers are his special love, and whenever he sees a beautiful flower he wants to make it a part of himself. He would breathe a flower in such a way as if he and the flower were loving each other.... The girl whom he loves is also a lover of Nature:

> so her friend, her companion, her lover was nature. She saw the sun declining wanly. In the dusky, cold hedgerows were some red leaves. She lingered to gather them, tenderly, passionately. The love in her fingertips

> caressed the leaves; the passion in her heart came to a glow upon the leaves.
>
> (*Sons and Lovers*, D.H. Lawrence, Wordsworth Classics, 1992)

Both Miriam and Paul seek emotional fulfillment from one another. In her company he gains insight and his vision goes deeper:

> They went into the garden. The sky behind the townlet and the churches was orange-red; the flower garden was flooded with a strange warm light that lifted every leaf into significance. Paul passed along a row of sweet peas.., gathering a blossom here and there, all cream and pale blue. Miriam followed.... (*Sons and Lovers*, D.H. Lawrence, Wordsworth Classics, 1992)

I would like to end this study with a most enchanting poem of D.H. Lawrence, reverberating with the beauty of Nature:

Red Geranium and Godly Mignonette

Imagine that any mind ever thought a red geranium
As if the redness of a red geranium could be anything
But a sensual experience
And as if sensual experience could take place
Before there were any senses.
We know that even God could not imagine
The redness of a red geranium
Nor the smell of mignonette
When geraniums were not, and mignonette neither
And even when they were,
Even God would have to have a nose
To smell the mignonette.
You can't imagine the Holy Ghost sniffing
At cherry-pie heliotrope.
Or the Most High, during the coal age
Cudgeling his mighty brains
Even if he had any brains: straining his mighty mind
To think, among the moss and mud of lizards and mastodons

To think out, in the abstract,
When all was twilit green and muddy,
'Now there shall be tum-tiddly-um and tum-tiddly-um,
Hey presto! Scarlet geranium!'
We know it couldn't be done.
But imagine, among mud and mastodons
God singing and yearning, in that dark green mess
Oh, for some other beauty, some other beauty
That blossomed at last, red geranium, and mignonette.

Works Cited

Lawrence, D.H., *Lady Chatterley's Lover* and *A Propos of Lady Chatterley's Lover*, ed. Michael Squires, Cambridge University Press, 2002.

Mackey, Douglas A. *D.H. Lawrence: The Poet Who Was Not Wrong*. Borgo Press, 2007.

Naheed, Qamar. *D.H. Lawrence: Treatment of Nature in Early Novels*. A.P.H. Publishing Corporation, New Delhi, 2008.

Oates, Joyce Carol. *The Hostile Sun: The Poetry of D.H. Lawrence*. Black Sparrow Press, 1973.

Paterson, John. "Lawrence's Vital Source: Nature and Character in Thomas Hardy" in U.C. Knoepflmacher and G.B. Tennyson, eds. *Nature and the Victorian Imagination*. Berekey, Los Angeles. London: University of California Press, 1977.

Pinion, F.B. *A D.H. Lawrence Companion: Life, Thought and Work*. London: Macmillan, 1978.

Wikipedia

Internet Sources:

www.counter-currents.com/tag/derek-hawthorne/page/4/

(Published in Counter-Currents Publishing-Books Against Time, Jan. 6, 2011.)

www.griseldaonline.it/../lawrence-ecological-consciousness-pissarello.html

www.victorianweb.org/authors/hardy/dinirjko.html

(written by Dr. Andrzej Diniejko, Senior Lecturer in English Literature and Culture, Warsaw University.)

9

The Battle of the Sexes: D.H. Lawrence and the Struggle for Modern Sexuality in *Lady Chatterley's Lover*

Charlotte Fiehn

Although Lawrence certainly considers the problem of sexuality in his other major novels—*Sons and Lovers*, *The Rainbow*, and *Women in Love* in particular—*Lady Chatterley's Lover* remains the most precise exploration of sexuality in the modern world. In Connie Chatterley, Clifford Chatterley, and Oliver Mellors, Lawrence develops the most extensive and the most precise portrait of struggling modern personalities and sexual identities. Connie Chatterley is the most clearly disconnected woman, literally emaciated by lack of physical sexual contact from her husband, Clifford and emotional sexual contact from the her sexual partners before Mellors. Clifford, likewise, represents the most precise portrait of the disconnected modern man. The Great War, the ultimate culmination of ideas, literally destroys Clifford, sending him home "more or less in bits" (Lawrence 1). Clearly, though, Clifford also embraces the world of ideas, the modern, and he chooses to disconnect himself from those who do not belong to his social class. Finally, in Oliver Mellors, Lawrence portrays a man disconnected from the world but capable of reconnection. In Mellors' transformation, as much as in Connie's, Lawrence shows a certain kind of sex, sexual connection, as the cure for modern disconnection. This paper, then, explores Lawrence's representation of sexuality as a problem of a distinctly modern, industrialized society, beginning with the development of his perspective in *Sons and Lovers*, *The Rainbow*, and *Women in Love*, but concentrating on its ultimate manifestation in *Lady Chatterley's Lover*. To demonstrate the final maturity of Lawrence's thoughts on gender and sexuality, too, this essay considers Lawrence resolves the modern sexual disconnect through his depiction of Connie and Mellor's sexual and gender-specific identities.

As Diana Trilling wrote in her essay on "Lawrence and the Movements of Modern Culture", sexuality for Lawrence is "nothing if not conditioned...by the full-scale emotions which he insisted upon both as its source and justification but also by the larger social purpose to which he thought that sexuality must minister" (3). This manifests, too, to some degree, in most of Lawrence's major novels. In *Sons and Lovers*, for instance, the first of Lawrence's major works and a novel that emphasizes emotional and even sexual jealousy between Paul Morel and his mother, Lawrence stresses a clear disjointure in the sexual relationship between past and present. Lawrence describes the relationship between Paul Morel's parents in detail to establish this, too. From his description of Mrs. Morel's dislocation, her sense of isolation from her husband, become relevant in establishing Paul's own alienation later. Chronicling the "Early Married Life of the Morel", that is, Lawrence describes the struggles between Arthur and Gertrude Morel in much the same language as he later describes those between Paul and his respective lovers. The first three months of their marriage are "perfectly happy" (*Sons and Lovers* 14) and a certain novelty applies to their relationship to one another. Lawrence notes that, for instance, "[s]he had never been "thee'd" and "thou'd" before" (14), implying the social disparity between husband and wife. He also highlights a kind of conscious unity. As Mrs. Morel accepts the novelty of a miner's life, seeing her husband as "noble" (14), he abstains from alcohol, signing "the pledge" (14) and "wore the blue ribbon of a teetotaller" (14). Yet, the appearances of their life are misleading. Mrs. Morel, in particular, has perceptions that become undone over time. She, for instance, believed that they lived "in his own house" (14). She also shows resilience with her "ladylike ways" (14) that cause her mother-in-law and sisters-in-law to mock her. In terms of intimacy, too, Lawrence describes a strange disparity and disjointure between husband and wife. She grows "weird of love-talk" (14) and tries to "open her heart to seriously to him" (14). This implies a degree of performance, of show, in their intimacy at first. Mrs. Morel notes him listening "deferentially but without understanding" (14), which "killed her efforts in a finer intimacy, and she had flashes of fear" (14). The more Mrs. Morel becomes conscious of the disparity between herself and her husband, the social and intellectual distances in particular, the more she becomes afraid and even angry. As her husband is "restless of an evening" (14), too, though, he finds that "to be near her" is not enough. Eventually, Mrs. Morel turns to her son, her child for consolation and feels, otherwise, "very lonely, miles away from her own people" (17), cleaving to her child because the presence of her husband "only made [her loneliness] more intense" (17). The result is "a battle between husband and wife—a fearful bloody battle that ended only with the death of one" (16). It is also a battle that ultimately involves each of the children born to them. As Mrs. Morel fails to make her husband not so "purely sensuous" (17) but also "moral, religious" (17), trying to force him to "face things" (17), she brings about a transformation in her children, especially in Paul.

Like the relationship between his mother and father, Paul's adult, romantic relationships with Miriam Leivers and Clara Dawes involve a great deal of uncertainty and conflict. In "Lad and Girl Love", for instance, Lawrence describes the disparity between Paul and Miriam as they embark on their doomed romance. Miriam reverts to a "sneer" (*Sons and Lovers* 180) and Paul feels resentment towards her, for the way she acts towards him. While they both avoid acknowledging "[t]hat there was any love growing between [them]" (180), Paul "thought he was too sane for such sentimentality, and she thought herself too lofty" (180). Lawrence also stresses that "both were late in coming to maturity, and psychical ripeness" (180), too, to the point that, eventually, their physical contact causes violent reactions in him: "if she put her arm in his, it caused him almost torture. His consciousness seemed to split. The place where she was touching him ran hot with friction. He was one internecine battle, and he became cruel to her" (191). Unable to maintain a relationship with either Miriam Leivers or Clara

Dawes, at the death of his mother, Paul finds himself, as John A. Taylor put it, "entirely alone" (380). Lawrence describes Paul "turned away...the last hold for him...gone" (*Sons and Lovers* 455). Although the pronouncement of Paul's fate, his likelihood of being able to achieve a positive relationship is negligible. As Thomas Jeffers argues in his study of *Sons and Lovers*, "[m]ind and spirit are patently what motivate Gertrude Morel once the work of her loins (conceiving, gestating, birthing) is done" (Jeffers 197). Considering the portrait of Arthur Morel, too, Jeffers argues that, "For all the beer and lack of vocational ambition.... Morel is not the melodramatically "bad father" who beats his wife and children and gambles away whatever money he doesn't drink" (197). Beyond the "flashes of violence" (197) that Arthur does exhibit, the disparity between Paul's parents, creating a model for Paul's own struggles, arises from Mrs. Morel's "disillusioned standoffishness" (197) and her own clinging to the intellectual, a life in the mind, in the abstract, which paves the way for modernism.

In *The Rainbow* Ursula experiences a similar sense of disjointure. She finds, for instance, that "[h]er life was always only partial...never did she live completely" (*The Rainbow* 309) as she endeavors to establish a career for herself and so displaces herself. The partiality of her life is such that she lacks a meaningful expression for "the anguish of her youth and her young passion and yearning" (309). Instead of finding a meaningful way to express her sexuality, as Connie Chatterley and Oliver Mellors do, Ursula's sexuality does nothing but inform her isolation. Although "[s]he called to him from her heart wherever she went, her limbs vibrated with anguish towards him...radiating force of her soul" (309), she does not know who he is, "where did he exist?" (309). Amidst the "constant bad news of the war" (309), too, Ursula feels as if the world is "a hurt, a hurt, a hurt against her" (309). The result, Lawrence explains quite clearly: "in this state", he emphasizes, "her sexual life flamed into a kind of disease within her" (309). She has limited release through a homosexual relation either. Her sexuality, not expressed in any viable heterosexual context either, then, becomes a quite literally destructive force.

Her sexuality ultimately causes feel pain as she continues to try to be "sensitive" (309). After the sexual encounter with Skrebensky, too, after which she becomes pregnant, Ursula is no less free. Indeed, she returns home even less alive and even less her own agent. She is "faint, dim, closed up" (448). She can "scarcely speak or notice...as if her energy were frozen" (448). Her experience of pregnancy, her first awareness of it, also suggests a kind of diseased state. As "weeks crawled by in apathy" (448) and she continues on "inert, without strength or interest" (448), she becomes "stricken under the pain of herself and of him" (448), the pain "like a flame that took hold of her limbs and body" (448). The developed image positions Ursula as if she is "tied to the stake" (448). She experiences a sense of "wonder" but even the world is part of "flaming hours" (448) and the flames are all-consuming, "licking her and devouring her" (448). As Lawrence explains, though, the flames are both destructive and "good" (448). They represent the dual creative and destructive force of Ursula's sexuality and of sexuality in the modern world in general. Of course, Ursula's submission and her epiphany, which occur in the novel's final chapter, occur too late to bring about a meaningful union with the father of her child. Even as Ursula asks herself, at last, "[w]as it not enough that she had her man, her children, her place of shelter under the sun?" (449), even as she sees that she "would marry and love her husband and fill her place simply" (449), seeing her mother "in a just and true light" (449), confessing herself and submitting, giving "her limbs to the bondage" (449), it is too late and he is married (457).

In *Women in Love*, although Lawrence conceives her after a different fashion, Ursula has moved on from the events of *The Rainbow* to accept a second epiphany of sorts. She has understood that her first acceptance was not enough; that she endeavored to force the idea of a man in her life, of a meaningful relationship, when she had rather to accept the possibility less divisively; she had to be more passive still to conform to Lawrence's ideal. In the opening chapter and the discussion between Ursula and Gudrun, Gudrun is the one who claims that "[t]he man makes it impossible" (*Women in Love* 3) and the prospect of children ["I get no feeling whatever from the thought of bearing children" (3)] is essentially unappealing. Ursula appears far more receptive both to marriage and to the prospect of children. In effect, this foreshadows that Ursula's relationship with Rupert Birkin will be the more successful of the two. Gudrun's relationship with Gerald Crich, overwhelming in its self-destructive because of disparity of intention and nature. As Carolyn Tilgham suggests in her study of *Woman in Love*, however, one of Lawrence's principle objectives is to unravel the "conventional and tightly woven associations of sexual desire and middle-class heterosexuality" (90). Indeed, as Tilgham suggests, Lawrence "sets himself the task of divorcing desire from heterosexual coupling...to challenge their repeated conflation in the bourgeois values that structure British courtship rituals, marriage, and home life" (90). The principle method of achieving this end, though, is through the way in which Gudrun and Crich attack each other and, by extension, Ursula and Birkin. An unconventional pairing emerges: Ursula and Gudrun's relationship, their familial connection, leads to the opportunity for Rupert Birkin and Gerald Crich to form their attachment. As the conversation between Ursula and Birkin demonstrates at the end of the novel, the unconventional association between Birkin and Crich exposes the limits of the conventional heterosexual relationship, as Ursula and Gudrun, respectively, formulate their connections. "It's a bitter thing to me" (*Women in Love* 495), Birkin says and Ursula asks whether it is "that he's dead" (495). She offers herself as consolation, "[y]ou've got me" (495) and asks "[a]ren't I enough for you?" (495). Lawrence allows Birkin's confession, then, to destroy those conventions Tilgham refers to in her study. The relationship between the two men does not conform to the standards of any kind of courtship rituals and it has no conventional result, no overt sexual or domestic connection. Yet, Birkin recognizes the potential for deeper connections between individuals, men and women, when he declares that "I wanted a man friend, as eternal as you and I are eternal" (495). As Tigham argues, "[t]he substitution for heterosexual coupling" is very much "unfettered, "uncoupled" heterosexual marriage" between Birkin and Ursula, which then gives way to the impeding of social values and expectations through the supplementing of the "newly defined heterosexual relationship with an implicit textual approbation of the homoerotic desire felt by Birkin for Gerald Crich" (90). At the novel's conclusion, although Birkin admits the capacity for isolation, that he "can live all [his] life without anybody else, any other sheer intimacy" (496), a "complete, really happy" (496) life depends on more profound connections, an "eternal union" (496) that transcends conventions.

If transcendence and redefinition are the focal points of *Women in Love*, however, with *Lady Chatterley's Lover*, Lawrence offers a solution to the overwhelming struggle between men and women and the relentless challenge to sexuality in the modern world. While overt homoerotic or homosexual elements emerge in *Women in Love* through Birkin's desire for "another kind of love" (*Women in Love* 496), *Lady Chatterley* exposes that the idea in a more universal and predominantly heterosexual focus with its examination of the relationship between Connie Chatterley and Mellors. In *Lady Chatterley's Lover*, Lawrence not only concentrates on expanding the modern context implied by *Women in Love*, but provides a clear solution to the problem of disconnection. Indeed, *Lady Chatterley's Lover* opens with a distinct declaration about the state of the world. As a means of grounding hid discussion about the potential for "eternal union" (*Woman in Love* 496), that is, Lawrence lays claim to time and space of the modern world. "Ours is essentially a tragic age" (*Lady Chatterley's Lover* 1), his narrator declares; "we are among the ruins, we start to build up new little habitats, to have new little hopes" (1). The immediate context of this novel, of course, is the First World War. For Lawrence, the war was a war of ideas, the final proof of the destructive power of ideas, especially their destructive power acted upon people. Although industrialization is an element of modernism and a product of ideas as well, the first image of destruction is a man, Clifford Chatterley, "[h]is hold on life was marvelous" (1) and the irony in this decidedly apparent. "He didn't die" (1), though, Lawrence stresses. Instead, he becomes accustomed to his new form: "the bits seemed to grow together again" (1). Although "the lower half of his body...paralysed forever" (1), leaves him incapable of having a sexual relationship, Clifford is perhaps disconnected even before he experiences physical paralysis. Notably, Clifford "professed to like Wragby" (11), which means that he has a connection to the house which is "a long low old house with brown stone" (10), surrounded by the view of the "chimney of Tevershall pit, with its clouds of steam and smoke...trailed in utter hopeless ugliness for a long and gruesome mile" (14), the "willful, blank dreariness" (14). More than this, Clifford also has a horror of anyone who is not of his class. The tradesmen, the people who populate Tevershall village and the mines are distant from Clifford. Lawrence notes, for instance, that "[t]here was no communication between Wragby Hall and Tevershall village, none" (11) and "[n]o caps were touched, no curtseys bobbed" because the colliers, the miners, "merely stared" (11) and the tradesmen "nodded awkwardly" (11). All of this disconnection feeds into the sense of how Clifford is in physical relationships anyway, at least somewhat by choice. "Of physical life", Lawrence stresses, Connie and Clifford "lived very little" (14). Stressing the modern nature of Clifford and also Connie's disconnection, the problem of sexuality in the modern world, Lawrence also describes Clifford's lack of interest in sex and his desire for knowledge. Feeding the "strange denial of the common pulse of humanity" (11), Clifford studied "the technicalities of coal-mining" (6) and he joins in with the war. Being "more upper-class than Connie" (6) and also at ease in "the narrow 'great world' that is, landed aristocracy society" (6), Lawrence stresses Clifford's isolation, somewhat deliberate, in his fear of "middle and lower class humanity" (6). His ambition also becomes significant, too, because it feeds into the sense that he isolates himself and he associates himself with the world of ideas that Lawrence himself, consistently in his major novels, identifies as destructive. Clifford's ambition and his reversion to writing stories that are "[c]lever, rather spiteful" (13) again stresses his intellectualism; as Lawrence clarifies, "the whole world of his being [is] in his stories" quite early on in the novel (13).

The problem of sexuality in the modern world has a powerful rendering in the portraits of Connie and Mellors, too, at first, before their relationship develops. Lawrence describes Connie on various occasions as disconnected and physically sickened by the lack of contact with the natural world. Her father comments on her lack of sexual contact from Clifford as essentially undermining Connie's femininity. He remarks that she is a "demi-vierge" (*Lady Chatterley's Lover* 15) and that she looks sickly, "getting thinner" (18), feeling a growing "restlessness" (18), which, of course, is a transformation that continues until she starts to visit Mellors. As she moves closer to a sexual relationship with Mellors, she also becomes more conscious of nature and the coldness of the various expressions of modernism. She recognizes Clifford as having a chilling effect upon her. His "prostrations made her go cold for head to foot" (115). Mrs. Bolton and "the sound of businessmen" (115) also cause her to "go cold" (115). Lawrence also stresses that Clifford's dependence on Connie is also largely responsible for the development of this coldness, the emotional and psychological problems that develop. As "nothing really touched him" (13) so Connie realizes that "she herself didn't really, not really touch him" (13). To some degree, she recognizes that Clifford is "a negation of human contact" (13). Clifford's negation also risks her own. She becomes uncertain of her own femininity. Although she achieves some release through her affair with Michaelis, some break from Clifford's "blind, imperious instinct to become known" (19), Michaelis is ultimately a kind of contrast to Clifford. Being "absolutely Bond Street" (19), Michaelis causes Clifford's "country soul" to recoil (19) but he is ambitious, a professional, a modern man; he is also "a hopeless outsider" (19). He also "followed blindly" and moves without noticing things, without having "contact with his surroundings" (22-23). Sexually, too, Michaelis feels confounded by expectation. He expects that Connie will hate him. He declares that "a woman is supposed to" (24) after a sexual encounter. As for Mellors, Lawrence describes him as, initially, "kindly, but distant" (114). Like Connie, he also looks "thin and ill" (114) initially. However, like Connie, and unlike

Clifford, Mellors also holds on to some greater humanity. He has "keen blue eyes" (114) and he looks at Connie; Lawrence gives the clear sense that Mellors is sensitive to the things around him, he is "sane and wholesome" (114) and he "looked at her" (114) as well; unlike Clifford and Michaelis, Mellors has the capacity to make connections even as he experience disconnection. To demonstrate how the problem of sexuality may resolve, Lawrence inevitably describes the physical relationship between Connie and Mellors in considerable detail. He stresses not just the sexual relationship, going into detail about the way in which Connie and Mellors have sex, but provides an almost philosophical aspect to their sexual encounters. In particular, he uses Connie's early doubts about her relationship to Mellors, her questioning of the situation, of her reaction to their sexual encounters, to probe the proper way for her, the female, to act. In their first encounter, for instance, Lawrence shows Mellors as dominant and active. Connie, on the other hand, demonstrates "a queer obedience" (117) and a profound submissiveness to the "soft, groping, helplessly delirious hand touching her body" (117). Even as Lawrence stresses Connie's struggles with her "tormented modern-woman's brain" (118) in this encounter, however, he reveals her optimum state: laying back, "quite still, in a sort of sleep, in a sort of dream" (118). In a sense, Lawrence leads Connie to experience a disconnection from her doubting, disconnected "modern-woman's brain" (118) through her submission to Mellors, giving herself up to Mellors and his own "mysterious stillness" (118). The submission leads Connie to start "realizing the depth of the other things in her" (137), recognizing "[a]nother self...alive in her, burning molten and soft in her womb and bowels" (137). She transforms gradually as her relationship with Mellors progresses, as she continues to give into him, becoming "flowing and alive now and vulnerable, and helpless in adoration of him as the most naïve woman" (137). Thus, Lawrence demonstrates the way in which submission for the female and a dominance for a male can lead to an optimal, creative, positive relationship. Connie's eventual pregnancy provides final evidence of her rejuvenation. She recognizes "the immense difference between having a child to oneself, and having a child to a man whom one's bowels yearned towards" (137). Her restoration to life is manifest in the way that "her womb, that had always been shut, had opened and filled with new life" (137).

Lady Chatterley's Lover represents the culmination of Lawrence's ideas about sexuality, though, and the problem of sexuality in the modern world. It stresses not just the disconnection of the individual but the consequence of disconnection and the potential method for reconnection. The consequences of disconnection particularly emerge in Lawrence's portrait of Connie. Like several of his earlier female characters, Connie feels burdened by her gender, "the agony of her own female forlornness" (115), as part of her disconnection. Lawrence also describes her "tormented modern woman's brain" (115) as giving her no "rest" (115), contributing to her sense of uncertainty and, particularly, her resistance to giving herself "to the man" (115). Connie also struggles to identify Mellors when first they are together. She questions what sort of man he is, "[w]hat sort of man was he, really?" (123), even feeling quite overwhelmed that she does not know him well ["Stranger! Stranger!" (128)]. Even as she experiences these manifestations of mystery—and Connie does recognize the mysteriousness of Mellors, the mysteriousness of his masculinity, though, Connie also feels a growing reconnection. She rediscovers the natural world, in a sense, as Mellors discovers her femininity. Although, initially, "[s]he did not understand the beauty he found in her, through touch with her living secret body" (127), she clearly comes to understand it, to eventually share in the secret, in the mystery; "the flame" (312) they share and acknowledge together at the novel's conclusion. The problem of sexuality, then, as Lawrence presents it, is that modern men, men exemplified by the likes of Clifford Chatterley, are physically and emotionally disconnected, without the means to recognize, to sense or otherwise perceive the mysteries of womanhood and the natural world. Similar disconnection emerges in the characterization of Paul and Mrs. Morell in *Sons and Lovers* and even that of Ursula and Gudrun *The Rainbow*. In Clifford Chatterley, the portrait of the modern man and the disconnected man are both more developed and more precise to apply the cultural dimension that the likes of Jae-Kyung Koh considers in an article on D.H. Lawrence's world vision of cultural regeneration. Indeed, as Koh stresses, the cultural connection, highly developed in *Lady Chatterley's Lover*, is to World War I and the "fundamental changes in postwar British and European society" (189). Lawrence stresses the war as also "a symptom of the final decline" and Clifford, as far as he is representative, standing in as the "inhuman mechanical determinism of the post-war period" (190). "Connie's world" (196), her isolation, also stands in as the indication of "an enclosed and barren" space (196) and a space that she overcomes through her pregnancy with Mellor's child and the removal of herself and the child from Clifford's influence. Mellors, too, as Koh argues, is the only character in Lawrence's fiction, who "has come through the war, but is able to move beyond the experience of destruction" (204). The final message of the novel on sexuality and gender, at least, is that, in Mellors, Connie, and their new connection, a "new set of values emerge" and the "possibility in postwar Britain of new kinds of relationships" (204) emerge.

The conclusion of *Lady Chatterley's Lover* is the affirmation that a meaningful sexual connection between men and women—"fucking" (312) in a creative fashion, with a man dominant and a woman submissive—allows even those who have experienced the ultimate devastation of intellectualism, of ideas, in the war, cannot only survive but thrive. Disconnected by modernity, by the war experiences as the ultimate realization of modernity and industrialism, individuals can nonetheless reconnect to nature, to a natural state of being, and to natural relationships if they give themselves up to the mystery of nature. More so than in any other of his novels, too, sexuality emerges in *Lady Chatterley's Lover* as fundamental to the continuity and sustainability of society; fundamental and positive if it involves male dominance and female submission. As Jeffrey Meyers argues in his essay on D.H. Lawrence and homosexuality, for Lawrence, the "intrinsic sexual nature [is] dual and not entirely male...male and female elements [being] in conflict, not in balance" (135). *Lady Chatterley's Lover* stands apart in its dealing with sexuality because it brings about a kind of balance between Mellors and Connie. The novel's resolution, in that sense, is beyond Paul's ambiguous state in *Sons and Lovers*, beyond Ursula's in *The Rainbow*, and certainly beyond both Ursula and Gudrun in *Women in Love*, allowing that Ursula and Gudrun in particular are modern women and largely incapable of the kind of submission that Connie achieves. The balance extends beyond mere sexuality, though, in this last of Lawrence's novels, because it also sees an affirmation of gender roles—an affirmation of Connie's submission, her passivity. Hers is the "Lady Jane" role in the end; she is an object for her male lover, a thing to be worshipped, certainly, but a vessel of his sexuality and the affirming force of his gender, too. She affirms his dominance and allows his continuity, his sustainability as a means of balancing the gender conflict that otherwise defines Lawrence's earlier pairings. *Lady Chatterley's Lover* stands alone in its depiction of a resolution for these conflicts, too, yet the benefit of comparing it with his earlier major works is substantial. In the end, comparison affirms and even expands understanding of Lawrence's final maturity, his final revelation of the potential for peace in the relationship between men and women in the modern age or, perhaps more accurately, beyond it, surpassing it. Most of Lawrence's writing, as Raymond Williams says, is "an antithesis to the powerful industrial thesis which had been proposed for him" (204). In *Lady Chatterley's Lover*, however, the reader sees Lawrence able to satisfy the "hunger for a new creative, life-affirming age" (Koh 205) by proposing how, with Connie and Mellors like Adam and Eve of a "new future" (Koh 205), a potentially post-modern age, may emerge through the creative energy of the male and female.

Works Cited

Jeffers, Thomas L. "*Sons and Lovers*, and the End of Sex." *The Hudson Review*, 52, (1999): 191-204. JSTOR. Web. 4 Aug. 2014.

Koh, Jae-Kyung. "D.H. Lawrence's World Vision of Cultural Regeneration in *Lady Chatterley's Lover*." *Midwest Quarterly* 43.2 (2002): 189. *Academic Search Premier*. Web. 6 Aug. 2014.

Lawrence, D.H. *Lady Chatterley's Lover*. Garden City, NY: Nelson Doubleday. 1928.

———. *Sons and Lovers*. New York: Barnes and Nobles Classics. 2003.

———. *The Rainbow*. London: Penguin Classics. 2007.

———. *Women in Love*. New York: The Viking Press. 1969.

Meyers, Jeffrey. "D.H. Lawrence and Homosexuality." *D.H. Lawrence: Novelist, Poet, Prophet*. Ed. Stephen Spender. London: Wiedenfeld & Nicolson. 1973. 135-46.

Raymond, Williams. *Culture and Society:* 1780-1950. New York: Columbia University Press. 1983.

Taylor, John A. "The Greatness in *Sons and Lovers*." *Modern Philology*, 71, (1974): 380-87. JSTOR. Web. 4 Aug. 2014.

Tilghman, Carolyn. "Unruly Desire, Domestic Authority, and Odd Coupling In D.H. Lawrence's *Women in Love*." *Women's Studies* 37.2 (2008): 89-109. *Academic Search Premier*. Web. 5 Aug. 2014.

10

The Problematics of Gender with Reference to the Philosophy of D.H. Lawrence

Jayeeta Ray

In one of his essays Lawrence articulated that the great relationship for humanity will always be the relation between man and woman. The relation between man and woman, woman and woman, parent and child will always be subsidiary. It is the relation itself which is the quick and the central clue to human life (*A Selection from Phoenix, Henceforth ASFP* 180).

Lawrence was not only focusing on the husband-wife relationship rather on a whole gamut of relationships he was conscious of the various social hurdles that hamper normal and healthy man-woman relationships and so he at certain turnings suggested a plane beyond the social setting 'Rananim' and at other times used metaphors of stars, birds, rainbow and so on to describe a perfect relationship between a couple. In most of the novels however, we can discern Lawrence puzzled with the conflicts, tensions that are intertwined in every relationship in a tangible social set-up.

D.H. Lawrence's major novels—*Sons and Lovers*, *The Rainbow*, *Women in Love*, *Lady Chatterley's Lover* brings into play a whole gamut of polyphonic voices lending the texts a dynamic perspective. This becomes clear from the novel, *Women in Love* where we can visualize a multiplicity of unmerged voices of different characters who represent various points of view lending the novel a 'polyphonic' dimension.

Lawrence was deeply involved with the reconciliation of the rival and warring elements—for instance in his non-fiction work *The Crown*, Lawrence brings into play the figures of the lion and the unicorn where through their fighting he allegorizes the fight between the two opposite forces. In Frank Kermode's work it is stated:

> The lion is our dark nature, the unicorn our light, the strife and equilibrium is the third of the trinity, reconciling the two eternities between which we exist... perfection lies in their balance of the two opposing tendencies or streams.... (51)

The polar opposites are evident in almost every novel of Lawrence where we find diametrically opposite characters coming together and then going asunder. The male-female polarity has been articulated by Ursula in *The Rainbow*.

Nevertheless, it was begun now; this was thus transformed as she desired physical consummation through male-female polarity. Passion and must go on, the passion of Ursula to know her own maximum self, limited and so defined against him. She could limit and define herself against him, the male, she could be her maximum self, female oh female triumphant for one moment in exquisite assertion against the male, the supreme contradiction (*TR* 281).

The multiplicity of perspectives that one comes across in the novel of Lawrence is worth noting. This is evident in Lawrence's *The Rainbow*. Ursula's partner Skrebensky comes across as an automation. He has no sense of individual identity but believes in the modern concept of collectivity. In his soul Skrebensky was dead for he represented the great, established idea of life. However, though the relation between Ursula and Skrebensky got aborted yet it benefited Ursula to a great extent for it was through her romantic experience with Skrebensky that Ursula had a good knowledge of herself as a female. This development of her feminine self helps her in her relations with the next man in her life—Rupert Birkin figuring in *Women in Love*. Skrebensky acts as a stepping stone enabling her to form better relationship with Birkin who appears in the next novel, *Women in Love*. Ursula is portrayed in many contradictory colours. She is painted as an unconventional woman in very conventional set-up. When Ursula reaches her adolescence and adulthood, she experiences the maternal oppressive measures from her mother Anna and tries to liberate herself from the conventional mores. Lawrence sets Ursula through a range of familial, professional and sexual experiences. As a 'new woman' she enters a University College for her higher education, works as a teacher in a man's world and has certain uncommon new experiences on account of which she even undergoes immense suffering. She is the 'new woman' caught in the net of world that is neither totally traditional nor totally modernized. That she can establish herself as a human being and that also in a period which was extremely male-dominated speaks volumes as an assertive woman.

In the context of social and material setting, the man-woman relationships assume different dimensions. Lawrence was working on analyzing the defects in the institutions of love and marriage, man-man relationship, husband-wife relationship and so on. In his letter to Thomas Dunlop in 7 July 1914, Lawrence makes some valuable comments on marriage and on husband-wife relationship.

> But you may be taking yourself inwardly apart from her, and leaving her inwardly separate from you, which is no true marriage and is a form of failure.... There is the real sharing of one life.... One must learn to love, and go through a good deal of suffering to get to it like any knight of the grail, and the journey is always towards the other soul, not away from it. Do you think love is an accomplished thing, the day it is recognized? It isn't. To love you have to learn to understand the other, more than she understands herself and to submit to her understanding of you (*Letters* Vol. II: 191).

Lawrence believed in certain unwritten rules for a couple to live successfully, for instance 'the husband shall have to love his wife completely and implicitly and in entire nakedness of body and spirit'. Such a vision of human relationship has been a dominant theme in his novels. Lawrence was strictly against the dominant-subordinate hierarchal system in a relationship. He was opposed to the leader-cum-follower relationship. So to him the new relationship should be based on "between men and women, and not the one up one down, lead on I follow, *ich dien* sort of business." This unequal status of the partners is visible throughout Lawrence's novels. In *The Rainbow*, Will appears to be totally overpowered and overwhelmed by his wife Anna and her husband was to her the unknown to which she was delivered up. She was a flower that has been tempted forth into blossom, and has no retreat. He had her nakedness in his power. And who was he, what was he? A blind thing, a dark force without knowledge. She waited to preserve herself (*TR* 157).

Ursula, the woman of the next generation feels a profound hatred for such an existence. She is a new woman with progressive ideas. To Ursula, love is a supreme thing. In the eyes of Birkin, love is rather 'a maintaining of the self in mystic balance and integrity—like a star balanced with another star'.

Birkin pleads that love is a creative act "where man had being and woman had being, two pure beings, each constituting the freedom of the other, balancing each other like two poles of one force, like two angels or two demons".

Birkin who is the spokesperson of Lawrence is against the female urge to possess and cling on to the male partners. Even Ursula it is found wants to bind Birkin in chains just as Miriam and an older version in the form of Mrs. Morel who wishes to chain Paul. In a man-woman relationship, Birkin does not believe in the practice of domination of one partner over the other. On the other hand, he feels that they should live in freedom together 'like two stars constellated together'. Birkin fails to accept woman as the Magna Mater, the Mater Dolorasa as in Birkin's previous love Hermione, who wishes to possess Birkin's body and soul.

The apprehension of the male to be subsumed by the female is a product of the masculine/feminine binary. The discourse of the two social constructs has political ramifications. This idea has been expressed by Judith Butler in her famous work *Gender Trouble*. Even recent theorists like Lacan have highlighted on the 'formulae of sexuation'. This formula gets reversed through certain slogans: 'woman is a symptom of man', 'there is no sexual relationship'. These formulas reduce women to an inferior status and make them mere objects. This gets somewhat overruled in the fiction of D.H. Lawrence.

Lawrence was obsessed with the male-female dichotomy. At many instances in his critical works he has compartmentalized the attitude of the two sexes where maleness is associated with thought and purpose and femaleness is identified with emotion. In his *Fantasia of the Unconscious*, Lawrence highlighted the difference between men and women. Lawrence stated:

> The whole mode, the whole everything is really different in man and woman. Therefore we should keep boys and girls apart that they are pure and virgin in themselves. On mixing with one another, in becoming familiar, in being 'pals' they lose their own male and female integrity. And they lost the treasure of the future, the vital sex polarity.... For the magic and dynamism rest on otherness. (*Fantasia of the Unconscious*; henceforth *FOU* 103)

Lawrence highlighted on spirituality and other-worldly plane but this he did through the channel of mundane, this worldly things. To Lawrence, sexual and physical passion gives way to something rather more mystical and mystified. Sex is a channel, a doorway into something else. This can be illustrated from the portrayal of such characters as Lydia Brangwen, Ursula Brangwen, and Connie Chatterley and so on.

The relations between men and women in marriage changed colours in Lawrence's novels. Christianity made marriage in some respect inviolate. Man and wife, a king and queen with one or two subjects, a few square yards of territory of their own is the perfect definition of marriage.

Marriage according to Lawrence is an institution that reminds each partner of their respective roles. Women are the signifiers of 'Law' and men of 'Love' as discussed earlier. Men it is seen display will but women should avoid to show will. In *Aaron's Rod*, Lottie as a woman and as a mother felt herself as the 'first great source of life and being, and also of culture. The man was but the instrument and the finisher. She was the source and the substance (*AR* 252). In Lawrence's works, men are found to show will but it is believed that women should avoid it. In Lawrence's short story St. Mawr, Mrs. Witt is possessed by a dominating female will and is doomed to self-destruction. Hermione in Lawrence's novel *Women in Love* is another case study of obdurate will power and obstinacy Lawrence's main focus is on polyphony or multi-voicedness. Lawrence is always viewing things from a pluralistic perspective. In the first version of *Studies in Classic American Literature*, the multiple voices come into play.

While discussing the multiple voices in Lawrence's works, it becomes relevant to state that Lawrence was concerned about the fact of relation between man and his universe at a particular moment and he expressed this through his essay, "Why the Novel Matters". Unlike Flaubert who complained that the novel 'stood away from life as from a leper', Lawrence explained that 'the novel is a perfect medium for revealing to us the changing rainbow of our living relationship' (*ASFP* 180-81).

The power equations involved in a relationship even more pronounced in Lawrence's novel *Aaron's Rod* where it is stated that:

> Practically all men, even while demanding their selfish rights as superior males, tacitly agree to the fact of the sacred life-bearing priority of woman. Tacitly they yield to the worship to that which is female...they conspire to agree that all that is productive, all that is fine and sensitive and essentially noble is woman.... (*AR* 252)

Discussing marriage, D.H. Lawrence very succinctly explains in his essay, "Study of Thomas Hardy":

> in marriage each party fulfils a dual function with regard to the other; exhaustive and enrichening. The female at the same time exhausts and invigorates the male, the male at the same time exhausts and invigorates the female. (*Phoenix* 241)

That both the sexes are in need of each other is evident from these lines. That the man needs the woman for his sustenance also comes out clear in the lines:

> He knows as very pure-bred thing knows that his root and source is in his female. He seeks the motive power in the woman. (*ASFP* 226)

Lawrence undergoes a profound realization of the male-female dual existence. He terms it the 'Two-in One, male and female' where neither the male nor the female is greater than the other. This becomes evident from the lines in *Aaron's Rod*:

> Two eagles in mid-air, like Whitman's "Dalliance of Eagles". Two eagles in mid-air, grappling, whirling, coming to their intensification of love oneness there in mid-air. In mid-air the love consummation (*AR* 167). In a nutshell, Lawrence stated the male-female dichotomy exists in doing, the female in being.
>
> The male feels proud of his maleness when he receives from the female an 'administration to his male being. Whilst he meanwhile gives her the gratification of himself'. (*ASFP* 23)

Lawrence is plagued by a constant self-division. He points out the joyousness of the adventurer who lands on a seashore after a challenging journey and is overjoyed by what he discovers there.

Shall I enjoy the strange motion of the stranger, like a pleasant sensation of silk and warmth against me, stirring unknown fibres? (*ASFP* 232).

In the essay from "Study of Thomas Hardy" he brings into focus the divide between the male and the female principle. While referring to the male, he focuses on the 'Love', the Spirit, the Mind, the Consciousness; a denying, a blaspheming against the Female, the Law, the Soul, the Senses, the Feelings' (*Study of Thomas Hardy;* henceforth *STH* 252).

That to Lawrence marriage was complete in itself. It was an urge of the 'being' for the relationship itself. To him the relationship was more vital than the other concomitants like the man and woman or children. Lawrence was advocating for the partners ability which would act as a signal for a better union. As suggested by Omendra Singh, the real marriage of man and woman happens when the man and the woman unite in the complete peace of their minds and their ego (Singh 45).

Lawrence's preoccupation with the need of marriage is evident from his talks with his friend McLeod:

> I think the one thing to do is for men to have the courage to draw nearer to women, expose themselves to them.... Because the source of all life and knowledge is in man and woman and the source of all living is in the interchange and meeting and mingling of these two. (Mailer 107)

Lawrence feels that the sexual urge is one of the most natural urges of the body though sex or the sexual act is not an end in itself. In "Look! We Have Come Through" he calls this urge as hunger:

> The hunger for the woman, alas! It is so deep a Moloch, ruthless and strong, 'tis like the unutterable name of the dead Lord, Not to be spoken aloud. (Carswell 24)

Lawrence elaborated on the nature of marriage of its strength and weakness in modern times. Writing to Catherine Carswell he alluded to the approaching happiness following her marriage.

In one of his letters, Lawrence wrote to Catherine Carswell:

> It is those who are married who should live life of contemplation together. In the world, there is the long day of destruction to go by. But let those who are single, man torn from woman, woman from man, men all together, separate obstinacy, is an enemy pure and simple. (*ASFP* 477)

The only way to solve the riddle of man-woman dynamics is for the wife to smother the serpent—advised Eve which is her, and for the man to talk himself out of his old arrogant Adam. Then they make a fair and above-board contribution called a successful marriage (*ASFP* 477).

However, just like with Lawrence no theory sticks. At one point in the novel *Women in Love* he insists on the fact of the vulgarity and coarseness of the fusion of the two sexes. Lawrence detested the habit of the sexes to merge, melt and absorb instead of retaining its individual being. This idea is found in his novel *Women in Love* or Lawrence was intensely passionate about the manner of love relationships.

Lawrence was taken over by his prophetic vision. As quoted in Frank Kermode's work, Lawrence's purpose was to show how the visionary is contained by the novelist; Lawrence's works present a multi-dimensional approach to social/economic and political life. Lawrence argued that art is not only essentially related to life but is modified by it even as it is capable of changing life. 'The novel' he declared is a perfect medium for revealing to us the changing rainbow of our living relationships (*ASFP* 180).

Against a fast transforming background of the industrial set-up and a changing of the socio-economic infrastructure, Lawrence attempted to capture the consequences of such changes on the human psyche and in turn on human relationships. The new adjustment between man and man, man and woman and man and his social surroundings required a new form, new experiments in technique and a new kind of language.

Lawrence was keen on maintaining a democratic relationship. To him the purpose and spirit of democracy was that the sexes should maintain a status of equality. Lawrence in his essay "Why the Novel Matters" states that "only in the novel are all things given full play" (*ASFP* 188). Like Bakhtin it may be also said in the case of Lawrence that Lawrence's novels express the inherent polyphonies of life.

Lawrence addressed and enunciated his theories, ideas and philosophies on love, marriage and life in short through a series of signs and images, symbols and metaphors. As addressed in Sheila Lahiri Choudhury's book he is described as 'the new tantric of Europe' whose recognition of the importance of man-woman relationship is analysed from the perspective of the Tantric philosophy. There has been unearthed a great similarity between the Tantra philosophy and Lawrence's ideas on the solar plexus especially in the concept of the Kundalini which is central to the Tantric philosophy or system. There has been found a link between the Tantric philosophy and Lawrence's concept of Kundalini as discussed in his *Fantasia of the Unconscious*.

The Rainbow becomes a signpost for each generation to describe the nature of their relationship. Thus, Lydia and Tom Brangwen not only perceive the rainbow but also are able to uphold it through their marital union. She [Anna] played between the pillar of fire and the pillar of cloud in confidence having assurance on her left. Birkin unaware of the other's (Ursula's) presence watch the reflection of the moon on the waters of Willey Green. Birkin's attempts top burst the image of the moon on the waters of the pond correspond to his desire to explode his fantasy of Ursula. It also reasserts the 'destructive-consummative' philosophy which is in effect a reinvention of the phoenix myth. The symbol of creation and destruction becomes manifested through the attempts of Birkin and Ursula to establish their relationship after getting burnt in the fire of their destruction. The promise of a rebirth or a renewed life is a pronounced theme in *Women in Love*. Lawrence through his deep relation with the Bible and his profound thinking on matters of sex, metaphysics attempts to reconstruct a new dimension of man-woman relationship.

According to Lawrence, the root of all problems is the duality within it. Lawrence was preoccupied with the resolution of the conflict through the idea of 'star-equilibrium' that in a way connotes freedom.

The balance maintained in a relationship is rarely attained. In the final novel entitled *The Lost Girl*, Lawrence presents a constant juxtaposition of opposites. To Lawrence, a 'one up one down' relation would mean an utter 'negation of life'. He felt that human beings are 'all bullies, all being bullied' (*Letters* 64).

Lawrence crusaded for a two-sided relationship. In the letter to Mrs. Hopkins dated August 19, 1912 he wrote that he believed in a two-sided relationship where the woman loves the man and is in turn loved by him. Here he even confessed that he believed in marriage.

Lawrence thus supports the institution of marriage which should be based on mutual give and take between man and woman. This concept of man-woman relationship is pronounced in almost all the novels of D.H. Lawrence including *Sons and Lovers*, *The Rainbow*, *Women in Love*, and *Lady Chatterley's Lover* and so on. He feels that married people ought to be sufficient to them. Lawrence it seems harboured a strong and a firm opinion on the development of a wider relationship.

One vital reason for the break-up between Connie and Lord Chatterley was not due to want of material prosperity but due to want of a vital and creative relationship between the husband and the wife.

Lawrence's emphasis on the blood knowledge comes out from his statements:

> My belief is in the blood...blood being wiser than the intellect. One can go wrong in the minds but what the blood feels is always true. (*Letters* 180)

To Lawrence man-woman relationship is of primary significance. At one point he wrote:

> A woman that I love sort of keeps me in direct communication with the unknown in which otherwise I am a bit lost. (*Letters* 21)

Woman likes to submit to the man who is confident and sure of himself. It is only when men are unsure of themselves that they become wilful and adamantine, fighting for woman's cause—in a way feminists.

The real trouble with women is that they must always go on trying to adapt themselves to men's theories of women, as they,

> Always have done when a woman is thoroughly herself, she is being what her type of man wants her to be. When a woman is hysterical it's because she doesn't quite know what to be, which pattern to follow, which man's picture of woman to live up to. (*ASFP* 393)

Both the sexes blunder in trying to place the partner in some particular frame. There have been many masculine theories of what women should be. But men run to type and it is the type not the individual that produces the theory of the 'ideal' woman. This becomes evident not only in the case of novelists like D.H. Lawrence but even Hardy in the case of *Tess of D'Urbervilles*, *The Return of the Native*, *Jude the Obscure* and so on.

> Men give them such abominable Patterns, child-wives, little-boy-baby face girls, perfect secretaries, noble spouses, self-sacrificing mothers, pure women who bring forth children in virgin coldness, prostitutes who just make themselves low, to please the men.... Man is willing to accept woman as an equal as a man in skirts, as an angel, a devil, a baby-face, a machine, an instrument, a bosom, a womb, a pair of legs, a servant, an encyclopaedia, an ideal or an obscenity; the one thing he won't accept her as is a human being, a real human being of the feminine sex. (*ASFP* 394)

This brings to our mind the heroine, Constance Connie Chatterley's belief in a much latter novel, *Lady Chatterley's Lover*.

Lawrence was sarcastic about the fast-changing notion of what a woman should be. To him, '...Men are fools'. He states how they spend ages trying to train the little boy-baby-face woman type but when they got her perfect, they desire for something else.

The moment they marry the little-boy-baby face, instantly they begin to pine for the noble Agnes, pure and majestic, or the infinite mother with deep bosom of consolation, or the perfect business woman, or the lurid prostitute on black silk sheets: or, most idiotic of all, a combination of all the lot of them at once.... When it comes to women, modern men are idiots. They don't know what they want, and so they never want, permanently what they get. (*ASFP* 396)

In *Sexual Politics*, Kate Millett argues that Birkin finds Gerald's mastery of the mare in *Women in Love* agreeable and also compares this to mastery of women. Birkin/Lawrence perceives the dangers of the will-breaking game, the deadly and fatal relationship that he shares with Hermione and next with Ursula, Birkin fights to death—the fight is in Lawrence's terms is a battle of wills. In the essay "On Lawrence's Hostility to Will Full Women" which figures in *Renewing the Normative D.H. Lawrence*, we get a discussion of the anti-Christian ways of behaviour.

The Faustian uses of mind and will as terminal powers, dominating and exploiting emotional life, would be Lawrence's version then of the anti-Christ.... The men and women who adopt this terminal mode in *Women in Love*—Hermione, Gerald, Gudrun, Loerke...they choose their own destruction (Spilka 151).

All the subtle dynamics of Lawrence's man-woman thesis has been done mostly through his novels which are rather experimental in character. Lawrence was keen to show how through mythical overtones as presented in *The Plumed Serpent*, 'The Woman who Rode Away', *Kangaroo*, *The Rainbow*, *Aaron's Rod* and so on the symbols of the eagle, the plumed serpent, rainbow, stars suggest a plane far away from the real world. They belong to a non-human realm. Lawrence hints to his readers that though the relationships are suggested through such remote symbols as stars, moon and so on. They are very much a part of this world with all the attachments of gender, class and other social constructs. Thus in spite of trying to remove human affairs to a heavenly or other-worldly level where no inequalities exist, the relationships fail to totally get rid of such social constructs. We need to see Lawrence exploring the field between the social and the asocial—the limits and the limitless. Lawrence who had been philosophically ruminating on these intellectual issues find an ample substantiation in his non-fiction works. However, an echo of these ideas is to be found in the novels.

Notes and References

Male-female Principle:

Lawrence conceives of two universal forces or principles or impulses operating in individuals and attacks Darwin, Spenser and Huxley who believe that life is one principle and not two. These two principles are simultaneously getting reconciled with each other and it is this reconciliation which is the essence of all creativity and growth. These two principles are described by Lawrence in terms that are symbolic. The first force is termed Female, Axle, Inertia, god and Father, Law, Nature, Judaism and Graecism, Darkness, Flesh, Body, Soul, Oneness or Monism, Form, Being, Furies and feelings. The second force is called man, Wheel, Motion, The Son, Love, Knowledge, Christianity, Light, Mind, Multiplicity or Pluralism, Formlessness, Knowing, Doing, Apollo and Consciousness. According to Lawrence, these forces are at work in every man and every woman. Thus the man may be termed "male" or "female" according to the predominance in him of either of these forces (Phoenix, 459).

Lawrence draws a lot from Nietzche, for according to Nietzche, male and female principles are responsible for life and creativity. According to him, the continuous development of art is bound up with the duplicity of the Apollonian and the Dionysian impulses which roughly correspond to Lawrence's Male and Female. Nietzche differentiated between the two impulses. The Dionysian impulse which is primitive, irrational and health giving and the Apollonian impulse which is the source of all that is rational, self-conscious and ultimately destructive (Nietzche, Frederich. *The Birth of Tragedy*. Included in O.B. Hardison Jr. ed., *Modern Continental Library Criticism*. London: Peter Owen, 1964: 227-28).

Interestingly, for Lawrence taking his cue from Hardy's metaphysic, he states that "there is no reconciliation between Love and the Law. The spirit of love must always succumb before the spirit of the law" (*Phoenix* 480). Slavoj Zizek, a Slovan philosopher has taken his cue from Lacan and elaborated on the thesis of psychoanalysis.

In Zizek's reading of Otto Weininger, a German philosopher is popular for his notorious anti-feminist and anti-*Semitic*, *Sex and Character.* In that work Zizek formulates that the sexual difference is predicated upon an association between subject and object. It is affirmed that men are active, noble spirits (or subjects) and women are passive, ignoble matter (or objects). As passive matter, women are dominated by sexuality. Thus woman's personalized sexuality is a product or an outcome of a universal and impersonal instinct, the one which governs her entire behaviour.

The proposal that Weininger makes is that 'woman is the sin of man'. She is produced by man and exists in so far as man embraces his own sexuality at the expense of his spirituality.

Works Cited

For the novels of D.H. Lawrence like *The Rainbow, Sons and Lovers, Women in Love, Lady Chatterley's Lover, Aaron's Rod* and *Kangaroo* abbreviations have been used: *TR, S&L, WIL, LCL, AR, K,* etc.

Boulton, T. James and Zyatuk George. *The Letters of D.H. Lawrence*. C.U.P., 1981.

Butler, Judith. *Gender Trouble: Feminism and the Subversion of Identity*. London: Routledge Classics, 2006, reprinted 2007, 2008 (twice).

Carswell, Catherine. *The Savage Pilgrimage: A Narrative of D.H. Lawrence*. London: Chatto and Windus, 1932: 24.

Choudhury, Lahiri Sheila. *An Alternative Gaze: Essays on D.H. Lawrence*. New Delhi: Chronicle Books, An Imprint of DC Publishers, 2008.

Draper, P. Ronald. *D.H. Lawrence*. London: The Macmillan Press Ltd., 1964.

Inglis, A.A.M. "*D.H. Lawrence*: Morality and the Novel" in *A Selection from Phoenix*. England: Penguin Books Ltd., 1936, 1971.

Kermode, Frank. *Lawrence*. London: Fontana Paperbacks, 1973.

Lawrence, D.H. *Fantasia of the Unconscious and Psychoanalysis of the Unconscious* (1921). London: Heinemann, Penguin, 1971 reprinted 1986.

———. "On Being a Man" in *A Selection from Phoenix*. England: Penguin Books Ltd., 1936.

———. "*Manifesto*" in *The Complete Poems of D.H. Lawrence*, Vol. I. London: Heinemann, 1957.

Mailer, Norman. *The Prisoner of Sex*. New York: New American Library, 1971, 107.

Meyers, Tony. *Slavoj ZiZek*. London: Routledge Taylor & Francis Group, 2009.

Singh, Omendra. *D.H. Lawrence. Prophet of New Life and Art*. New Delhi: National Publishing House, 1997.

Spilka, Mark. *Renewing the Normative D.H. Lawrence: A Personal Progress*. The U.S.A.: University of Missouri Press, 1992.

11

D.H. Lawrence and *Lady Chatterley's Lover*

Bhaskar Roy Barman

In this article I pick on D.H. Lawrence's last, many critics tend to say, 'poorly written' novel entitled *Lady Chatterley's Lover*. Many scholars, particularly Lawrence scholars, sort of feel inclined to avoid discussing in detail this novel, or rather rest satisfied by touching upon it when talking about the gamut of his literary work, characterizing it as a notorious novel. Its expurgated edition was published in 1928; it was published in full in England in 1960. The novel appears to me, I humbly confess, the most difficult of the whole gamut of his work to handle impartially, exploring and analysing it in intrinsic detail. We cannot bring ourselves to shut our eyes to the permeation of social evils and immorality and perversity into this novel. The hostilities his novels *Women in Love* and *Lady Chatterley's Lover* had evoked purport to have prejudiced and sort of jaundiced an impartial appraisal of the novel. These hostilities have evidently emanated from the awareness of the representation in the novel of the social truths and realities of which the readers of the novel have themselves savoured the taste.

D.H. Lawrence died in 1930 at the age of forty-five. Before he died he could see the expurgated edition of this novel published in 1928 and its unabridged edition published in Paris in 1929. Before his death he got aware of the hostilities aligned with it. With his death there has arisen a suspicion the hostilities gave rise to that he was a false prophet. People have started doubting of Lawrence's dignification of instinct over reason, of body over mind which was but "an aspect of primitivism which expresses itself in dance music based on the rhythm of kraal"

(1950: 754), the music peculiar to the village of huts enclosed by a fence in South Africa. But there is no denying the fact that his gospel happens to have descended upon the ears already tuned up to hearing it. 'The world he wrote for', writes John Drinkwater, "was morally sick, and it snatched eagerly at the new hope he offered. Civilisation had failed; civilisation had precipitated a murderous war; therefore we must rid ourselves of artificial thwartings and repressions; we must get back to a more elemental way of living. There was enough truth in this to make it seem almost like a revelation of a new Messiah, and it was reinforced by the teaching of Freud, which had just then influenced thought and behaviour" (1950: 754-55).

This necessitates a brief review of how he engineered the impression of prophetism on the minds of his readers; I cannot simply leave my readers conjecturing about this point of view attached to Lawrence.

The prophetic strain in Lawrence is partly ascribed to his relation to the mainstream of literary and cultural life in his day. Both his working class origin and his provincial background ganged up to sort of maroon him from the high culture of Edwardian and Georgian London. It suffices to say in this article with its thrust on *Lady Chatterley's Lover* that Lawrence somehow succeeded in marshalling the attention of the arbiters of literary and cultural taste and adopted, in order to keep it, the stance of the preacher and prophet. The occasional raucousness of his tone "is the index both of his sense of his urgency and importance of what he had to say and his despair at ever getting enough people to listen and understand" (2003: 66-67).

"More specifically", Gamini Salgardo writes, "Lawrence's first real contact with the world of ideas and vision in his own community in Eastwood would have been through a preacher, the Congregational minister, the Reverend Robert Reid, a close friend of Lawrence's mother" (2003: 67). The value of his background elicited two different phases of interpretation opposed to each other. T.S. Eliot and others represented the first phase by sneering at the value of Lawrence's background, labelling it "hymn-singing, tin-chapel pietism" (2003: 67), which implies it to be the crudest form of revivalist religiosity. Other critics who advocated the other phase went to the extent of describing the young Lawrence as having inherited a vital and comprehensive traditions. Lawrence, looking back, offer to treat his readers to a sure and neutralized view of his upbringing, as in 'Hymns in a Man's Life'. He writes:

> I think it was good to be brought up a Protestant: and among Protestants a nonconformist, and among Nonconformists, a Congregationalist. Which sounds pharisaic. But I should have missed bitterly a direct Knowledge of the Bible, and a direct relation to Galilee and Canaan, Moab and kedron, those places that never existed.... So altogether I am grateful to my 'Congregational' upbringing. The Congregationalist are the oldest Nonconformists, descendants of the Oliver Cromwell Independents. They still had a Puritan tradition of no ritual. But they avoided personal emotionalism which one found among the Methodists when I was a boy. (Quoted in the Preface 2003: 67)

The passage quoted above gives us to understand that his congregational background endowed Lawrence with two things of permanent importance which moulded his literary ideas and vision. It is owing to the stress his mother put on regular religious activity that the background, in the first place, oriented at an impressionable age to fundamental religious issues, opening his way to skeptical agnosticism and later to 'the very Lawrentian 'religion' of *The Plumed Serpent* and The Man Who Died' (2003: 67). The background, in the second place, by saturating his youthful consciousness, as the massage cited above suggests, the language and rhythm of the Bible, helped Lawrence to form the staple of his prose style, as the palms and hymns moulded the rhythm of the poetry. Lawrence himself writes about the influence of the Bible in his childhood in his introduction to The Dragon of Apocalypse, published in 1930:

> I was brought up on the Bible, and seem to have it in my bones.
>
> From early childhood I have been familiar with Apocalyptic language and Apocalyptic images: bit

> because I spent my time reading Tevelation, but because I was sent to Sunday school and to chapel, to Band of Hope and to Christina Endeavour and was always having the Bible read to me. (Quoted in the Preface 67-68)

It should be borne in mind that the debunking of the gospel that Lawrence advocated has not derogated his stature as an artist. Nearly all his writing encompassing, as it does, poems, travels, essays and fiction has established Lawrence as a man of genius. His novels—we have all perceived it—crepitate with energy so much so that one cannot help feeling that they must have been written under a feverish spell of creativity. They were to be sure. D.H. Lawrence himself spoke of how his creative impulse, his creative excitement, mesmerized him into writing novels. John Drinkwater informs us that "Lawrence once told Aldous Huxley that he had written 145 pages of a novel without knowing what it was about. He was incapable of revision. If he was dissatisfied he rewrote; all his major novels are said to have been rewritten three times" (755).

We cannot deny *Lady Chatterley's Lover* the status of a major novel, despite the label of notoriety attached to it I confide in my readers—in the belief that they won't divulge it to anybody else—that I know of a Bengali novelist now dead who purports to have put to use the subject-matter of *Lady Chatterley's Lover*, garbed in the garments of Bengal in a novel of his and became famous, though criticized. It's absolutely my own view; I won't be able to allude to any reference to substantiate it. I read this novel so many years ago and I know not of any critic comparing it to *Lady Chatterley's Lover*. I could discern some similarity between the two novels. I have referred to my impression of the Bengali novel in order to tell my readers that the influence *Lady Chatterley's Lover*, though it evoked hostilities and adverse criticism, imperceptibly streaked into the mental set-up of majority of writers throughout the world. I believe my readers agree with me that no one wastes their time on a poorly written novel.

I could not resist the temptation of alluding to D.H. Lawrence's Letters admirably edited by Aldous Huxley

1932, reference *The Concise Cambridge History of English Literature* (874), which presents itself as one of the most valuable autobiographies of modern times in order to substantiate what I have said about the popularity the novel has enjoyed since its publication.

The story the Letters reveal, full of humour though they are, is a tragic story, inasmuch as Lawrence's life was dominated by an unending and courageous struggle against two things: his own ill-health caused by tuberculosis, and 'the prudery of the public'. A pioneer in the management of sexual themes undoubtedly as he was, he found himself confronted with those self-appointed guardians of public morals, the pundits of the popular press, who have always preferred smoking-room stories. *The Rainbow*, his first novel, laid itself open to the wrath of those pundits of the popular press and they did succeed in getting withdrawn the publication of the novel! Thenceforth the hunt continued. *Women in Love*, too, invited the same wrath. George Sampson reproduces in capital letters the headlines welcoming *Women in Love*: "A BOOK THE POLICE SHOULD BAN: LOATHSOME STUDY OF SEX DEPRAVITY: MISLEADING YOUTH TO UNSPEAKABLE DISASTER" (2001: 874-75) and quotes the reviewer reviewing this novel under these headlines as saying '"I do not claim to be a literary critic, but I know dirt when I small it, and here is dirt in heaps-festering, putrid heaps which smell to high heaven."' The reviewers, the so-called literary intellectuals, reacted to *Lady Chatterley's Lover* by saying that a landmark of evil was produced—George Sampson quotes this comment—by '"the bearded satyr and world-famous novelist who has prostituted art to pornography"' (875). Apropos of D.H. Lawrence and *Lady Chatterley's Lover* George Sampson writes:

> if Lawrence had lived to a normal old age, he would have found himself as revered a literary figure as Swinburne or Hardy, some of whose work provoked as mush indignation among Victorian reviewers. And he would have found himself wealthy beyond the dreams of Arnold Bennett, if he had lived to draw the massive

> royalties from the Penguin edition of *Lady Chatterley*, the film rights from *Sons and Lovers* and all other rights from radio, television, paperbacks and school editions. (2001: 875)

Before we deal with *Lady Chatterley's Lover* in some detail, we must needs acquaint ourselves with the situation contemporaneous with the work of Lawrence and that of other novelists writing between the two world wars.

The period between the two world wars, to be more precise, between 1914 and 1939 boiled with literary activity culminating in the production of many excellent novels by Lawrence and other major novelists, James Joyce for example. I should like to tell my readers beforehand James Joyce will figure, albeit slightly, in my present discussion, for both the novelists, internationally acclaimed though they are, took on literary and social oppositions valiantly, without giving up on their constructs in the face of the social oppositions and hostilities. By drawing on the comparison between the two I can, I think, help my readers and myself, too, to dip deep to the heart of *Lady Chatterley's Lover*.

Leave it be. The history of the literary activity obtaining during the period referred to is largely a history of the novel and there is nothing surprising about it. The period characterized itself by chaos, economic, moral and intellectual. Consequently, the material the writer had to grapple with was so missed up and muddled as to necessitate a form needed to give a shape to it, a form capable of cataloguing all kinds of ideas and experiences. The novel was the form itself. We should refresh our conception, our understanding of the novel. We are all more or less acquainted with one of the famous definitions, first phrased by the French critic Abel Chevalley, and later subscribed to by E.M. Forster. The novel is a fiction in prose of a certain length. "What could be looser? So the novel became a sort of hold-all and usurped the place once held by tighter mediums of expression: the drama, the essay, the longer poem. The writer was emboldened in his choice by the knowledge that rising standards of education had created a new public which might jib at literature offered neat, but could be induced to swallow it in the guise of fiction" (1950: 752). The novel is not a recent genre. It has a long history to boast of. Below is the history of the development of the novel which first originated in Italy as novella as a short tale as in Boccaccio's 'Decameron'.

It is in the 17th and 18th century that novel was contrasted with romance as being something shorter and as having more relation to real life.

In England the beginnings of the novel can be mapped out in verse romances popular in the Middle Ages. In the sense that a novel describes a development of character through a narrative, it has been argued that Chaucer's '"Troylus and Cryseyde" is the first true novel' (1996: 413). Prose romances of this kind commanded popularity. The sixteenth century witnessed the production, under Italian influences, of several collections of short tales such as, for example, Painter's 'Palace of Pleasure'. Lyly's 'Euphues'[1] exercised a considerable influence on the prose style of the period. Sydney's 'Arcadia', another romance as famous as Lyly's 'Euphues', has provided stylistic attractions. Thomas Nash's picaresque[2] novel, 'The Unfortunate Traveller or The Life of Jacke Wilton' (1594) brought up a new note of realism which influenced Defoe and Smollett. In fact the seventeenth century was dominated by the romance type of fiction.

Defoe can justly be called the first English novelist because of the fact that all his works possess a quality, completely new in English literature, of an imaginative realism and his delineation of characters verges on realism. The eighteenth century, beginning with Defoe, turned out to be the great age of novel. It should be mentioned in this connexion that "there are elements of this development in the 'Coverley' papers of Steele and Addison with their skilful character drawing" (1996: 413). Alongside of Defoe may be mentioned Samuel Richardson, Fielding, Sterne.

A new element made itself noticed towards the end of the eighteenth century through the inauguration of the novel of terror by Horace Walpole with his *Castle of Otranto* (1764). To this time also belongs the didactic novel exemplified by Codwin's *Caleb Williams* (1794).

The success of Walter Scott, whose novels introduced a new breadth of historical writing with a much greater skill in character drawing overshadowed both these tendencies reifying the characteristics of the romantic revival. Jane Austen, writing at the same time, as she did, belongs in subject-matter to the eighteenth century, though her skilful penetration and thoughtfulness resemble many of the elements of the modern period.

The modern popularity of the novel, inaugurated by Walter Scott, was kept up in the writings of Dickens, Thackeray and other Victorian novelists. The greatness of the Victorian age was more amply and fully demonstrated in this branch of literature than in any other. The Victorian novel, allowing for its having lacked the distinction of the greatest eighteenth century novels, cultivated breadth and a greater subtlety. The period of transition between the Victorian and the twentieth century novel was dominated by Henry James and Joseph Conrad by bringing, as they did, a new style and shapeliness from very different backgrounds and by doing away with much of the over-elaborate detail and padding associated with the lengthy novel.

To cut this discussion short, let us pass on to the twentieth century.

The first half of this century marked itself out as the period of experimentation in the hands in particular of James Joyce and Virginia Woolf who researched new methods of communication and conventions of writing, fleshing out in their respective ways the stream of consciousness or interior monologue technique. The writings of D.H. Lawrence look ignited by a passionate desire to reform society and introduce new ideals by exposing, as in *Lady Chatterley's Lover*, the false values of society.

As I have said earlier, I shall touch upon James Joyce's novel Ulysses to show how the novels categorizing social evils fall a victim to the wrath of literary and intelligentsia. When he began to write Ulysses in 1914, James Joyce harboured a determination in his mind to valiantly put, police notwithstanding, everything in 'my novel' (1950: 753). Yes, police had something to say about it, at the instigation, I venture to opine, of the literary intelligentsia. The literary intellectuals could not hold patience to wait for the novel to be completed to lash out at it. The serial publication of the novel was stopped by the American court. The complete work was published in Paris, and 'there was an interval of nearly twenty years before the authorities allowed it to be published and sold in England' (1950: 753).

There is some difference between *Ulysses* and *Lady Chatterley's Lover* in treatment of theme and style. The consensus of opinion today categorizes *Ulysses* as a comic work, the term 'comic' being used in its very widest sense, and *Lady Chatterley's Lover* is a direct insinuation of the social evils obtaining at the time of the writing of this novel.

Ulysses, in point of style, sculpts a transitional stage between the realism of Dubliners and the symbolism of Ulysses and is conceived of, so to say, as the entrance-hall of Ulysses, "Stephen Dedalus, as closely based upon the author as Paul Moral upon Laurence in *Sons and Lovers*, being the hero of *The Portrait* and the Telemachus of its successor" (2001: 878).

It is the time we should pass on to dealing with *Lady Chatterley's Love* critically, before concluding this article.

The novel *Lady Chatterley's Lover* begins with the novelist's assertion that follows, which purposes to prepare the readers for the whirlpool which the circumstances have forced upon the female protagonist, Connie Reid, the maiden name and Constance Chatterley, the marital name.

> Ours is essentially a tragic age, so we refuse to take it tragically. The cataclysm has happened, we are among the ruins, we start to build up new habitats, to have new little hopes. It is rather hard work: there is now no smooth road into the future: but we go round or scramble over the obstacles. We've got to live, no matter how many skies have fallen. This was more or less Constance Chatterley's position. The war had brought the roof down over her head. And she had realized that one must live and learn. (2013: 07)

The passage has introduced us to Connie Reid, the female protagonist of the novel. She was brought up in the atmosphere of cultured bohemianism of the upper-middle class. "Her father was the once well-known R.A., old Sir Malcolm Reid. His mother had been one of the cultivated Fabians in the palmy, rather pre-Raphaelite days. Between artists and cultured socialists, Constance and her sister Hilda had had what might be called an aesthetically upbringing" (08). She with his sister tasted the thrill of sex experience. Their father could sense, when his two daughters came home for the summer holidays of 1913, they had had sex experience. But he took it easy, because he was himself a man of experience and "let life take its course" (08). The daughters themselves were not daunted by such experience. "In the actual sex-thrill within the body, the sisters nearly succumbed to the strange male power. But quickly they recovered themselves, took the sex-sensation as a sensation, and remained free" (09). In 1917 at the age of 23 she marries Clifford Chatterley. "Clifford Chatterley was more upper-class than Connie. Connie was well-to-do intelligentsia, but he was aristocracy. Not the big sort, but still it. His father was a baronet and his mother had been a viscount's daughter" (12). After they have spent a month's honeymoon, he is sent over to war to return paralysed from the waist down and impotent.

On returning from the war, Clifford makes himself a successful writer and has many intellectuals flock to the Chatterley mansion, Wragby to the consternation of. Connie growing gradually isolated. The vaunted intellectualism associated with the literary rigmarole proves to Connie empty and shallow. She is aware of a growing restlessness which is 'taking possession of her like madness'. "Vaguely she knew herself that she was going to pieces in some way. Vaguely she knew she was out of connexion; she had lost touch with the substantial and vital world. Only Clifford and his books, which did not exist...which had nothing in them! Void to void. Vaguely she knew. But it was like beating her head against a stone" (22). To relieve herself of the torture of the isolatedness, she has recourse to a brief and dissatisfying affair with a visiting playwright, Michaelis. He fails to satisfy her Connie longs for real human contact and, failing to find it, relapses into despair. All men seem scared of true feelings and true passion. She feels herself alienated and distanced from Clifford, who has been octopussed all around by a meaningless pursuit of a success in his writing and has surrendered himself to his obsession with coal-mining, which sort of nauseates Connie and physically distances her. A nurse, Mrs. Bolton her name, is hired to look after the needs of the handicapped Clifford as a subterfuge for Connie to be left more independent and for Clifford to get deeply clinging to the nurse, his manhood freezed by an infantile reliance.

To fill in the void of Connie's life arrives Oliver Mellors, newly returned from service in the army to be appointed a gamekeeper on Clifford's estate. Though Mellors keeps himself aloof and derisive, Connie cannot help feeling curiously drawn to him by his innate nobility, grace and by his purposeful isolation and the undercurrents of natural sensuality. He manages to keep her at a safe distance at several chance meetings under the plea of the class distance between them, but at chance meeting at a hut in the forest they have sex. Though the sex continued on several occasions, Connie keeps a distance between them by remaining profoundly separate from him. Notwithstanding their physical closeness.

One day it so happens that when Connie and Mellors are having sex in the woods, they experience simultaneous orgasms. This turns out for Connie to be a revelation and makes her begin to adore Mellors, leading her to feel that they have been connected on some deep sensual level. She professes herself proud to believe that she is going to be pregnant with Mellors' child, he being a real, "living" man, unlike the emotionally-dead intellectuals and the dehumanized industrial workers. They feel themselves growing together, drawn closer on a primordial physical level, as are woman and man emotionally guided....

Connie goes away to Venice on a vacation. When she is away in Venice Mellors' old wife returns and spread the scandal around out of vengeance, resulting in the firing of Mellors from his job by Clifford and institutes a lawsuit seeking divorce from Mellors. Connie returns and, apprised of the situation, confesses to Clifford to having been pregnant with Mellors' baby, but Clifford, even hearing this confession, refuses to divorce her.

The novel ends with Mellors working on a farm and waiting for his divorce to be effected, and Connie living away with her sister, hopefully waiting for an opportunity for them to live together.

In *Lady Chatterley's Love*, Lawrence, as the story of the novel suggests, shows himself determined to grapple efficiently with the problem of creating a resurrection story literally phallic, with a real man bearing the phallus. The sort of man assigned with the task of bearing the phallus is required to be a freed man, a man who has succeeded in throwing off the fatal chain and in isolating himself from the mob. In this novel Lawrence returns to his early archetype of non-conformity in the person of the gamekeeper, a kind of hermit, safeguarding his garden of Eden. The hermit figure presented in the gamekeeper is not wholly satisfying, though. It is not possible to ascertain whether the hermit is escaping to or from life.

> Let us search for the phallus-bearer in *Lady Chatterley's Lover*.
>
> 'Ours is essentially a tragic age, so we refuse to take it tragically'

Thus opens the novel, as we have got to know, "with a stiff upper lip, mouthing the post-war platitudes" (1979: 179):

> there is now no smooth road into the future...we've got to live, no matter how many skies have fallen...one must live and learn.

The cataclysm Connie had found herself confronted with and had so easily acclimatized herself with was the paralyzing from the waist down of her husband Clifford with whom she enjoyed a honeymoon that last only a month. The marriage, the honeymoon, the embarkation, the wounding and the return of Clifford, "are all given in a brief paragraph of three sentences (as below) in a tone which is resigned to a point of flippancy..." (1979: 179):

> Then he went back to Flanders: to be shipped over to England again six months later more or less in bits. (2013: 07)

Our normal sympathy that might have been aroused for Clifford seems deliberately suppressed. The question why doesn't Clifford's body matter to Connie?, tugs at our consciousness, when we take our mind off Connie for a brief while. Does the novelist want our attention focused on Connie and her dallying with the gamekeeper? But the novelist does not economize on the delineation of the character of Clifford. 'His (Clifford's) hold on life', we are told to begin with, "was marvellous. He didn't die, and his bits seemed to grow together again. For two years he remained in the doctor's hands. Then he was pronounced a cure, and could return to life again, with the lower half of his body, from the hips down, paralysed forever" (2013: 07).

The space, by having got Clifford hamstrung and by having reduced to rubble Connie's world, slows just a little for a flash-back to the childhood of Connie and her sister Hilda before the war broke out, when nameless young Germans entered into their relationship.

> However, came the war, Hilda and Connie were rushed back home again after having been home already in May, to their mother's funeral. Before Christmas of 1914 both their German young men were dead: whereupon the sisters wept, and loved the young men passionately, but underneath forgot them. They didn't exist anymore. (11)

Our responses again stand inhibited by its tone. But the irony here goes around with an account described at some length of the sexual relationships which the German young men had established with the sisters. Their attraction had been intellectualized through their passionate talk. The sex thing entailed no giving, no submission, which would have threatened the girl's freedom. The sex was exploited and indulged in to experience, so to say, a sort of primitive reversion. "There was no interchange, only a loss on both sides, of privacy for the woman and of manhood for man. They failed to exist for the girls in the last analysis, failed to impinge on their womanhood" (1979: 180).

As for Clifford, he gives unto Connie an intimacy which lies beyond sex. This intimacy has grown, not out of manhood, strength and purpose, but out of weakness and dependence.

> A man needed support and comfort. A man needed to have an anchor in the safe world. A man needed a wife. (14)

The energies of Clifford who has defrauded Connie of her own body are let be poured into the void at the centre of him wherein resides his maleness and human warmth.

There comes to the relief of Connie defrauded of her own body by Clifford the gamekeeper, Mellors. They were not thrown together facilely, though. At first Mellors is hostilely cautious, keen on maintaining his privacy and freedom. He seeks refuge in the wood which safeguards him against the outer world in which he had endured much, especially at the hands of women.

The descriptions of the woods are linked with wider themes. Connie's anticipation coupled with her half-fearful eagerness, as she hurries through the jungle, propelled forward by a desire to meet her lover is got across in richly suggestive description of the wood. She cherishes Mellors in her heart of hearts, for he responds to her primarily as a woman and hands her back to life at the sought-after level of her being by connecting her to the freshness and fertility of the woods with the result that her knocked-down body is reactivated with life and that she vibrates with a sense of creativeness.

The woods they choose to make love are inundated with a profusion of blossom and buds while Clifford busies himself in piloting his 'weird wheeled ship' of civilization through these 'last wild waters' and leaves a wake of destruction.

For Mellors, his relationship with the woman, Connie is, is the core of life. It bestows upon him the strength of convictions, which emboldens him into desiring to "make people pause from earning money to look at themselves and see what the toil has done to them, to make them aware of beauty, to 'pull down Tevershall and build a few beautiful buildings'" (1979: 190).

'They ought to learn', quotes Keith Sagar, "to be naked and handsome, and to sing in a mass and dance the old group dances, and carve the stools they sit on, and embroider their own emblems. Then they wouldn't need money. And that's the only way to solve the industrial problem, train the people to be able to live and live in handsomeness, without needing to spend" (1979: 191).

But Mellors entertains no illusions about living such a life, conscious as he is of the fact that there is little or nothing that he or anyone else is able to do single-handed. This "was not, still is not, the programme of any party or the creed of any church. Civilisation has become the very evil it should seek to destroy, in whose destruction it should, for the present, take its very purpose" (191). Mellors' vision is, to be frank, utopian, rather, starry-eyed. He is not quite sanguine about his expectations, though.

'There's bad time coming', Keith Sagar again quotes, "there's a bad time coming! If things go on as they are, there's nothing lies in the future, but death and destruction, for these industrial masses. I feel my inside turn to water sometimes, and there you are, going to have a child by me. But never mind. All the bad times that ever have been, haven't been able to blow the crocus out: not even the love of women. So they won't be able to blow out my wanting you, nor the little glow there is between you and me" (1979: 190).

We have got assured that Mellors and Connie will shelter the glow and believe in it, because that glow is not but a romance; it is 'love in its manifestation', in the words of Keith Sagar, "from genuine desire to tender love, love of our fellow men, and Love of God" (191). It is "love, joy, delight, hope, true indignant anger, passionate sense of justice and injustice, truth and untruth, honour and dishonour, and real belief in anything" (1955: 233). "It is the hope for a dying civilization" (1979: 191) and is phallic.

And Mellors is the phallus-bearer.

Notes

1. Euphues is prose romance, divided into two parts, the first part entitled *Eupheus: The Anatomy of Wits* published in 1578 and the second part entitled *Euphues and England* in 1580. 'The plot of each is little but a peg on which to hang discourses, conversations, and letters, mainly on the subject of love' (1996: 183).

   It is owing to its peculiar style out of which the term 'Euphuism' has been coined, that 'Euphues' has become famous. This peculiar style is characterized by the excessive use of antithesis pursued, sense notwithstanding, and emphasized by alliteration and other devices, and by the use of allusions to historical and mythological personages.

2. Picaresque, a term derived from Spanish 'picaro' meaning 'a rogue', applied to a class of romances dealing with rogues and knaves.

Works Cited

Drinkwater, John (1950). *The Outline of Literature*. George Newnes Limited, Strands W.C.2, UK.

Eagle, Dorothy (1996). *The Concise Oxford Dictionary of English Literature* (Second Edition); Oxford University Press, Oxford.

Lawrence, D.H. (2013). *Lady Chatterley's Lover*: Fingerprint Classic: An Imprint of Prakash Books India Pvt. Ltd., New Delhi.

Moore, H.T. (Ed.) (1955). *Sex, Literature and Censorship*. Heinemann, England.

Sagar, Keith (1979). *The Art of D.H. Lawrence*. Vikas Publishing House, Ghaziabad, UP.

Sampson, George (2001). *The Concise Cambridge History of English Literature*. Cambridge University Press, South-Asian Edition by Foundation Books, New Delhi.

Salgado, Gemini (2003). *A Preface to D.H. Lawrence* (First Indian Edition), Pearson Education (Singapore) Pvt. Ltd., Indian Branch, New Delhi.

12

Instability of Form and Modernity of D.H. Lawrence's *Sons and Lovers*

Arpa Ghosh

D.H. Lawrence's *Sons and Lovers* (1912) never fails to intrigue and impress. It sets outs to make a certain statement in the grand tradition of the Victorian novel. It does something more.

Sons and Lovers is a novel with strong autobiographical elements. In persuasive ways, Paul Morel is Lawrence himself. Mrs Morel is a fictional prototype of Lawrence's dominating mother, while Walter Morel, a representation of his father. The narrative voice of the novel is located somewhere between omniscient and limited narrative. In the Victorian realist tradition the novel may be perceived as a triptych: the story of the first generation Morels, Paul's relationship with Miriam followed by his relationship with Clara. The three women in Paul's life can be conveniently categorized as mother, angel and whore. The unhappy ending of the novel with Mrs Morel dying of cancer and Paul ending his relationship with Miriam and Clara is yet not tragic. He is alone but moves towards light rather than darkness, ready to begin a new phase of his life. "Turning sharply, he walked toward the city's gold phosphorescence. His fists were shut, his mouth set fast" (Lawrence 1913: 511). The closure then is both tied up and open-ended; tied up in the sense that it marks an end of the only relationship that Paul ever values—his relationship with his mother, and open-ended in the way *Bildungsromans*, or coming of age novels, a modern rather than a Victorian genre, are open-ended.

At the same time the triptych stereotypes are heavily problematized. The mother is presented in a sexualized manner, and there is more than a hint that she is deeply attracted to her son (Lawrence 1913: 261-62). The angel (Miriam) is also an incubus who is accused of sucking the life out of Paul (Lawrence 1913: 237). The whore (Clara) flagrantly disobeys the stipulations of Christian marriage by taking up a lover and yet never really forgets her husband and finally returns to him.

As Frank Kermode argues in his essay "The Writing of *Sons and Lovers*" (Rylance 1996: 21) the novel is shaped not so much by an unfolding plot narrative (in the Victorian tradition) as it is by a pattern of 'symbolic and structural variations from episode to episode'. For example, Paul's rejection of Miriam is actually a rejection of the stifling love that he associates with his mother. Mrs Morel's obsession with her second son is a continuation with her obsession with her first. From point of view of status, Clara with her feminist leanings and the uncouth working class Baxter Dawes are next generation replications of Mrs Morel and Walter Morel. Paul's movement away from them denotes his emotional distancing of himself from the working-class locus of his parents.

Kermode also notes that Lawrence's technique of 'over-painting' especially in the depiction of Miriam is apt for depicting a reality that stresses ambiguity, instability, repetition and bias, often at subconscious levels. Kermode shows how with peculiar vulnerability and honesty, in the Miriam-Paul sections the narrative speaks in spite of itself. Constantly accused by Paul of sucking life out of things, Miriam is at the same time shown to be a girl anxious to learn about life, to enjoy it. This double consciousness, first encountered in the portrayal of Walter and Gertrude Morel, makes itself more vividly manifest in the portrayal of Miriam. Paul tells her: "You don't want to love—your eternal and abnormal craving is to be loved. You aren't positive, you're negative. You absorb, absorb, absorb, as if you must fill yourself up with love, because you've got a shortage somewhere" (Lawrence 1913: 268). This is an exceptional instance where a Victorian narrative device is turned on its head. Unknown to himself Paul reiterates his mother's grouse against Miriam:

> "She exults—she exults as she carries him off from me", Mrs Morel cried in her heart after Paul had gone. 'She is not like an ordinary woman, who can leave me my share in him. She wants to absorb him. She wants to draw him out and absorb him till there is nothing left of him, even for himself. He will never be a man on his own feet—she will suck him up.' So the mother sat, and battled and brooded bitterly. (237)

And yet, in the hen-coop scene, a very different picture of Miriam emerges:

> As he went round the back, he saw Miriam kneeling in front of the hen-coop, some maize in her hand, biting her lip, and crouching in an intense attitude. The hen was eyeing her wickedly. Very gingerly she put forward her hand. The hen bobbed for her. She drew back quickly with a cry, half of fear, half of chagrin.
>
> 'It won't hurt you', said Paul.
> She flushed crimson and started up.
> 'I only wanted to try', she said in a low voice.

'See, it doesn't hurt', he said, and, putting only two corns in his palm, he let the hen peck, peck, peck at his bare hand. 'It only makes you laugh', he said.

She put her hand forward, and dragged it away, tried again, and started back with a cry. He frowned.

'Why, I'd let her lake corn from my face', said Paul, 'only she bumps a bit. She's ever so neat. If she wasn't looking how much ground she'd peck every day.'

He waited grimly, and watched. At last Miriam let the bird peck from her hand. She gave a little cry—fear, and pain because of fear—rather pathetic. But she had done it, and she did it again.

> 'There, you see', said the boy. 'It doesn't hurt, does it?'
> She looked at him with dilated eyes.
> 'No', she laughed, trembling. (159)

The gap between Paul's accusation (a mirror-reflection of Mrs Morel's accusation) and Miriam's actual hesitant desire to savour life experiences is subtle and not easily fathomable. But the double consciousness of Miriam as nun and Miriam as friend and complement to the artistic growth of Paul is a narrative force that is interminably at work. Though the narrator at one point makes an observation that is tantamount to the pronouncement of a sentence:

> And she was cut off from ordinary life by her religious intensity which made the world for her either a nunnery garden or a paradise where sin and knowledge were not, or else an ugly, cruel thing. (274)

Paul's emotional dependence on her and her unstinted encouragement of his art is also faithfully and honestly reproduced:

> A sketch finished, he always wanted to take it to Miriam. Then he was stimulated into knowledge of the work he had produced unconsciously. In contact with Miriam he gained insight; his vision went deeper. From his mother he drew the life-warmth, the strength to produce; Miriam urged this warmth into intensity like white light. (196)

Like Sterne's *Tristram Shandy*, D.H. Lawrence's novel begins long before his birth. But unlike Sterne's shifty, devious narrative that is keen to challenge the emergent eighteenth century master-text that authorizes the narrator's voice, Lawrence narrative voice, at least in the first section, is an authoritative, omniscient one very much in Hardy's tradition. Methodically the protagonists, young Mrs Morel and Mr Morel, are introduced, their courtship and marriage elaborately narrated. The first instances of post-marital disillusion of the young wife are also charted with an eye for minute detail and in a style that faintly recalls George Eliot's style of chronicling marital discord in the Lydgate-Rosamond sections of *Middlemarch*.

However, soon the discrepancy is evident. Mrs Morel, though backed by authorial sympathy, when actually in action appears to be a hard, relentless and exacting woman. To the father's passionate nature she is the 'logical' foil. Her relations with her husband are described in the most hard and discomfiting language:

> Nevertheless, she still continued to strive with him. She still had her high moral sense, inherited from generations of puritans. It was now a religious instinct, and she was almost a fanatic with him, because she loved him, or had loved him. If he sinned, she tortured him. If he drank, and lied, was often a poltroon, sometimes a knave, she wielded the lash unmercifully.
>
> The pity was, she was too much his opposite. She could not be content with the little he might be; she would have him the much that he ought to be. So, in seeking to make him nobler than he could be, she destroyed herself, but lost none of her worth. She also had the children. (Lawrence 1913: 25-26)

In spite of dearth of family sympathy, Walter Morel is described in warm, ruddy terms. He is a man constantly associated with the fire that cunningly offsets the coldness of his wife:

> He [Walter Morel] went downstairs in his shirt and then struggled into his pit-trousers, which were left on the hearth to warm all night. There was always a fire, because Mrs Morel raked. And the first sound in the house was the bang, bang of the poker against the rake, as Morel smashed the remainder of the coal to make the kettle, which was filled and left on the hob, finally boil. His cup and knife and fork, all filled and left on the hob, finally boil. His cup and knife and fork, all he wanted except just the food, was laid ready on the table on a newspaper. Then he got his breakfast, made the tea, packed the bottom of the doors with rugs to shut out the draught, piled a big fire, and sat down to an hour of joy. He toasted his bacon on a fork and caught the drops of fat on his bread; then he put the rasher on his thick slice of bread, and cut off chunks with a clasp-knife, poured his tea into his saucer, and was happy. (Lawrence 1913: 38-39)

The much-quoted passage delights by its warm association with food, fire, restorative drink and happy solitude. Walter Morel's instinctive approach to life is stressed more than once.

He is a charming dancer and nifty with his tools. On rare occasions his children enjoy his company. Morel is shown to be a child of nature, his aggression an uncontrollably violent reaction to his wife's subtle and intellectual coldness. In this famous scene where the rift between Morel and his wife takes a nasty turn over the severing of William's locks (Lawrence 1913: 24-25), the narrative is ambiguous. William's soft shorn curls have closer associations with his father's vitality than with his mother's cold rage. As H.M. Daleski has perceptively put it: "The weight of hostile comment which Lawrence directs against Morel is balanced by the unconscious sympathy with which he is presented dramatically, while the overt celebration of Mrs Morel is challenged by the harshness of her character in action" (Rylance 1996: 46).

The same ambiguity is to be noted in Lawrence's portrayal of Miriam. Miriam is introduced very much in the Victorian realist manner as a girl more inclined towards spirituality than sensuality, deeply influenced by her mother's self-abnegating virtues:

> Her great companion was her mother. They were both brown-eyed, and inclined to be mystical, such women as treasure religion inside them, breathe it in their nostrils, and see the whole of life in a mist thereof. So to Miriam, Christ and God made one great figure, which she loved tremblingly and passionately when a tremendous sunset burned out the western sky.... (Lawrence 1913: 177)

As the second part of the novel unfolds the reader is uncomfortably aware of a chasm between the narrator's perspective and Paul's attitude towards Miriam. Paul accuses her of sucking the life out of things. And yet in her company his soul is 'warm'. In a superbly complicated narrative Lawrence shows how, as a result of his mother's influence, Paul's natural affinity towards Miriam gets cramped. Quite early in his life Paul acknowledges that he needs both Miriam and his mother to encourage him in his artistic pursuits:

> "A sketch finished, he always wanted to take to Miriam. Then he was stimulated into knowledge of the work he had produced unconsciously. In contact with Miriam he

> gained insight; his vision went deeper. From his mother he drew the life-warmth, the strength to produce; Miriam urged this warmly into intensity like a white light" (208). His mother's influence was to make him 'quietly determined, patient, dogged, unwearied.' (198)

By his own admission Paul admits that contact with Miriam allows him to grow as a painter. Yet he never desists from accusing her of draining him of vitality. The gap between authorial perspective and Paul's opinion evident in Lawrence's depiction of Walter Morel, the father who in spite of his warmth and vitality becomes an outsider in his own home is true of Miriam's portrayal as well.

And yet such shifts are not dishonest. Rather they are impressionistic. Though, Victorian in structure and ideology (the primacy of the male perspective), *Sons and Lovers* is modern in spirit. Paul's description of his painting gains relevance in this context:

> It's because there is scarcely any shadow in it; it's more shimmery, as if I'd painted the shimmering protoplasm in the leaves and everywhere and not the stiffness of the shape. That seems dead to me. Only this shimmeriness is the real living. The shape is a dead crust. The shimmer is inside really. (201-02)

What Paul describes here is the throb and immediacy of an Impressionistic painting. Just as the painting is keen to capture the here and now of the moment in all its richly layered complexity even if it means the flouting of symmetry and accuracy, so too the narrative within the confines of Victorian linear, realist form strives to capture the multi-faceted truth of the moment. Instead of a plot moving forward in neat linearity, there is a series of doublings. Miriam, though hated by Mrs Morel, actually bears a strong resemblance to her in the way she lays claim over Paul's love. Paul's rejection of her is his rebellion against his mother to whom he feels shackled. Clara in her superiority and initial feminist leanings and her husband Baxter in his uncouth drunkenness, recall Mrs Morel and Walter Morel. Rejecting Clara and leaving behind the couple, Baxter and Clara, in his broken quest for a future could be Paul's second rejection of his parents.

Sons and Lovers begins at the nodal point of the economic and social interface between mining community and the Morel family. The major link Walter Morel, the breadwinner, however is ostracized from the family by the instigations of the mother. Gradually, a single life—Paul Morel's life—emerges from it. The life that emerges develops into a consciousness, and from then on, there is a constant tussle between the realist narrative of working class life and the stream-of-consciousness narrative of the artist's life. Fighting out of the working class Paul Morel gives shape to his mother's desire only to find himself alone, isolated, derelict. In Graham Holderness's words:

> The most significant 'absence in the realism of *Sons and Lovers* is this suppression of the bourgeoisie. Despite the fact that the novel alludes to the middle class as Mrs Morel's proper home, and points to it as the ultimate goal of social mobility and moral improvement, it is not actually depicted there—not presented, as it is in *The Rainbow* or *Women in Love* or *Lady Chatterley's Lover*. In *Sons and Lovers* there are miners, but no mine owners...there is a clear and concrete dramatisation of working class life, but bourgeois society and culture are firmly excluded from the compass of the novel's social world. (Rylance 1996: 143)

The novel ends in a vacuum with the onus of finding a new community completely on Paul, now that his mother is dead. Even while the mother had been alive, Gertrude Morel had no clear idea of the life outside and beyond the mining community she was forced to inhabit. In such a scenario, realism is hopelessly inadequate as a technique to depict reality. But at the same time complete dependence on stream-of-consciousness is bound to muddle the issue, as it is difficult to locate class positions in stream-of-consciousness narratives, a charge that Lukacsian realists often lay at the door of modernists. A novel that begins as a class conflict, especially in the depiction of the dysfunctional Morel marriage where a woman of a slightly higher class marries a working class man with disastrous consequences, gradually shifts to a narrative recording an artist's growth and coming of own. With disarming honesty Lawrence shows how when he rejects his father's class, he rejects not only the virility and vitality, but also the certainty that goes with it. And yes, the narrative technique is all about showing the shimmering, protoplasmic immediacy of the moment as it subsumes the past even while denying it and trickles forward to the future. In a letter to Rachel Armand Taylor Lawrence wrote:

> My mother was a clever, ironical delicately moulded woman of good, old burgher descent. She married below her. My father was dark, ruddy, with a fine laugh. He is a coal miner. He was one of the sanguine temperament, warm and hearty, but unstable: he lacked principle, as my other would have said. He deceived her and lied to her. She despised him—he drank. (1910)

Later, a more bitter note can be detected in the poem he wrote about his parents' unhappy marriage:

> My father was a working man
> And a collier was he,
> At six in the morning they turned him down
> And they turned him up for tea.
>
> My mother was a superior soul
> A superior soul was she,
> Cut out to play a superior role
> In the god-damn bourgeoisie.
>
> We children were the in-betweens
> Little non-descripts were we,
> Indoors we called each other you,
> Ouside it was *tha* and *thee*.

These autobiographical pieces make it amply clear that Lawrence was not only scarred by childhood experiences, he was also keenly aware of the class connotations of his childhood trauma. Yet, when his fictional prototype Paul abandons the mining community at the end of the book, he leaves it static and unchanged. His father and his friends are portrayed throughout as spontaneous, 'natural' creatures. Miriam's family has dimensions of the fantastical in that they are farmers more closely aligned to the sun as opposed to the sunless, industrial existence of the miners. In this way Lawrence simplifies yet fails to ignore the class issue that returns to haunt him. One of the first novelists to emerge from the working class Lawrence is yet unable to write the great proletarian novel, increasingly shifting focus from the outer to the inner, from the objective to the personal and the subjective. In his essay "Individuality and Society in *Sons and Lovers*" John Goode points out:

> Of course, Paul is, like Lawrence himself, very exceptional, but it is only possible to realize the whole truth of a social world in fictional terms through the exceptional man; the character who is realized as 'average' in a novel can only, obviously, embody part of the truth. *Sons and Lovers* is a portrait of the artist as a young man, but the portrait can stand for the landscape of a whole epoch. In the particular case, it is the only way in which the epoch can be recorded since it is an epoch in which the working class emerges not as a class but as separate individuals nurtured and uprooted by the new aspirations and opportunities offered by the post-Forsterian 'democracy'. (Rylance 1996: 125)

Lawrence's age marks the rise of the new individualism, of the cracking of old moulds. By means of narrative technique and style Lawrence holds this up. In the final count *Sons and Lovers* shines in its credo of honesty and commitment to the exigencies of the artistic text.

Notes

1. All textual quotations have been taken from *Sons and Lovers*. D.H. Lawrence, Great Britain: Penguin Books, 1948. First published, 1913.
2. My understanding of the critical aspects of *Sons and Lovers* has been enhanced by *Sons and Lovers: Contemporary Critical Essays*. General Editor: Rick Rylance, New Casebooks, NY: Palgrave Macmillan, 1996.

13

Autobiography as Trajectory of Sublimation: D.H. Lawrence's *Sons and Lovers*

Reena Mitra

"Lawrence is incomparably the greatest creative writer in English of our time...he is one of the greatest creative writers of any time;...."[1] says F.R. Leavis, underlining the characteristically singular genius of the novelist pertaining specifically to his art of rendering human relationships and of implementing technical innovations that facilitate this depiction. In his first novel, *The White Peacock* written in 1911, Lawrence is observably naive and uninitiated, preoccupied with cultivating an assimilation of his own experience into "literature", keeping in view the literary conventions of the genre. With *Sons and Lovers* (1913) he arrived at a completely uncircuitous treatment of his personal problems distinguished by an unrelenting absorption in the autobiographical. The emotional disorder which earlier marred his personal relations has, in this novel, been sublimated and manifested in creative art clearing his complexes forever.

The theme and motivation for *Sons and Lovers*, we are aware, arose from a compulsive exigency gripping the mind of the author and the eventual completed work offered an appeasing discernment in his understanding of the particular predicament he sought to come to terms with. Lawrence's statement certifying his later work, *Women in Love* as being "all analytical—quite unlike *Sons and Lover*s, not a bit visualized"[2] is incidentally an expository comment on the latter novel itself and on its creative thrust and definitive concern. Insights into and explorations of life are perpetrated but there is little characteristic individuality in the personages of Lawrence's world who convey intuitional and instinctive truths more than distinctive individual specificity.

D.H. Lawrence incontestably wrote his novels "out of the stuff of his own experience"[3] as Stumpf and Scott put it. From the very initial years of his writing Lawrence was determined to transcribe life in the strains of his own personal experience and *Sons and Lovers* is generally assessed by critics as the most autobiographical of his novels steeped deep in all that transpired in his own life. Paul Morel, the protagonist of this work, is an intimate parallel to the early Lawrence himself. Also, his travels form the basis of many of his later novels like *Kangaroo* (1923) and *The Plumed Serpent* (1926) which were directly inspired by his visits to Australia and Mexico, respectively. Commenting on Lawrence's personal approach to the novel, David Daiches observes that the former projects his novels from the very centre of his own passionate experience so that they act out, sometimes tentatively, sometimes fiercely, sometimes desperately, his own deepest insights and forms of awareness, and the lyric and dramatic modes interpenetrate each other.[4]

Lawrence, the son of a coal-miner was born and brought up in Nottinghamshire, a small and unassuming village in Eastwood. It was while studying in University College in Nottingham that he took to a career in writing after teaching for a few months. His novels are concerned with alleviating the severity of the predicament of modern man confronting the clampdown on natural instincts and emotions by the complexities of industrialization with its base motives, its run after materialistic gains and its disastrous mechanization of human conduct. They are persistent efforts at showing man a viable escape route from the desensitization of life that had crept into personal relationships for it was these relationships that he explored in the context of the larger social background.

Mark Schorer, in his essay on *Lady Chatterley's Lover*, observes that Lawrence initially subscribed to the realistic practice in the writing of fiction but soon realized that his approach was incompatible with what he sought to do in his later novels like *Sons and Lovers, The Rainbow, Women in*

Love, etc. Schorer refers to these novels as psychic dramas in which primary human impulses rather than human personalities struggle and embrace, and they end with heroes who have made a journey of the soul and whose regeneration puts them beyond the conditions of that social world out of which the novel as we have known it has always come and in which it has always been rooted.[5]

Despite the erratic artistic quality of Lawrence's writing which has often been pointed out, his novels have always been lauded for the immense vibrancy and vigour that emanates from them. Vividness and intensity in depiction is what characterizes *Sons and Lovers,* a work very close to Lawrence's heart and one which engages us with what Rodney Hillman calls "the living quality of the novelist's rendering of actuality."[6] Firmly entrenched in an authentic historical and social milieu it achieves a rare cognizance of and a receptiveness to the minutiae of living. Scenes like Walter Morel at breakfast or cutting fuses with his children watching closely with rapt attention, of Mrs Morel ironing clothes, of Paul going to obtain his father's emoluments and Paul and Miriam on the swing stick to the mind like burrs. The first two scenes convey the warmth and vigour of Morel; Mrs Morel's apparently simple scene of ironing registers through Paul her lack of "fulfilment" in matrimony as well as her own vibrant dynamism; the fourth is a scene conveying Paul's discomfiture in his social environment arising from his consciousness of superiority; and the "swing-scene" exposes the essential incompatibility between Paul and Miriam. These quotidian activities of the Morel family through apparently routine in their occurrence are loaded with implications that change one's perspective to the "narrative", if one may call it so. And, it is to Lawrence's meticulous structural co-ordination of vivid and significant details that the novel owes its coherence and impact.

Much of *Sons and Lovers* indisputably stems from Lawrence's own understanding of and encounter with life as he lived it and it was for him a painful experience to overcome the personal immediacy of all that had transpired in his various relationships while trying to incorporate almost all of it in his novel. In a letter written on October 26, 1913, he referred to his difficulties and inhibitions in writing this largely autobiographical work: "one sheds one's sicknesses in books—repeats and presents again one's emotions, to be master of them."[7] Arriving at a state of "emotion recollected in tranquillity"[8] with relative success was for Lawrence a major exercise. However, parallels with and digressions from biographical particulars are of interest more to the biographer than to the literary critic whose enquiries must be in terms of the coherence and credibility of the novel. However the reader's consciousness of the personal circumstances under which the novel was written may enable him to discern the more rewarding aspects of a study of the work.

Lawrence, in his later life, it is interesting to note, realized that justice had not been done by him in his portrayal of his father in *Sons and Lovers*. He also revised his sizing up of his mother after the publication of the novel: "I would write a different *Sons and Lovers* now; my mother was wrong, and I thought she was absolutely right."[9] The point at issue here is how incontrovertibly and plausibly have the Morels been depicted in the novel. That the unsettled duress and anxiety under which Lawrence's perception of his parents was forged has unfavourably influenced his depiction of the Morels in this fictional work can well be established by an unbiased exploration of what really transpired in his life.

The conflict and the persistent bickering between Lawrence's parents is a significant externalization of the conflict within himself. His father was a totally non-intellectual, illiterate miner and an incorrigible drunkard but was generously endowed with a vibrant and rich discernment of life; his mother, intellectually inclined, spiritual in her proclivities and rather sophisticated in her demeanour, was "cut-out", as he himself realized later in life, to play a higher role among the bourgeoisie. The first meeting between the two parents is winsomely depicted in the first chapter of *Sons and Lovers*:

> the dusky, golden softness of this man's sensuous flame of life that flowed off his flesh like the flame from a candle, not baffled and gripped into incandescence

> by thought and spirit as her life was, seemed to her something wonderful, beyond her.[10]

Despite the fact that initially, Gertrude Coppard, representing Lawrence's mother, found Walter Morel, a fictional portrayal of his father, "full of colour and animation...so ready and so pleasant with everybody"[11] and he, in turn, realized that he "melted away before her...that thing of mystery and fascination, a lady",[12] the marriage was not a happy one and something was unsparingly destroyed in the father. The children could not escape the consequences and became inextricably involved in the hostilities between the parents in *Sons and Lovers*. In actual life, too, the ever-widening schism between Lawrence's father and his mother perpetuated disaster and discord in the family. Lawrence, too, as one of the offsprings was intensely affected by it. In his depiction of this collision in *Sons and Lovers*, however, he fails to be fair to his father and the balance is always in favour of his mother.

Lawrence's mother's class-consciousness in being superior to her husband and the people around in the Bottoms, which comprised six blocks of miner's dwellings, filtered down to her son. Coming from the working class he harboured the rancour of his class-consciousness. In his novels, never did he applaud the bourgeoisie or show his express approval of anything it did. Lawrence was also a strong non-conformist for he had been bred in the practice of being at variance with the established Church conventions. Walter Allen, frowning on his non-conformist stance and his percipient consciousness of his social stratum, observes:

> the nonconformist attitude, combined with a rancorous class-feeling, does give rise to a nagging, intolerable tone of moral superiority which make him appear at times a latter-day Carlyle.[13]

In form and structure, *Sons and Lovers* conforms to the conventions of the autobiographical novel that prevailed at the time of its writing—1913. Comparisons extemporaneously creep in and one is inclined to compare it with Bennett's *Clayhanger* (1910) and Dickens' earlier novel, *David Copperfield* (1849-

50). Bennett, however, views his characters from a vantage point and remains relatively detached; Dickens, if it had not been for the passionate outburst in the second chapter of his novel, would have kept his "deep sense of abandonment"[14] and his consciousness of being "banished" by his parents, more particularly by his mother, to himself. Lawrence, very different from these two novelists, maintains a much greater proximity to his characters, and we strike an immediate cord of close relationship with them through the sheer directness and urgency of his communication. Lawrence, strictly speaking, does not use the stream-of-consciousness technique and yet he enables the reader to see and understand the individual characters through flashes of apprehension, through divination and insight. Their existence, "their essential livingness"[15] is conveyed through bold strokes that are reminiscent of Hardy's depiction of characters like Gabriel Oak and Michael Henchard. There is an incontestable full-bloodedness in the way persons, places and scenes are depicted and underlying them is a world of meaning, thematic and representative. The quotidian here becomes vital as it slips into the symbolic. Calderwood and Toliver, referring to Alan Friedman's views in his essay, "The Stream of Conscience", state that a fictional event, however insignificant and routine it may appear to be, is essentially, not just an aspect of plot but "a moment in the creation of self".[16] Expatiating further on Friedman's observations on fictional theory they proclaim that "in their responses to events, characters define both their experiences and themselves as well".[17] So, the relation of characters to their milieu and their circumstantial context provides an insight into the characters themselves.

Also, what is of consequence in Lawrence's novels is not the dramatic potential available in his scenes and characters but the feelings the latter have towards one another, that is, the involved *interplay* of emotion, fervour and passion, all leading to a realization of instinct and proclivity. As Joseph Warren Beach puts it,

> His (Lawrence's) all-embracing intention is, seemingly, to show the materialization in human lives of the elemental life-impulse—we might say the procreative

> instinct, but I think he would object to having it defined so narrowly—the welling up into conscious life of the great subterranean waters of unconscious vital force.[18]

Much importance is given by Lawrence to the feelings of people, especially feelings representing a lack of connection and a disintegration of forces meant to flow together. And also, as Beach puts it, "the offs & ons of sexual attraction are marvellously presented".[19]

In the main, yet, a new comprehensive vision of experience, seems to have emerged in the modern novel, as also in Lawrence's works where moral implications are not totally precluded from the flux of experience depicted. The novel as a genre is competent enough to portray not only the outer world of action but also the inner world of character and, as observed before, the relation between them. Lawrence's *Sons and Lovers* conforms to this "narrative" interaction—if we may call it so—between the subjective and the objective domains of life. What one needs to explore in it as an exercise in criticism is the organization of experience in terms of "the full, expanding interaction between the inner world and the outer".[20] The focus is on experience as structure—a full, unfurling, open experience not to be confined by anything that restricts the self but to be taken as what Alan Friedman calls "a flow, a journey, a process".[21]

Lawrence's evocation of the "journey" of the Morels and the portrayal of their home, based clearly on his own experiences in life, offer one of the most touching depictions of the miseries and blissful raptures known and lived through by the family. *Sons and Lovers*, a novel largely autobiographical in its content, is believed to have been written by Lawrence out of sheer inner compulsion to seek relief by expelling the rancorous experiences of life from his system and there by purging his system to arrive at equilibrium and peace. As Middleton Murry shows in his book *Sons of Woman* (1931), Lawrence was a persecuted and harassed soul for forty-five years of his life and his works are an expression of his misery and frustration during that period. According to E. Albert, the most perceptible feature of Lawrence's protagonists in his novels is that they all bear a pronounced resemblance to their creator. Paul Morel in *Sons and Lovers*, and Birkin in *Women in Love* are, for example, clear reflections of the author himself, who being a hyper sensitive individual reacted sharply and consequently, suffered greatly. His parents were never blessed with marital harmony and the home environment was always vitiated with estrangement and disputes. Disgusted with the barbarous and savage behaviour of his father, Lawrence on the rebound, came very close to his mother. She, too, with no sense of fulfilment in her marriage started pinning her faith increasingly on her children, particularly David Herbert Lawrence, for emotional satisfaction and for the actualization of her aspirations. The closeness and mutuality that grew between mother and son took on an unhealthy complexion and rendered Lawrence incapable of forming a salubrious and stimulating relationship with other women. This made Lawrence a timorous psychopath. He met and fell in love with Jessie Chambers when he was sixteen but his mother-fixation hindered stability and emotional fulfilment in this relationship. After being together for nearly a decade they finally separated. This excruciating experience of a failed relationship lay heavy on Lawrence who sought a catharsis in his practice of the literary art. Thus came *Sons and Lovers*, an imaginative reckoning of the painful experience he had gone through in life. The major characters and events of this novel have a close parallel to their originals in Lawrence's life.

Lawrence and his sister, Ada, have both given us written evidence that Walter and Gertrude Morel were modelled on their parents, Arthur and Lydia Lawrence, respectively, for an impetuous personal urgency had furnished the subject matter and the stimulus for *Sons and Lovers*. A great deal of what Lawrence remembers with such intensity in the novel and renders with such fidelity in it was once existent and real for he recalls with such verisimilitude the details of the scenes and relationships depicted. In fleshing out the personalities of the parents as incorporated in the novel, Lawrence keeps in mind that his father was "only a collier" with "nothing praiseworthy about him"[22] whereas Ada always considered him a handsome man. Lydia Lawrence came from a middleclass background but was conscious of her relative social and intellectual superiority to her husband, Arthur. There is reference to her once having been forsaken by a sophisticated youth. Later, when she met Arthur Lawrence she was instantly drawn towards him and was overwhelmed by his irresistible humour and spontaneity. The marital life of the Lawrence's, however, was never quite happy for despite efforts on both sides no reconciliation was possible between the civility and finesse of Lydia and the boorish uncouthness of Arthur, between her middle class values and his uninhibited vigour and gusto bursting forth to meet life in the raw. Arthur was not carved out for poetry and religion but Lydia, spitefully, often subjected him to discussions on these serene subjects and this exasperated him no end. On such occasions Arthur reacted rather strongly by either behaving crudely at a party or by coming home drunk. Often a fight between the spouses ensued and the children were stunned into intimidation. All this is faithfully depicted in *Sons and Lovers*.

Lydia Lawrence could not take her husband's gross and barbaric behaviour for long. After being disenchanted with a marital tie she had plentiful hopes from, she turned in desperation to her sons who replaced their father in her affection and concern and became central to her obsessive world comprising, primarily, her sons, Arthur and David who became in *Sons and Lovers*, William and Paul Morel, respectively. In real life Arthur, Lydia's eldest son, was her favourite and she looked towards him for a respectable future. Unfortunately, however Arthur died in London at a very early age but the void so created was soon filled up by David, that is, Paul in the novel. Like his fictional counterpart David, too, was sickly and had a bout of pneumonia at the age of seventeen. This brought his mother and him very close in liaison and it was in this mutuality that they actualized each other. It is a transcript of this reality that is conveyed to us in what *Sons and Lovers* has to offer the readers.

Miriam in *Sons and Lovers* represents Jessie Chambers whom Lawrence met in 1901. Initially, Jessie was rather uncomfortable with what Lawrence had written about their relationship in the Paul-Miriam episodes in the novel and it was at her instance that much of it was rewritten under her guidance.

She felt that the poignancy of the mother-and-son relationship should have been conveyed with greater fidelity and truthfulness. Convinced that she had a clearer recollection of their times spent together Lawrence submitted to her supervision in his writing the novel with the least of fictionalization. It is now largely accepted that the entire "Lad-and-Girl Love" chapter and bits of "Strife in Love" and "Defeat of Miriam" conform to notes supplied by Jessie Chambers.[23] Jessie, however, was dissatisfied with the recast novel, too, as she resented the glorification of the protagonist's captivity by his mother, who had destroyed the adolescent tenderness that existed between Paul and Miriam in the novel. In a letter to Helen Corke she wrote, "The Miriam Part of the novel is a slander".[24]

Jessie, a year younger than Lawrence, was a girl who, like Miriam in *Sons and Lovers*, visualized herself as straight out of a Walter Scott novel. Endowed with an unmistakable literary bent of mind, she spent time with Lawrence reading romantic poetry and some preferred works of fiction. She was also a discriminating critic of Lawrence's drafts of his novels and of his paintings and contributed much to his works by way of an unbiased censure.

Clara Dawes of *Sons and Lovers* has no single original on whom she is modelled. Jessie Chambers, in her record of Lawrence's personal life, avers that Lawrence, in his portrayal of Clara drew traits from three different women; yet, these women remained only inspirations for, in the main, the depiction of Clara is primarily an imaginative one. Other girls at the Jordan's too, are not very factually presented as they are shown as far more respectable than they really were.

Not only did the major characters of *Sons and Lovers* have originals in Lawrence's life but the places referred to and the incidents that took place were also transcripts of what actually took place. Bestwood is the fictional name given to Eastwood, Lawrence's birthplace, where he spent his early years observing the mining activity around. Added to this is the realistic description of the Breach which is substituted by the Bottoms in the novel where mostly all incidents take place.

The given illustrations of parallels between what transpired in Lawrence's life and what we witness in the novel gives irrefutable evidence of the novel being an autobiographical work and yet, one must not err by taking it as a mere record of events that really occurred in the author's life till the time of his mother's demise. Eliseo Vivas warns one against any total identification one may seek to make between what really transpired in Lawrence's life and the succession of events as recorded in the novel. We need here to pay heed to Lawrence's own advice to the reader of his novels: "Never trust the artist. Trust the tale."[25] He was certainly cognizant and aware of the fact that he had set out to write a novel and not an autobiography and yet one cannot overlook the autobiographical element in it.

That Lawrence wrote *Sons and Lovers* to lay the ghost of his rankling past behind is a matter of general acceptance but it is of importance to bear in mind that he has a certain world-view to project in it and wishes to re-write and elucidate his own life and that of his parents in the light of that stance. He explores in the work the complexities and convolutions of human relationships, particularly the man-woman relationship in its myriad forms. In the novel, the marital harmony of Walter and Gertrude Morel is destroyed because the latter, in her dominant role, shows little regard for "the divine otherness" of her ebullient husband and assumes a kind of superiority that decimates a healthy relationship in marriage. The Paul-Miriam relationship breaks down because of Miriam's thrust on spirituality and her denial of the demands of the body; Paul and Clara fail to clinch their relationship and attain happiness together because their "love" lacks depth. Most importantly, Paul proves to be miserable failure in life for his mother-fixation allows him no space to secure his own independent happiness with a girl of his own choice.

Lawrence's narrative design in *Sons and Lovers* provides him with a powerful means of cognition and an equally firm grasp of the world around him. In fact, the manner and modes of perception which his chronicling adopts help us arrive at an aesthetic interpretation of reality or what is generally understood as artistic truth. "Artistic truth is life's truth aesthetically interpreted.... It is a result of cognition set down in a work of art."[26]

Augustine's memoirs, *Confessions*, written between 397 and 400 AD, devised the convention of transmitting experience into narrative, human activity and conduct into textual self-portrayal and termed the end product "autobiography". The autobiographical process is a re-construction in words of all that came to happen in the author's life and a re-creation of his personality, viewed with the wisdom of hindsight. This exercise in depiction enables the autobiographer to establish his true identity and give us a veracious picture of himself. Such a work beginning in self-depiction is concluded with a more thorough knowledge of the self. "Self-portraiture...is a synonym of self-knowledge."[27]

Lawrence's *Sons and Lovers*, however, is not an autobiography by definition but the fictional stance chosen for this *bildungsroman* is one that lays bare with relative honesty aspects of the personal life of the author. Besides, in the ultimate analysis, it remains a blend of autobiography and fiction with autobiography giving the specificity and solidity of facts to flights of imagination. Lawrence chose to covertly unveil certain facts of his life in this novel for a personal catharsis that would finally enable him to bury the past and start life afresh like his protagonist, Paul Morel. Like Gladys in Sally Morgan's *My Place* he seems to be telling himself, "There's no point in digging up the past, somethings are better left buried."[28] So, in writing *Sons and Lovers*, Lawrence clearly sought relief from the great emotional stress, tumult and uneasiness seething within him as remnants of his individual past and the autobiographical content of the novel afforded him a strategy for coming to terms with life and with himself.

Notes

1. Leavis, F.R., "Lawrence and Art", *D.H. Lawrence: Novelist* (Harmondsworth: Penguin Books Ltd., 1955, rpt. 1973), 18.
2. Cited in Leavis, F.R., "Lawrence and Tradition", *D.H. Lawrence: Novelist,* 114.

3. Stumpf, John and Scott, Jon C., *Notes on Twentieth Century English Literature* (London: Coles, 1971), 72.
4. Daiches, David, *The Novel and the Modern World* (Chicago: University of Chicago Press, 1960), 141-42.
5. Schorer, Mark, *Modern British Fiction: Essays in Criticism* (New York: Oxford University Press, 1961), 298-99.
6. Hillman, Rodney, "D.H. Lawrence: *Sons and Lovers", Notes on Literature* (London: The British Council), November RP 13 (161).
7. Moore, Harry T., ed., *Collected Letters of D.H. Lawrence* with an Introduction by Moore, Vol. II (London: Heinemann, 1977).
8. Wordsworth, William, *Preface to Lyrical Ballads* with Introduction and Notes by C.T. Thomas (Madras: Macmillan, 1981), 23.
9. Cited in Hillman, Rodney, "D.H. Lawrence: *Sons and Lovers*", *Notes on Literature*, 2.
10. Lawrence, D.H. *Sons and Lovers* (New Delhi: Rupa, 1999, rpt. 2010), 12.
11. *Ibid.*, 11.
12. *Ibid.*, 12.
13. Allen, Walter, *The English Novel* (Harmondsworth: Macmillan, 1954, rpt. 1970), 358.
14. *Ibid.*, 165.
15. Smith, Frank Glover, *D.H. Lawrence: 'The Rainbow'*, Studies in English Literature Series (London: Edward Arnold, 1971, rpt. 1978), 1.
16. Calderwood, James L. and Toliver, Harold E., ed., *Perspectives on Fiction* (New York: Oxford University Press, 1968), 344.
17. *Ibid.*
18. Beach, Joseph Warren, *The Twentieth Century Novel* (New Delhi: Kalyani Publishers, rpt. 1988), 371.
19. *Ibid.*, 375.
20. Friedman, Alan, *The Turn of the Novel* (New York: Oxford University Press, 1966), XV.
21. *Ibid.*, XVI.
22. Cited in Paul, Rajinder, *Sons and Lovers: A Critical Study* (New Delhi: Rama Bros., 1975, rpt. 2014), 156.

23. E.T., Jessie Chambers, *D.H. Lawrence: A Personal Record* (New York: Cambridge University Press, rpt. 1980).
24. *Ibid.*
25. Cited in Leavis, F.R., "Lawrence and Art", *D.H. Lawrence: Novelist,* 34.
26. Novikov, Vassily, *Artistic Truth and Dialectics of Creative Work,* English Trans (Moscow: Progress Publishers, 1981), 14.
27. Olney, James, ed., "On Writing Autobiography", *Studies in Autobiography* (New York: O.U.P., 1988).
28. Morgan, Sally, *My Place* (Fremantle, Western Australia: Fremantle Arts Centre Press, 1987), 123.

14

Psychoanalysis and D.H. Lawrence's *Sons and Lovers*

Enkelena Shockett

Modernism (1914-1927) was a cultural shift where the changes in society, politics and technology, and slackening family, local and religious ties became the focus of the then literature; representatives of *Modernism* conceived as the value for human person only the education with Christianity; also in this context, I could state out that the liberal humanism weakened a lot. Hence, the fathers of atheism (*Marx, Freud* and *Nietzsche*) were read thoroughly and declared as highlights to follow. Some modernist writers rendered as follows: *James Joyce, Ezra Pound, T.S. Eliot, Virginia Woolf, D.H. Lawrence* and more, privileged themselves in establishing and developing the Modernist literature; nonetheless individually they set up their respective cannons due to literary contributions of which we all are aware of.

As the paper focuses on *Sons and Lovers* as a Freudian novel my intentions will enhance my projection on how to measure the development of the stories and characters in the whole text and also how to evaluate the poetics utilized by D.H. Lawrence. Turning back to this novel I could state that it tells the story of Paul Morel, a young man and budding artist. From this point, I also state that it obviously explains the semi-autobiographical nature of this masterpiece. Hence in a few words I could imply that when you have experienced *Sons and Lovers* you have lived through the agonies of the young Lawrence striving to win free from his old life. Generally, it is not only considered not only as a paramount and evocative portrayal of working-class life in a mining community, but also an intense study of family, class and early sexual relationships.

A few more historical details on this novel highlight that Lawrence began working on the novel in the period of his mother's illness, and often expresses this sense of his mother's wasted life through his female protagonist Gertrude Morel. Letters written around the time of its development clearly demonstrate the admiration he felt for his mother—viewing her as a 'clever, ironical, delicately moulded woman'—and her apparently unfortunate marriage to his coal-miner father, a man of 'sanguine temperament' and instability. He believed that his mother had married below her class status. Rather interestingly, Lydia Lawrence wasn't born into the middle-class. This personal family conflict experienced by Lawrence provided him with the impetus for the first half of his novel—in which both William, the older brother, and Paul Morel become increasingly contemptuous of their father. And the subsequent exploration of Paul Morel's antagonizing relationships with both his lovers, which are both incessantly affected by his allegiance to his mother point out the deep and thoughtful stand of Lawrence on making vivid the picture of the family context. In addition, the title *Sons and Lovers* had reinvigorated Lawrence into vehemently defending his novel and its themes as a coherent work of art, which cradles between a *great tragedy* and a *great book*—in a few words a novel that mirrors the tragedy of thousands of young men in England, hence the interpretation of the characters penned by Lawrence design stereotyping individuals regularly encountered in reality.

A Freudian Reading of the Novel

As the novel *Sons and Lovers* is qualified as a Freudian novel it is worth discussing it from the point of Psychoanalytical view. Stated so I rather prefer to start with rendering the opinions and statements, which certainly drive our researches on *Sons and Lovers* to the realm of Psychoanalysis as a theory and literary method and praxis as well. In this light I could reckon the contents of both Parts, which make up the whole novel.

In Part I, we encounter a brief description and inset of Paul's parents, the father's gaiety, "has that single-minded veracity of impression which was consistent" (Kermode, Frank 1973). At this point, Paul Morel is distinguished for his caressing voice and he speaks of author's language of tenderness. Moreover in this part we encounter also Miriam otherwise Mrs. Morel who is locked out by an angry husband; and under a great moon she buries her face, and returns to the house smeared with pollen—an almost miniature of Elisa in *Chrysanthemums* of J. Steinbeck. Beside this scene we discipline ourselves into interpreting other scenes which transcended and caught up into other symbolic modes which resonate no damage at all to the relations of acts and persons who amazingly perform in the text conceived in its entity: I obviously reckon the moment when the blood of the mother harshly struck by her husband drops into the baby Paul's hair. This boy sleeps with his mother and lovingly cleans off all the mire off her shoes.

In a few words, I could explicitly state that episodes of everyday life will tell their own story better when the entire narrative context is capable of assuming large symbolic meanings. And an understanding of how this worked is remarkably qualified as a breakthrough of D.H. Lawrence into the American literature.

Observing closely the relationship Paul-Mother we perceive the perspective that Miriam will become highly disputable as a character involved in Paul's family context. Chosen as a sexual partner the acts of Miriam position Paul into an unresolved discrepancy between the novel treatment of two themes "the crippling effects of a mother's love...and the 'split' between kinds of love, as represented by...Clara and Miriam". In this light, we notice the various treatment of the two parental characters. In addition viewed from the above perspective I opinion out my stand on this novel as means of coming to understand a situation where understating has not been achieved in ordinary experiences. And this poses the matter that *Sons and Lovers* makes up a very special case and its relation to reality is highly curious and as it is considered as the first Freudian novel in English by which Graham Hough means a workshop in which the author put his *personal trauma* as well as a *catharsis* achieved by re-living an actual experience. However, Mark Schoner and Mark Spilka have positioned this novel as a technique and form, which resonate autobiographical narration of Freudian self-analysis and self-transcendence.

Regarding Miriam I allow myself to position her not only as a rival but also in some ways a double defined into the rejection of her for her mother, which unquestionably is also a rejection of the mother.

In Part II, we perceive Paul Morel to become a very powerful narrator. And this nonce-technique according to Louis L. Martz points out in fact the author's habitual method to confront the text again and again. And the representation of Miriam is highly effective and due to this finely achieved. Jessie Chamber did not like Miriam as she has noticed something wrong in her attitude to the non-human or animal—in few words she has found in her the right person to reduce men or nail them strongly. However the confusions of Paul have colored her image so strongly that we smell his condemnation and rejection of her up to the level of failure. Therefore the only woman who could please him that far would be someone unknown and it is precisely this unknown female identity that keeps him sexually vital. Further more 'his sex in the head' lights him up so much that produces a kind of sacrifice from the part of Miriam who decides to change her identity and push Paul into the experience with death. At this point I could add that Miriam possesses two faces, the vital and sensitive often snubbed by Paul; and the timid, possessive features, which make her resemble Mrs. Morel. However I believe you all understand that both become visible at the same time.

Regarding Clara I could state that she is a very sustainable mother substitute. The first thing Paul does after having love with her is to clean her boots. And this sexual satisfaction produced from the relationship with Clara established a sort of his separation from life. In this vain, I could also make clear that she is produced for night and as such should be considered. This makes probably a reason for Paul to fight her husband Dawes and comes into terms with the married couple. Unfortunately the death, which dominates his sex, manifests itself in the same chapter as the fight when his mother confesses her cancer.

Viewed from this point I could explicitly state that Paul has developed a very sensitive emotional maturity, which makes slightly uncomprehensible the pathos concealed in the whole novel, although we accept it intuitively and also its implications as well. Nonetheless the hatred of the father and too much love of the mother are the *leit-motifs*, which spin up the texture of the novel. However the complete understanding of *Sons and Lovers* depends on deciphering the enigma and our knowledge of evolutionary theory. Yet without Freudian psycho-sexual theories we cannot understand Paul's distortions which "is so great that it preludes all mating is not only prejudicial to the individual's true happiness, but may lead to an atrophy of all initiatives. Paul constantly associates his feeling of death with his inability to mate and that too is psychologically sound" (Draper, R.P. 1970). According to Freud, we comprehend that parental influence regularly determines the mating impulse. And the child's attachment to the parent of opposite sex becomes the prototype of all later love relations. Certainly this causes a sort of jealousy of the parent of the same sex that all children seem to entertain conscious and unconscious fantasies in which rival parent is either killed or removed. At this point a disturbance of the balanced influence of both parents upon a child follows and abnormal concentration upon the beloved parent provoking in this manner neurotic disturbances on Paul. And Paul experiences a simultaneous passion of love and hatred, which makes up a very well-known psychological fact. This constant juxtaposition of love and hatred looks like obsession. And this juxtaposition certainly produces the narrative text and affords the identity characters who perform in order to develop balance or arrangement.

However, Paul is nonetheless a projection of the author's own personality and the arrangement of love feelings transcendent he revolves and the three women he loved: his Mother, Miriam the shrinking mystical creature, and Clara Dawes altogether determine his destiny. At this point, the narrative is more impressionist, colorful and ambitious. In a few words the Freudian system is weighted towards determinism. Paul is described with his axiom that unconscious processes cannot become conscious, therefore modifiable without therapist's aid, which is doomed. The vital context is a fluid system that is fully indeterminate. When the individual cannot make the correct and life-enhancing choice, this state is judged. And the issue of life and death are fully worked out in the texture of events and the road to salvation run along the edge of the abyss, where Paul stands, when his mother died and when he started to establish his double rejection of Clara and Miriam. Hence, Paul is caught in dual focus.

At this point, I could say that he is caught also in the neurosis pattern called repetition compulsion from which there is not escape. However as a vital hero Paul is threatened to death, because of the difficulty of the human relationships he has thrust upon him in childhood and develops on his own in early manhood is a sign of how to keep the Self alive in the turmoils of life as the novel ends.

Paul is the proper hero of *Sons and Lovers,* because he holds and uses the freedom in a greater measure compared to the other characters. As long as the whole narrative text (the book) is entitled an autobiographical narrative, it is worth connoting it as an expression and reflection of Lawrence's life, till his mother died. And Paul as a character is a dominant one and as such his vitality is stronger and his awareness of vital issues is finer compared to Lawrence, who has produced him narratively. This certainly establishes a sort of paradox, which gets clear by Paul's story. Paul forces his agonized relation with Miriam to the final issue of sexual union and then he leaves her only when he is satisfied that they are too much at emotional cross-purposes to marry. He is entirely dominant in the affair with Clara before drawing into *a nuit blanche* of grief, because of his mother's death, although he copes with his mother, since she gets ill. Even the ending of the novel points out Paul's nature, which contains vitality, that reflects his freedom so his fate remains indeterminate *au fond*. His freedom also involves alienation and isolation from the world and we perceive this concern when he experiences his mother's death—a condition to which he has exposed his Self.

Conclusion

Concluding I could yet stress out that *Sons and Lovers* as Julian Moynahan has addressed to us obviously spins up D.H. Lawrence a sort of neurotic case history for Paul is both accurate and comprehensive. And in spite of the fact that the author took issue with Freudians on two points: on the primary of the sexual impulse and the value of bringing neurotics to a conscious awareness of repressed instincts and drives, this certainly figures out the author's psychological outlook is what makes the novel matter. In this venue I would state that we notice three *formal orders or matrices* define the deep structure of *Sons and Lovers*. The first matrix is autobiographical narrative; the second matrix is narrative taken from psychoanalytical theory; the third is a narrative advancing an attitude otherwise called *vitalism*. Finally "the indeterminacy of the novel is resolved as the autobiographical narrative weakens and as the vitalism of the novel which does not coincide with the Freudian matrix, triumphs over it" (Murfin, R.C. 1987).

The question relates to what is implied by *vitalism*. Hence, I could explain in the line of Moynahan that it means a belief that the human Self cannot finally be determined by outside, environmental forces, the belief that passionate being is good and that the only dispassionate, life-defying being is evil. This makes the reason why the author has described a conflict between the instinctual, communal life of the men, and the material inspirations of the women.

The expressive means which each of these three forms of narrative is represented can be partially differentiated. The first is represented through painstaking richly detailed rendering of the naturalistic surface of the ordinary life in both expository and dramatic terms. And the psychoanalytic scheme is pointed out explicitly through an interpretative commentary; however it is largely implicit as it is conceived as an underlying pattern in the autobiographical narrative. The vital context informs soundly the naturalistic narrative and it is pointed up through specific narrative comment. Psychoanalysis and Lawrence's kind of *vitalism* have many points in common as readings of experience.

The novel shows how "the men worked and the wives aspired to escape the drudgery of the working class life". In addition I could say that as long as the novel highlights both gender escapist languages, the novel manages to transmit something incisive about class and gender division. At this point however, I could make clear that as we perceive the conflict(s) confined within a system which gives breath to a deadly smothering of women by a male-dominated society. Furthermore, as long as we frame everyday experience derived from reading *Sons and Lovers*, we position ourselves into the realm of authenticity explored in the novel. Hence nonetheless self-discovery becomes developed and imagination established the paradigm achievers of self-definition. That is how we measure the development of the main protagonists in the novel and also pose questions, which matter significantly because they open up perspectives out of which we certainly apply a multiplicity of readings—psychoanalytical reading of the novel becomes the focus of this paper.

In this light, I could conclude that the *self-fulfillment* of the protagonists, therefore, should be viewed from the unconditioned relationships and moral demands which go beyond the *Self*. In addition, the novel presents the *Freudian Oedipus imbroglio* in almost tragic completeness.

At last I could end up this research by stating *Sons and Lovers* is a record of a family and of a pathos of its complex relationship and in general D.H. Lawrence's novels offer a sort of fierce antagonism, which he displays. And the conflict he attempts to exhibit and make it to us comprehensible enough. Furthermore, this stand comes out from his obsessive love for his mother differently called "Oedipus complex".

Works Cited

Alexander, M. (2007). *A History of English Literature*. Second Edition. New York: Palgrave Foundation.

Drapper, R.P. (1970). *D.H. Lawrence: The Critical Heritage*. Great Britain: Routledge & Paul Ltd.

Holler, C. and Klepper, M. (2013). *Rethinking Narrative Identity: Persona and Perspective*. Amsterdam: John Benjamins Publishing Company.

Kermode, F. (1973). *D.H. Lawrence*. New York: The Viking Press.

Mchale, B. (1993). *Postmodernist Fiction*. New York: Routledge.

Murfin, R.C. (1987). *Sons and Lovers: A Novel of Division and Desire*. Boston: Twayne Publishers.

Qafleshi, E. (2008). *Sa pranë...përmes Hermeneutikë letrare*. Tiranë: GEER.

14

Women in Love: Between the Old and New

Mehar Fatima

While struggling to understand the curiously emerging consciousness in women, men, their societies, and nature, D.H. Lawrence voyages through a peculiar space and time wherein he encounters the "vanishing apparitions" of the old, making way for something new to come. *Women in Love* struggles to live through the transition of multitude; of chasm, secrets, dreams, ambitions, fantasy, imagination, fear, madness, silence, chaos, anarchy, and void amidst the shadows, crossing between the past and future.

The title of the novel may have startled its new modern readers into a moral, social, and a slight psychological inquisitiveness. Despite its apparent romantic connotation, the novel is precisely neither about women nor love. It is for us to measure through our interpretation and criticism of the novel, so as to determine the underlying assumptions and its meanings. Meaning making is yet another discourse. *Women in Love* has ability to prove its author's tremendous literary artistic credibility, displaying his newly invented modern writing techniques. It is Lawrence's masterwork and is one of the most significant novels of the modern era. However, difficult to apprehend, it creates a wider scope for the readers to analyze the novelist's art in the work of fiction. The interpretation of the novel depends upon different and varied perspectives granting to reflection of its essential themes. Contrary to the traditional literary fashion; the complexities of structure, a unique writing style, lucid narrative technique, psychological depiction, along with philosophical insight and rich symbolism arouses profound interest in the study of Lawrence's matchless work in the light of the emerging times. Lawrence boldly abandons the customary plot and liner narrative practice in favour of extraordinary new scenes and tales, which are ostensibly fragmented; however, they have strong links within, which join the destiny of characters together. Nevertheless, the characters in their disjointed personalities become highly symbolic. The structure and development of the characters intensely articulate Lawrence's loud thinking of the notion of civilization's modern progress and his assumption about man-woman relationship.

The novel begins with the Brangwen sisters, Ursula and Gudrun, "working and talking" (Lawrence 1980: 1) in their father's house in Beldover. Lawrence with his subtle implication says that "They were mostly silent, talking as their thoughts strayed through their minds" (Lawrence 1980: 1). The exploration on the psychological development of the characters, especially women, becomes the basic element of the novel in progress. These thoughts were about marriage. Gudrun views marriage, as a comfortable practice of the traditional past, which may '"Possibly" be "undesirable, but bound to be an experience of some sort"' (Lawrence 1980: 1). It could be perhaps a source of self-fulfillment. But Ursula asserted that the experience of marriage is '"More likely to be the end of experience"' (Lawrence 1980: 1). The two sisters were in search of something beyond romance in matrimony. They were not able to keep themselves connected to the practice of their counterparts from the previous age, and were preparing for bold experiments. They felt a strong temptation to avoid, as if the results of the first temptation have not been received happily. "In their hearts they were frightened.... *Nothing materializes!*" They were beginning to feel dissatisfied with the modern air. "Everything withers in the bud" (Lawrence 1980: 2-3). There could be something yet to come? Nigel Kelsey observes: "The questioning nature of Gudrun's and Ursula's opening dialogue accumulates in intensity as the questions themselves accumulate; definite feelings of emptiness, fear and loss" (Kelsey 1991: 141-42). These dialogues assemble questions; some old and some new, pertaining to a feminist thought, deemed necessary to be answered. Whether marriage was still a natural desire to be fulfilled or the changing society was constructing it again in its own way was left to be a lived reality. In the absence of no other choice, women could depend on the oblivious hope. This hope, to see what has never been witnessed before could create something new in contrast to the old representatives of the earlier Victorian marriage. In Mrs. Chrich some problematic images of matrimonial tie remain disturbing until the end. She seemed to have lost much in the locked relationship of absolute annihilation, living only to reflect the loss and fear. Therefore, the objective curiosity lingered on. Each of the women and men was tortured with subjective desires.

Secrets of the mind and heart coiled in darkness, of relationships within and with others. The presence of the dead could be felt through "vague scent of sap and of spring..." (Lawrence 1980: 9). Each one of the characters wished to be alone in order to exercise the innate power of their "free will", away from the enclosures and "tightness" (Lawrence 1980: 8) of the others. Sometimes there are evident feelings of mutual sufferings, regrets of returning to consciousness, to seek for new existence, but they know not of its existence. Yet they must move forward. The subconscious feelings; mingled with love and hate, become an energetic force which carry forward the novel in the development of relationships. Lawrence declares:

> You mustn't look in my novel for the old stable ego of the character. There is another ego, according to whose action the individual is unrecognizable and passes through, as it were, allotropic states which it needs a deeper sense than any we've been used to exercise, to discover....

Going deeper, through psychological cadence, he makes it very difficult for his readers to study the characters on traditional set patterns. It is from the outer to inner self as well as intensely within.

> ...like as diamond and coal are the same pure single elements of carbon. The ordinary novel would trace

> the history of the diamond...but I say "diamond, what! This is carbon." And any diamond might be coal or soot, and my theme is carbon. (Kirkpatrick 1979: 708)

Adopting the "carbon theme", Lawrence builds a world of relationships. A relation between Ursula and Birkin, makes Ursula vulnerable of the fact that he would accept her only on his own terms. His repulsion of marriage matches with that of Ursula's. They fail to appreciate the ring that would bind them. They asserted to embrace a new matrimonial conjunction, ensuring each other's essential freedom. Lawrence was making a new meaning of love by establishing a union between the couple where each obligates to the other though sustaining the integrity of the person. Ursula tries to strike a balance between her independent consciousness and her newly acquired love for Birkin. It is her desire to evolve beyond matter to pure energy. We look for this balance between Gudrun and Gerald. It is a challenge for Gudrun, who is a creative artist, possessed with self-motivated talent to go beyond perfection, to reconcile with Gerald, the industrial magnate. Rejecting his swiftly aging Victorian father's munificence, Gerald blindly dictates the family's honoured industrial coal mining system. He could not possibly find natural connections with others on the terms of mutual respect. His soul was trapped, his freedom was caged. Gudrun and Gerald were of the same form of kinetic energy. Their establishing bond was a combat of the mortals; supremacy verses dominance. "The bond was established between them" a silent bond "in that look, in her tone. She made the understanding clear—they were of the same kind, he and she, a sort of diabolic freemasonry subsisted between them. Henceforward, she knew, she had her power over him. Wherever they met, they would be secretly associated. And he would be helpless in the association with her. Her soul exulted" (Lawrence 1980: 114). No reconciliation of any sort could be possible between the two lovers; "the mutual hellish recognition" was finally met in Gerald's cold death and destruction. They tragically transformed their competence for vigorous sexuality into dreadful lust; lust for power. Their tragic bondage was originated in contaminated awareness of their minds. Love, thus becomes execution and chasm of despair. Lawrence writes in his foreword to the American edition of *Women in Love*, "We are now in a period of crisis. Every man who is acutely alive is acutely wrestling with his own soul." The period of crisis amounts to the critical existence of the present. Lawrence leaves no one behind. The "wrestling" here is not only between two bodies but between the bodies and souls. We can feel the void somewhere, everywhere; an expression of the First World War, though we don't find any direct mention of it anywhere. It simply is rampant in the air, the actions, the food, and thoughts. In response to the multi-faced catastrophe of the Great War, one could sense the growing aspirations longing for change. Nothing could remain still, neither human nor nature.

Wendy Perkins rightly scrutinizes, "The interchanges between men and women in *Women in Love* are complicated by the historical moment of the novel, an age where individuals no longer turn to society for advice on forming relationships" (Perkins 1992: 233). They abscond from the old to the new ones, perhaps in an attempt to rejuvenate, the two love stories of four people through corresponding proportion from different social standings and professions. Ironically, love could be means to salvation. Ursula and Gudrun fall in love with Rupert Birkin and Gerald Crich respectively. Birkin ended his stormy and rather idealistic relationship and psychological struggle with Herminone. A sensual association with Minette and Gerald was dissolved to make space for the new one. The budding relationships, the dreams and imagination of the two pairs could not be kept safely inclusive. The two men had a world of their own. There was intuition, inclination, and instinct. One reciprocated the other's love, idea and feeling. While the pairs, Ursula and Birkin continue to resist in idea and feeling, but their love culminates in an acceptable semi harmony. Gudrun and Gerald are seemingly able to hold on to their affectionate relationship, but it all ends in a fatal consequence of Gerald's death in the snowy Alps. Life and death becomes another theme. Lawrence connects and compares Gerald to the white moon, the Alps, and the Arctic snow wildness. Other things that attribute him are cold, chilly, despair, and frantic. Gerald and Gudrun actually belong to the same psychological framework, creating conflicts and intersections of willpower, ending in death. Contrastive portrayal of Birkin and Ursula survives the story. Though physically unfit, an opposite of Gerald, Birkin endures the burden of Life Force; an animating spirit instilled into man, and Ursula, calm, milder and more fragile than Gudrun are acutely alive man and woman, creeping into sensibilities, allowing Lawrence's craftsmanship to dramatic demonstration of struggles between the bodies and souls.

The readers fail to receive an affirmative nod from the character's long yearnings for an answer to their questions, because Lawrence believes "that experience is equivocal, ambivalent, and that there are no clear answers or wholly adequate resolutions" (Keith 1985: 192). None of the characters are essentially evil; it is their indisposition to define themselves in opposition to each other which obscures tranquility. The most astonishing part of the novel is the inability of marriage to complete a relationship, resulting in the triangle of desire. Birkin refuses to accept the completeness of the man-woman matrimonial relationship in the absence of his male friend, Gerald. He laments that he could not find an eternal union with his own gender to achieve completeness and contentment. Roland Barthes writes, "To interpret a text is not to give it a (more or less justified, or more or less free) meaning, but on the contrary to appreciate what plural constitutes it..." (Barthes 1974: 5). The indeterminate ending and incompleteness of the human correlation sum up Lawrence's artistic genius. It highlights the fact that this story of the early modern time was still in its period of revolutionary evolution, shaping the modern time. It perhaps remains a confession of the coming days. The novel moves ahead, sympathizing and reflecting the human course to its readers. And they too consciously comprehend the existence of the living reality. The incompleteness becomes a central component in the state of transition.

A part adieu to the fully accomplished world and a part effort to be reborn into a new becomes a significant theme of *Women in Love*. We discover Lawrence in search of some hope from the remains of the shattered individuals in the universal crisis. They are rescued and redeemed through love. Rupert Birkin wishes to create the future after a determined desire of one's own heart, echoing Omar Khayyam's serene imagination:

> Ah Love! Could thou and I with Fate Conspire
> To grasp this sorry Scheme of Things entire,
> Would not we shatter it to bits—and then
> Re-mould it nearer to the Heart's Desire!
>
> (Omar Khayyam 2000: 81)

So we find Lawrence balancing between hope and despair, exploring and combating new feelings in newly emerging world in order to apprehend them, a journey to an indefinite, encompassing everything and piercing into the innermost sensations of mankind. He was questioning possibly if "the water gleamed and the opposite woods were purplish with new" (Lawrence 1980: 28) why can't we? Lawrence has a charm of his very own. He corresponds with reality, with truth.

D.H. Lawrence's plans, techniques, and presentations diverge untamed. The task of interpreting his art becomes difficult. One has to come within reach of it with wider sympathies and elasticity. It is possible that we may be reading or studying his work erroneously. We may be self-conceited with hostility and resentfulness. Interestingly, the critics have never been happier with Lawrence's inquisitive works for many reasons of their own. Their Lawrence is an intensely distressed artist who articulated his mania into artistic expression which the instrument of modern psychoanalysis can help decipher. The allegations of preaching are no surprise, which is in fact preaching to the converted. They may like to go back without knowledge "and be like a savage" (Lawrence 1980: 40). The moment any philosophical artist discovers the truth and brings it forth, he has to bear moralizing charges. His observation and its assertion become painfully didactic. The ultimate truth may not be easy to digest as soft and tender well cooked meat. It is simply because his stories are not cooked at all, but a genuinely lived reality. Lawrence is his own critic. He places criticism above interpretation. His criticism is rooted in an understanding of the author's intentions. He believes that the aim of criticism is to highlight the intended meaning and application of the received meaning to the pulsating life through varied and powerful emotions. His canvas is hugely spread across civilizations, accommodating a large variety of perspectives constantly evolving and highlighting the modern dilemma. Lawrence's works give form and shape to the obsolescence. Jack Stewart studies Lawrence's expression of a painter's image in pure words, substituting visual images with written rhythm and harmony, investigating art movements such as expressionism, primitivism, and futurism in the novel. Lawrence's impressionistic diagnosis is also widely recognized. He united the world into the oneness of colour and light. His works are tremendously prolific and bitterly satiric. *Women in Love* bears witness of his rebellious and radical views. Lawrence regarded nature and intimate physical pairing of human bodies as a powerful therapy to contest with the evils of modern industrialized civilization. Here we can see a peculiar vision of every soul and an exalted eminence of warmth and fullness and of rich visualization. Some question his later works which evidently miss the early manners, but whatever is amiss is replaced most artistically by his convincing assertion, inner visualization and passionate conviction. The change of style from old to the new marks the evolution of metaphysical view. His shifting thoughts exhibit his universal change of attitude, carrying forward the new thinking towards progressive path. His works record his experience of his new vision. In his writings may be found the future of complete modernism.

Psychological interpretation reveals the hidden treasures of mind where obscure realities become visible through the verbal expressions, yet the language could not seize much significance. The inability of language to hold the content has been seen through Ursula's "inarticulate and inaudible" cry, "and she flushed deeply, between her desire and her wincing Confusion" (Lawrence 1980: 14). Communication gap created chaos and bewildered wilderness. Language was not enough anymore; it was beginning to lose the assumed value and cultural worth. The intended message could not be delivered and hence was not decoded. They remained suspended in the thin air, absorbed in nature, adding to the present vacuum-leading to anarchy.

There could be witnessed a radical shift in art and literature. Everything and everybody could not fit with ease in the conventional concept without being neutralized. The various nature of the shift could be noticed in aesthetic and cultural sensibilities. Proceeding and receding within the drawn scale was becoming a dynamic norm, as if time itself was caught between the old and something new. The aspiration for something new was throbbing in *Women in Love*. The characters were held struggling to escape but knew not where to, were yet visible far and wide and consistently. This was peculiar indeed, of the moving epoch. There was a loss of the well-established, stable, and meaningful cosmos. The ordered Victorian world was slipping away in its obsolete form, withering shape, and fading colour. Lawrence undoubtedly seemed sensitive to the loss both in his sense and perception, though he could not wait motionless and had to sway away in order to discover what was to come next. His concern was neither the gone past nor a complete future but he lived along with his art in the devastating present. This present was the workshop or the breeding ground for a new world in progress, evolving at a bidding speed and energy. His contemporary time of utter futility, living through some comprehensible and achievable dreams, ambitions, fantasy, imagination, recognized fear, sane madness, talking silence, organized chaos, anarchy, and void was making sense to the consciousness. Rejecting the completely expected optimism, Lawrence tries to a pessimistic view of the existing civilization, living through an apparent apathy and moral relativism; throwing away the old burden of morality parameter. *Women in Love* captures a momentous period of transition in fascinating ideas, striking images, lucid style, commanding language, and dramatic narrative.

Works Cited

Barthes, Roland (1974). *S/Z*. Trans. Richard Miller. New York: Hill and Wang, U.S.A.

Bell, Michael (1991). *D.H. Lawrence: Language and Being*. Cambridge University Press: Cambridge. UK.

Dube, Wolf-Deiter (1983). *Expressionists and Expressionism*. Trans. James Emmons. Geneva: Skira.

Kelsey, Nigal (1991). *D.H. Lawrence: Sexual Crisis*. London: Macmillan.

Khayyam, Omar (2000). *Rubaiyat of Omar Khayyam*. Trans. Edward Fitzgerald. New Delhi: Rupa Publications.

Kirkpatrick, D.L., Lawrence, D.H. and James Vinson, ed. (1979). *Novelist and Prose Writers*. London: Macmillan.

Lawrence, D.H. (1980). *Women in Love*. New York: Penguin Books.

———. "Morality and the Novel." *Study of Thomas Hardy and Other Essays*. ed. Bruce Steele. Cambridge: Cambridge University Press, 1985: 171-76.

Leavis, F.R. (1995). *Lawrence and Art*. Shanghai: Shanghai Art Publishing Press.

Perkins, Wendy. "Reading Lawrence's Frames: Chapter Division in *Women in Love*". *The D.H. Lawrence Review*. 1992: 229-49.

Ross, Charles L. (1991). *Women in Love: A Novel of Mythic Realism*. Boston: Twayne.

Sagar, Keith (1985). *D.H. Lawrence: Life into Art*. London: Viking Penguin Books.

Stewart, Jack (1999). *The Vital Art of D.H. Lawrence: Vision and Expression*. Carbondale: Southern Illinois University Press.

16

End of Another Home Holiday: In the Light of *Rasavada*

Ratri Ray

Lawrence's works, steeped as they are in human emotions, seems to cry out for an analysis according to *Rasavada* which is a theory that is based on human emotions. But no attempt, so far as is known to the writer, has been made in this direction. The present article is an attempt to analyse his poem *End of Another Home Holiday* according to *Rasavada*. It is being assumed that the reader will have a working knowledge of this theory. Its intricacies will be clarified as and when necessary. Much has been written on his poems but critical opinions will not be cited unless strictly relevant, for no critical study resembles one according to *Rasavada*. This theory looks at a work as an autonomous whole, independent of politics, etc. But not independent of the outer world since the *rasas* are generated in the *asraya's* heart as a response to external stimuli. Lawrence himself had said:

> Even the best poetry, when it is at all personal, needs the penumbra of its own time and place to make it full and whole.[1]

Only the immediate penumbra, however, might be relevant for *rasavada*, not the socio-political condition or the personal life of the poet. But all this will become clear as we proceed, hoping the reader will enjoy the exercise.

The beginning of the poem is devoted to nature. He has started to fell homesick even before he has left home. He anticipates a long absence and wonders when next he will see the moon sinking behind the sycamore tree at the end of the garden and,

> When will the scent of the dim white phlox
> Creep up the wall to me, and in at my
> Open window?[2]

How very strong and delicate his sense of smell is! The phlox is a flower that has hardly got any smell. Anyway the *rasa* we get here is definitely *Prakriti-rasa.* This is not one of the canonical nine. It is a modern *rasa*, firmly established by Bharatendu Harishchandra. Since, canonical or not, it is an important *rasa* in the present context, it is necessary to give a little explanation. The delight derived from beholding the beauty of nature, or the opposite terror at her might, all kinds of emotions generated by nature can be called *prakriti-rasa*. Its *sthayi* is *rati* because man has from the very beginning looked upon nature as his companion. Very after in other *rasas* (sringara etc.), nature exists as the *uddipana* (stimulant). Here it is not so for in this *rasa* nature herself is the *alambana* (fundamental determinant). It is by nature that the *rasa* is generated, so naturally she is the *alambana*. This scholar argues that the description of nature is poetry immerses us in delight, therefore definitely, this delight is *rasa*. Many other modern scholars have supported him. Bharatendu argues that it is a *rasa* that can be experienced in two ways: directly by a man on seeing nature, as well as indirectly by reading nature described in literature. Now we are such that cannot tell a cow slip from a harelip unless Wordsworth is there to hammer it home to us, but Lawrence's phloxes send their fragrance even to us—we experience *Prakriti-rasa* of high order. The phloxes are the *alambana* and the poet is the *asraya* (recipient). So, if the flower is the *alambana*, what is the *Uddipana*? It is Lawrence's consciousness that his holiday has ended, he is going away for he does not know how long.

The sound of the bell mentioned in the next line is manmade, but it has become so much a part of nature in the context that there can be no hesitation in including it within our *rasa*-experience. The trotting at the pony is also included as part of nature, which, indeed, it is.

So, within this *rasa*-experience we get *caksusa* (visual) *ghranaja* (olfactory) and *sravya* (auditory)—all three kinds of perception and the *rasa*—experience lasts for the entire section. It begins (*udaya*) with the half-moon sinking behind the sycamore tree and ends twelve lines later with the sound of the train. In the middle lines, it establishes itself (*pusti*) and firmly comes to an end (*santi*). In lyrics it is possible, indeed it is easy to have this *rasodaya*, *pustiu* and *santi* spread over a long-time as here.

But the poem has just begun. It goes on to generate another powerful *rasa*. The pet sees the light under his mother's door and the poem changes its tone utterly. The poet is guilt ridden at leaving her.

> That she should love me so
> She so lonely, greying now!
> And I leaving her
> Bent on my own pursuits.[3]

In this and the next two stanzas the poet is indirectly writing of his love for her. Indirectly, because he does not say as he does earlier, in line eleven, addressing his home, "ah suddenly I love you". Love here is too deep and too intense to be made light of in verbal expression. He cannot talk about it is so many words. Yet there is no doubt that this intense love touches us deep inside. Without doubt this is a *rasa*-experience. But which *rasa*, *sahrdaya* reader, which *rasa*? Certainly not any of the canonical ones. Here we have to turn to that scholar of scholars, Abhinava Gupta, who tells us of *sneharasa*. This is the counterpart of *Vatsala rasa* (of which more later), for the parents love for the child is *Vatsala rasa* and this love is the child's love for his parent. This is a *rasa* about which scholars have not bothered at all. Abhinava Gupta is one and the other is Sri Rupa Gosvamin. But he has not talked about it from the point of view that interests us. It is relay surprising because he devotes eighty-four slokas to vatsala splitting and re-splitting hairs in *Bhakti-rasamrta-sindhu*, but he has nothing to say about *sneha-rasa*. Elsewhere, in a different context altogether he has included it within *samartha rati* which is one of the divisions of *Sringara*, he says:

Aruhya paraman kasthari prema ciddipadipari
Hrdayari dravyannesa sneha ityabhidhiyate

When love increases and expands the conscious-
Ness and melts the heart then it is called *sneha*.[4]

This is what Abhinava Gupta has called love for one's parents. He calls it the tenth *rasa* with *ardrata* as its sthayi (permanent emotion). It is undeniable that in the poem heart has expanded and melted here. These lines are very fine examples of this *sneha-rasa*. It is surprising that other scholars have neglected it. Had Tulsidasa written a pada or two about young Krishna's feelings when he went to Mathura and set his parents free then scholars would perhaps have woken up to it. Tulsidasa has written enough about baby Krishna in all conscience, one or two about a teenage Krishna would not have come amiss. Anyway, we have Abhinava Gupta and Rupa Gosvamin to encourage us.

So here again we have another *rasa* experience with the poet as the *asraya*, and his mother as the *alambana*. The light under her door and of course the coming separation are the *uddipana*. The poet's self-reproach, his guilt are powerful *saricari* (transient) bhavas. It is generated, established or nourished and ends (*udaya*, *pusti* and *santi*) in three stanzas, a total of fourteen lines. No mean achievement to sustain a *rasa*-experience for so long. Many a sonnet there are that cannot do as much.

The next section gives us the experience of another *rasa—vatsala rasa*, the *rasa* that is the counterpart of *Sneha*. *Vatsalya* or parental love is its *sthayi*. It is time to write a few sentences about it, as has already been threatened. It was first mentioned by Narayana Pandita and later affirmed by his grandson Vishwanatha Kaviraja. His description of it is really memorable because of the economy of phrasing and felicity of expression. *Sphutari camatkaritaya vatsalanca rasari viduh* (its wonderful expression gives it the name *Vatsaa*). Sri Rupa has written a chapter of eighty-four Slokas about it, writing about all imaginable (and for fetched or plain unimaginable) varieties of it. Here we have the beginning of this *rasa* very quietly, with a picture of the rain wetting the roots of the grain and then the moon riding high and carefree in the sky. Then comes the heart breaking picture of the mother.

Frail and sad, with gray, bowed head,
The beggar—woman, the yearning eyed
Inexorable love goes begging.[5]

This *rasa*, in this instance, is accompanied with sadness, whereas *vatsala* is usually a *rasa* whose expression is a joyful one. Yet there can be no doubt that we experience *rasa* here. Outside of Lawrence the only sad evocation of this *rasa* is one that I do not want to remember, it is so painful. I refer to the scene in which Cordelier meets her when he is restored to sanity—this as well as the later scenes. This kind of comparison is anathema to me. It does justice to no one, neither to the poets, nor to the critic. But it is very rare to find *vatsala rasa* steeped in sadness outside of Lawrence. If the reader rejects this reference (it is not a comparison) with high indignation I will be the first to agree.

The next stanza carries on the *rasa*-experience, but this time another element is added to it, the element of nature. We have here both *prakriti* and *vatsala*, with *vatsala* dominant. We are offered a series of three images succeeding each other—all from nature, all about *vatsala*.

The wild young heifer, glancing distraught
with a strange new knocking of life at her side
Runs seeking a loneliness.[6]

It is incipient *vatsalya bhava* that prompts the heifer to hide when giving birth. But at least the heifer is a conscious animal. The next two instances Lawrence takes are from more instinctive life—that of a grain sending down roots in the soil and of an egg getting ready to hatch. He could have taken a mother duck or something like that but no it is an egg he takes to give an example of protective motherly love. It is not surprising that Auden should say:

> Whenever (Lawrence) forgets about men with proper names and describes the anonymous life of a stone, waters, forests, animals, flowers his bad temper and his dogmatism immediately vanish and he becomes the most enchanting companion imaginable.[7]

In this stanza we find a few extremely farfetched example of *vatsala rasa*. In fact they are so farfetched that it is difficult to call them examples of it. One can accept the heifer readily enough, but imagination does rather boggle at the grain an egg:

> The little grain draws down the earth, to hide.
> Nay, even the slumberous egg, as it labours under the shell.
> Patiently to divide and self-divide
> Asks to be hid and wishes nothing to tell[8]

But though the concept is farfetched it is undeniable that one experiences the ineffable delight that *rasa* experience gives and it is not plain and simple *prakriti rasa*. Protective and anticipatory precautions are there that argue *vatsala rasa*.

Strangely enough, though the next stanza gives an abstract instance of motherly, love, it seems to be far more comprehensible and acceptable than the grain and the egg. A completely abstract figure is imagined to have come and established tearful contact with the poet.

> Piteous love comes peering under the hood
> Touches the clasp with trembling fingers.[9]

This is no concrete, actual figure, it is purely imaginary, yet the poets imagination is so strong as to have invested this non-existent figure with more concreteness than the grain and the egg.

But the end is not yet. The final section of just one nine lines stanza is still left and in it the poet goes back once more to nature, creating *prakriti rasa* unmixed with *vatsala*. It describes that harsh mournful cry of a corncrake that evokes self-blame in the poet.

Yes, the poem is definitely a *rasottirna* poem. It affords us the experience of three unfamiliar *rasas*, *prakriti*, *sneha* and *vatsala*. We have it repeatedly a wonderful mixture of these *rasas* and let it be noted that the word "wonderful" is not being loosely used here. It is used in the sense of *camatkara*. The *rasa*-experience is known as *lokattara-camatkara-pranah* —an experience which is based on a wonder that goes beyond the world and in Lawrence's case we get it repeatedly. Indeed, he himself has written at length on wonder, on its being a quality that bathes things with the light that never was on sea or land. This encourages me to mention the Sanskrit concept of *camatkara* let not the reader be apprehensive that I am going to inflict on him Ksemendra's ten kinds of *camatkara*. I will instead quite just half a sentence of Abhinava Gupta, for in this case that much is enough.

> ca tripti-vyatirekena-avicchinno
> bhogabesa ityucyate.

What is called *camatkara* is an uninterrupted (*acchina*) state of immersion (*avesa*) in an enjoyment, characterized by the presence of a sensation of inner fullness (*tripti*).[10]

It is a concept with which Lawrence would have agreed because he says very much the same thing.

The poem is not long enough to justify a discussion of its *arigirasa*, but there is another question which is relevant in this case. The poem is a melancholy one. Whatever *rasa* is evoked, and there are no less than three in this poem of only sixty-three lines, every time it is steeped in melancholy. So what happened to the *Brhmasvada-sahodara* delight that is promised to us as *rasa*-experience?

Yes, the experience is a sad one but can it be denied that it affords an intense, mind expanding experience? What if it is sad? Abhinavagupta has told us:

> anandaghanam asvadyate. Tatra Ka duhkhasanka?
> -it is a blissful experience. Where is the fear of sorrow in that?
> Where indeed?[11]

Notes

1. Hough, G., *The Dark Sun*, Penguin Books, rpt. 1961: 223.
2. Wain, John, ed. *The Oxford Library of English Poetry* (Vol. III): 317-18. All the quotations will be from this edn.
3. *Ibid.*, 317.
4. Das, Khudiram, *Vaisnava Rasa*. Prakash, Bookland, Kolkata, 1993: 236.

5. *Ibid.*, 318.
6. *Ibid.*
7. Auden, W.H., *D.H. Lawrence* in *the Dyer's Hand and Other Essays*, New York: Vintage Pubs., 1990: 289.
8. Op. cit., 318.
9. *Ibid.*, 318.
10. Sethuraman, V. ed., *Indian Aesthetics*. Macmillan, 1992: 47.
11. Acarya Abhinavagupta, *Abhinavabharati*, Gaekwad Oriental Series. Baroda, New Delhi, pp. 1-292.

17

Interrogating Psycho-cultural Dynamics in the Plays of D.H. Lawrence

Beena Agarwal

Synthesis of opposites including social and psychological, carnal and spiritual, temporal and contemporary, individual and social, moral and pragmatic constitutes the comprehensive canvass of literary sensibility of D.H. Lawrence and it inspired him to pour out his vision in his novels, poetry, short stories and even in his plays with equal profundity and dexterity. The fact is well acknowledged that Lawrence's dramatic vision got lesser recognition and acknowledgement as compare to his novels and short stories. However, it can safely be established that like his poetry and novels, his dramatic art was directed to discern serious conclusions about the hidden terrains of human consciousness that quite often results in exploration of the dilemma of human existence in context of the inevitable socio-cultural environment. Inspired by such a paradigm of human existence, Lawrence conceives the patterns and paraphernalia of his dramatic plots beyond the formal adherence to dramatic strategies and theatrical mechanism. He constitutes his dramatic structures with dexterous manipulation of rich symbols to make invisible, visible and to present abstract realizations as a part of concrete reality.

Lawrence witnessed neglect and hostile criticism for his plays but with the production of his three popular plays *A Collier's Friday Night*, *The Daughter-in-Law* and *The Widowing of Mrs. Holroyd*, he touched the pinnacles of success. With the presentation of them in Royal Court Theatre in 1968, his identity was established as a modern dramatist of immense possibilities. His other popular plays are *The Fight for Barbara, The Merry-Go-Round, Touch and Go* and *The Married Man.* He used the art of theatre to explore the intricacies of human consciousness in context of "decisive experience of love, of family, of working life" (Raymond 9). It suggests that he contextualizes human consciousness in relation to the real life experiences. To explore psychological depth of social reality, he makes extensive use of symbols. About the richness and suggestiveness of his symbols, it is said, "His plays contain unconscious symbolism and through symbols, he presents the unconscious in man, which is unknowable only through symbols" (Nath 168).

Lawrence in his dramatic works constructs a comprehensive patterns of dilemmas working on human consciousness. He contextualize them placing the interrogations of human existence amid the prevailing network of social consciousness. He proceeds with the assumption that man can hardly escape the influences of social forces as they contribute in the formation of human psyche. To present the synthesis of conscious and unconscious and to project the abstract reality through concrete reality, he makes extensive use of rich symbols. Accepting the need of symbols in creative art, in his essay, "The Dragon of Apocalypse" and the volume *Fantasia of Unconscious* he reveals his views on the significance of symbols. It enhances the possibilities of emotional vigous, spontaneity and suggestiveness beyond the traditional domains of 'cause and effect relationship' in context of theatrical cannons expounded by Aristotle. With these symbols beyond the burden of cannons, he attempts to explore the mysteries of human nature that encounters the challenges of survival. It was an inevitable necessity of his art and sensibility because for his preoccupation with unconscious, the inner mystery of human adjustment at the various stages. He states:

> The Business of art is to reveal the relation between his circumambient universe with living moment. As mankind is always struggling in the toils of old relationship, art is always 'ahead' of the 'time' which themselves are far in the rear of the living moment. (Anthony 108)

It suggests that socio-cultural context are basis of the formation of psychological realities as Lawrence has projected them through the multi-level conflicts affecting the consciousness of his characters.

The idea of 'struggling with innerself' and 'living moment' inspired him to construct a complex web of symbols related to the unconscious state of human mind. Regarding the significance of unconscious symbols, he admits:

> Symbols are organic units of unconsciousness with a life of their own, as you can never explain them away because their value is dynamic, emotional, belonging to the sense consciousness of body and soul and not simply mental. (Beal 115)

Lawrence develops the structures of his plays only to comprehend the unknown realities of human psyche. In this respect in Lawrence's plays the symbols are employed not for artistic excellence and aesthetic elations only as it is evident in the plays of Tagore, "...Tagore creates a prison of symbols without genuine vitality and life, which is the primary criterion of literature" (Desai 153). For Lawrence symbol is not a need of artistic mechanism only but "an organic unit of consciousness with a life of their own" (*The Dragons of Archtypal* 157). He further elaborates the purpose of symbols to realise the aims of artistic creation:

> A complex of emotional experience is a symbol. And the power of symbol is to arose the deep emotional self, and the dynamic self, beyond comprehension.
> (D.H. Lawrence, *The Dragons of Archtypal* 158)

D.H. Lawrence used theatre to expose the dilemma of human survival witnessing a clash of invisible forces of Individual compulsions of desires and derives in the backdrop of established norms of social order. In this respect individual vs. society emerges as a leitmotif in his plays. However the distinction of his vision lies in the fact that he no longer searches the external realities but makes efforts to uncoil the hidden tangles of human psyche. This effort in the history of theatre inaugurated the era of psychological plays of multiple dimensions that subsequently culminated in the revolutionary theatrical practices of O'Neill Tennessee William, Samuel Becket and Strindberg Lawrence being influenced by Freud's idea of 'libido' and sexual instincts in all his writings promotes the idea that 'sexual impulses' are beyond the domain of socially governed morality principles. At the same time, man can't survive in absolute isolation to protect his innerself that is very well expressed in several of his characters who revolt against the irresistible social constructs. It assumes the form of negation, irritation, and the repression of social impulse, such a state of psyche makes a man lonely and miserable. In one of his letter addressed to the psychologist Dr. Trigant Burton, he mentioned:

> What ails me is the absolute frustration of the primeval societal order. I think societal instinct much deeper than sex instinct and societal repressions much more devastating. There is no repression of sexual individual, comparable to the repression of societal man. (Aldous Huxley 512)

The conflicting pulls of sexual instincts and social impulses constitutes the cardinal core of the plays of Lawrence.

Lawrence's celebrated play *A Collier's Friday Night* is a dramatic accounts of the conflict of the various phases of human relationship. The local of the play is the filthy atmosphere inside a collier's family. The crisis is born out of the maladjustment of Mr. and Mrs. Lambert who live in the filthy surroundings making their living with the drudgery of Collier's work. In the perpetual war of the parents, children suffer with the basic insecurity but support their mother for their emotional support. Father becomes isolated in his own family and suffers because of this exclusion. Like Mrs. Miriam of *Sons and Lovers* mother dominates the personality of her sons and encourages them to emancipate themselves from the filth of Collier's job. She tries to inculcate in them the spirit of sophistication and refinement. The divided family values hinders the emotional, biological and mental growth of son. When son, Earnst grows up and comes in contact of Maggie, mother feels frustrated and hostile in an unconscious way. Earnst becomes more and more weak and miserable with the dominant influence of mother. His conflict becomes internalized. His conflict becomes the conflict of choices. He finds helpless to reconcile his sexual desires and the irresistible impact of the dominant passions of mother. In her conquest of Earnst's soul, she rejects both Maggie and Lambert. Mother and son are lost in their webs of confusions. In *Collier's Friday Night*, characters prefer to survive in the darkness of night and darkness of pit. It is symbolic of their own life force. They unconsciously intends to seek a shelter in the darkness of night. Gertic accepts, "I like Friday night" (476) and Earnst speaks about the pavement where "it's so dark down there". Mother is apprehensive on the realization how Maggie got down "at night like this". Maggie prefers dark nights because "you can wrap yourself up it". It suggests the idea that different characters react to darkness in context to the realization of the darkness of their unconscious self. Mother makes efforts to dispel darkness but it is of no avail. In *Collier's Friday Night* "(Darkness) stands for the naked intimacy of the Collier's in the pit where they live in instinctive and intuitive life" (Nath 171). The darkness is related to the real life and the light is a symbol of the absurd and obscure crudity of modern materialistic world. The pit and darkness become a mechanism to survive in the protective zones. It reminds of O'Neill's idea of "Saloon" (Dark Wine Shop) presented in the play *Iceman Cometh*. It is an assertion of the natural biological life force. Lawrence through the clash of motives tries to justify that the modern rationalism of Industrial World can't compel the individuals beyond the calls of blood consciousness of instinctive behaviour. Mrs. Lambert suffers because she makes desperate effort to deny the call of life force. Her negation is expressed in the form of terrible pain that she bears in preventing her son going to pits. It prepares a strong dramatic situation because both the mother and son emerges 'spilt self' in their own way and it culminates in the form of their terrible tragedy. In the face of negation of Life Force, 'spilt self' creates frustration and its expression becomes more and more evident in sexual relations. In *Sons and Lovers*, Lawrence makes a categorical confession:

> The fact that he might want her as a man wants to woman had in his been suppressed into a shame. When she shrank in her convulsed coiled torture from the threads of such things, he had wined to the depths of his soul. And now his purity presented over their first one kiss. It was if she could scarcely stand the shock of physical love, even a passionate kiss then he was to striking and sensitive to give it. (*Sons and Lovers* 179)

In this respect in *Collier's Friday Night*, the images of night invariably associates with the images of death. For him the real understanding of life requires the understanding of death. Earnst disease and his unconscious drift towards the darkness of death is a symbolic manifestation of the horrors of denial of life force. In the play there is one suggestive occasion when Earnst and Maggie are left alone in the house when the mother proceeds to the market. It is an unconscious declaration of freedom from the damaging domination of mother. However mother image still grips his consciousness and instead of making love to Maggie, he seeks safer rescue in the form of reading a book of French verse. He turns out to be an escapist, she seems to thrive on his unconscious. It is evident that at unconscious level his act of burning of the loaf symbolizes his attempt to release himself from the hold of the mother. As soon as she looks a burnt loaf, she feels herself defeated by Maggie, "I always said she was deep one" (578). She becomes revengeful to protect her innerself in the form establishing her absolute control on Earnst's self. As a foil to the all absorbing passion of Mrs. Lambert, Mr. Lambert's desperate acts of shouting, growling and thumping suggests his helplessness to survive with his instinctive behaviour in modern Industrial social order. Mrs. Lambert calls Mr. Lambert "a hippotamus" and this image of wild beast symbolizes the savage maleness that civilization intends to crush. In fact the conflict of the ideologies of Mr. Lambert and Mrs. Lambert is a conflict of biological life force or socially constructed forces. His work in the pit is a natural response to his innate rhythm of life that is impossible to be re-modulated with the images of the sophisticated social order. The absolute identification with the darkness of pit suggests the absolute obedience to the life force that can bring salvation. The rational and idealizing principle are worthless without rhythm to ensure insecurity. Lawrence admits, "Physical life is a disordered corruption against which he can fight with only one weapon, his fine aesthetic sense, his feeling for beauty, for perfection for certain fitness which sooths him and gives him an inner pleasure, however the corrupt the stuff of life may be" (Lawrence. *Phoenix* 312-13). It is not the dilemma of an individual but demotes a comprehensive range of dilemma of existence. The creeping edifice of culture and the biological life force are at cross roads. In this respect Mr. Lamberts struggle for existence no longer remains the dilemma of an individual but it becomes a parable on obscurity the existence of man. It is said:

> He stands for a rhythm that is different to the greediness of the rational, the idiosyncrasies of culture and idealism. He carries in him the image of darkness in coal pit to which he runs from the house and from which he runs to the pub. His life in the pit symbolizes the ascent and descent of sexual rhythm. It may be a rhythm of death and life or sleep or awakening. (Suresh Nath 173-74)

In *Collier's Friday Night* as a foil to the idea of pits, 'rose' is projected as anti-symbol to realize the purpose of the play. Earnest is given a rose by her girlfriend. Mrs. Lambert does not like the act of accepting the rose. The idea of acceptance implies the effort of triumph on the sensibility of the son that would have been a challenge to mother's own internal insecurity that she unconsciously looks for in her son. Neillie, Earnst sister on the contrary is excited on the idea of rose because she had a realization that Eddie will "have the rose and all, to rejoice the cockles or his heart at this time" (503). In the subsequent scene of *Collier's Friday Night*, rose becomes a symbol of vital dark force. Earnst act of accepting rose from a college girl suggests the idea that inspite of mother's devouring effect, he retains his own life force and it is in proximity with the rhythm of life. However Neillie's act of taking away the rose again signifies her passion for the life force that was being thwarted in the life of Earnst. She retains the rose herself. Being torn between the conflicting pull of ideas, Earnst is reduced to the position of a "miserable pawn" dwindling between the expectations of her mother and her beloved Maggie. Lawrence establishes that in the network of familial relationship, man like Earnst survive with fractured psyche proclaiming the annals of eternal doom. Lawrence distinguished between the "literature of repudiation" and the literature of negation. Self-consciousness in man that is to be found in modern man "absolutely concerned with the disintegration process of his own psyche" (Anthony Beal 115).

In this respect, with the profound web of symbols, D.H. Lawrence endeavors to expose the issues of existence in marital relationship and its subsequent transmission to children that is gradually revolutionizing the expectations of the organized familial relations in the shifting paradigms of industrial world.

The idea of complexity of Industrial World as a burden to human existence obsessed Lawrence and led to the genesis of the play *Touch and Go.* Beyond the domains of external physical realities, he explores some serious issues that obstruct the process of self-consciousness. Besides of the horrors of Industrial world, he also constructs the fragmentation of human psyche under the creeping shadows of war. He finds war "an aweful process finally strangling us into Oblivion like the leaves of trees" (Lawrence. *Letters* 1956). War leads to the feeling of absolute helplessness born out of the apprehensions of annihilation reflecting the speculations of nothingness. Like Ernst Hemingway, Lawrence has a realization of futility and the triumph of the spirit of killing in the wake the upsurge of war. For him the 'term' war includes the war of nations as well as the Labour and capitalists. In the story *Fox,* he mentions how Henry, the protagonist has not sophisticated ideas about love, nature or social consciousness. Loving and killing are simultaneously operating on his consciousness. He makes a confession regarding the feeling born out of war. To quote:

> The war has a great explosion of society and all its forms assumptions, a sundering of man, like but of shrapnel of flying apart from each other out into a void and there drifting. (Keith Sagar 106)

In the play *Touch and Go*, war emerges as an striking symbol. War is closely related to the class war in the Industrial world. A glooming shadows of Industrial World leads to strife and absence of stability but it can lead to the formation of a new social order of constructive ideologies, new understanding.

In the play *Touch and Go*, Gerald Barlow, the Kingpine of mine owner survives with the burden of two problems. His conflict is personal as well as impersonal. In professional life, he has to face to the ordeal of the strike of mine workers and in personal life his passions for his sweet heart. Gerald resolves his emotional strife with his sweet heart Anabel by "hating almost to madness" (*Complete Plays* 337) for hate is a "real process". Side by side he is hopeful that strikers would make serious struggle and with creative struggle they will be able to have new hope and new struggle. The plan *Touch and Go* develops an idea that struggle has a strong creative force. Lawrence defines bullying or struggling as the desire to superimpose one's will upon another person. However the struggle must have definite conviction for its effective implementation. For the issue of salary, minors go for strike but their action remains futile without the force of conviction. Without conviction, struggle is meaningless. It is only the creative struggle that yields to meaningful results. Strikes without purpose are like 'Touch and Go'. To settle down the problem of labours and masters, it is inevitable to resolve the differences of soul. In spite of destructive impulses the purposeful strike and war work as creative and constructive force implying possibilities of improvement. He accepts:

> After the war the soul of people will be so maimed and so injured that it is horrible to think of. And this shall be the new hope that there shall be a life, wherein the struggle shall not be for money or power, but for individual freedom and common efforts towards good. (*Letters of D.H. Lawrence* 220)

Lawrence in *Touch and Go* in order to capture the vehemence of passions of workers makes experiment with unconventional language to synthesize the force of suppressed emotions. He presents such horrible images that are difficult to project in the direct expressions. It was also an effort to revolutionize the existing theatrical idiom. The labour leader William Houghton in the act I, uses symbols to expose instinctive death with their being reduced to almost automatous and rhythmless machines. He says, "You bleat a bit like a sheep in the bog."

Barlow and Wallsall make a number of compounds, such as they keep niggers in South Africa and there you'll be kept. And every one of you'll have a little brass collar round his neck, with number on it. You won't have names any more (*Complete Plays* 325).

He further admits that they are "just pit ponies that stop down fill they are blind and take to eating coat-slack for meadow grass, not knowing the difference" (361). Winifred Gerald's sister loves the wolf with its terrible fierce backbone and does not feel sorry for the 'goat'. The 'goat' and 'wolf' images reflect the idea of devouring and clash of power struggle that is the essential for the survival and industrial societies. Oliver finds goat like "a wrong sort of clergymen" (399) and is apprehensive that the goat will be killed by the wolf. He denotes the idea of power struggle between the capitalists and labour class and the death of goat is a symbolic representation of decay of the labour class.

In the background of power struggle, Lawrence manages the conflicts in man and woman relationship. Anabel aspires for the love of Gerald. The companionship of Gerald is the dream of her life but unfortunately they become the victim of jealousy without the anticipated presence of a lover. She is jealous of Gerald's friend Oliver and makes an affirmation of his all absorbing passion "Gerald had a passion for me. But he loved you" (337). Gerald fails to respond her passion and thwarted passion converts into resentment, denial and resistance. As an alternative for her passion, she escapes with Norwegian to Dar's where jealousy survives with the passage of time. Such alternatives help to come out of savage passion and to redefine the new life conditions. In April 1913, Lawrence wrote to A.W. Mclord:

> And I am sure that only through a readjustment between men and women, and making free and healthy of this sex, will she get out of her present atrocity. (Keith Sagar 35)

Sex relations in the modern societies are no longer unifying process. Sex is creative force that can encourage the lady like Anabel to search out new patterns required for the human survival. In *Phoenix II*, D.H. Lawrence admits:

> In the present social set up then, sex is no longer "a great unifier" and has become positively a "great divider". The slogan of modern society seems to be "Don't trust anybody with their real emotions. Trust them with your money, even but never with your feelings. They are bound to temple of them." (Lawrence 1968: 49)

In this respect Lawrence in *Touch and Go* accepts that in personal relations the industrial values float as significant variable. Individual for his survival must be very careful about it. The faith in personal relations beyond money-centered value, it is essential to inculcate faith and religion based on social structure. Mr. Barlow by his denial of struggle, represents death principle. Colliers fail to wage a genuine struggle which can open the door to a new life. Mechanization of human behaviour and human affairs is a serious hazard to human existence.

Lawrence's another well-known play *The Widowing of Mrs. Holroyd* is a dramatic account of the persistent disharmony and conflict in marital relationship. In this play Mr. Holroyd appears as a typical collier surviving in shabby surrounding with the savagery of shouting and growling. His manners are shunned by Mrs. Holroyd who shares sophisticated manners. To avoid the nagging of his wife, Holroyd use to take shelter in New Inn. The children were disgusted with the havoc like conditions of his family. Children one day finds their father being involved with the drunkard hussies. This information was brought to the mother who was busy in replacing lamp glasses over the frame. The action of preserving flame with glass lamp becomes an unconscious manifestation of her efforts to protect her own self beyond the obsessive behaviour of her husband. In the play lamp glass almost becomes an illusion in which she intends to survive to protect herself. However the illusion turns out to be in disillusionment with the information of children. In T.S. Eliots term Lawrence applies an appropriate